# PRINCIPLES OF METAL CUTTING

**G. Kuppuswamy**
Associate Professor
Manufacturing Engineering Division
Indian Institute of Technology
Madras 600 036



**Universities Press**

**Universities Press (India) Private Limited**

*Registered Office*
3-6-747/1/A & 3-6-754/1, Himayatnagar,
Hyderabad 500 029 (A.P), India
e-mail: *www.universitiespress.com*

*Distributed by*
Orient Blackswan Private Limited

*Registered Office*
3-6-752, Himayatnagar, Hyderabad 500 029 (A.P), India

*Other Offices*
Bangalore / Bhopal / Bhubaneshwar / Chennai /Ernakulam
Guwahati / Hyderabad / Jaipur / Kolkata /Lucknow
Mumbai / New Delhi / Patna


First published 1996
Reprint 2008, 2009, 2010, 2012, 2013

ISBN: 978 81 7371 028 5

Typeset by
Access Centre, Secunderabad 500 003

*Printed at*
Graphica Printers and Binders
Hyderabad 500 013

*Published by*
Universities Press (India) Private Limited
3-6-747/1/A & 3-6-754/1, Himayatnagar,
Hyderabad 500 029 (A.P), India

# Contents

# Preface

Today, knowledge of metal cutting or machining is important in several areas of manufacture, such as process planning, selection of tools and operation parameters, machinability data, economic analysis, etc. There is a growing trend to include a course on this subject at various levels, ranging from postgraduate to undergraduate and diploma levels. This book aims to fulfil the requirements of beginners for a fundamental knowledge of the concepts in the theory of metal cutting.

The book begins with an introduction comprising types of cutting and types of chips. The tool geometries of machine reference system, orthogonal tool reference system and normal tool reference system, and the interrelationship between them are discussed in Chapter 2. Chapter 3 deals with the chip formation mechanism in orthogonal and oblique cutting.

Chapter 4 presents the relationship between various forces involved in orthogonal cutting, through Merchant's circle diagran. It also includes a detailed discussion on dynamometers used for the measurement of cutting forces.

The thermal aspects of machining along with different types of wear are covered in Chapter 5. Other aspects like the significance and general principles of cutting temperatures are also discussed in detail. The common tool failure mechanisms typical to carbide tools/inserts, and tool-life analysis are dealt with in Chapter 6.

Chapter 7 dealing with machinability elucidates machining economics through adequate number of solved examples. The types of cutting fluids and grinding fluids along with their functions, advantages and disadvantages are included in Chapter 8.

Chapter 9 deals with the properties and development of various types of cutting tool materials. The significance of basic types of chatter—forced and self-excited vibration—is described in Chapter 10.

Chapter 11 on surface roughness discusses the effect of tool geometry and various cutting parameters on surface furnish. Chapter 12 deals with types of chip breakers.

Chapter 13 outlines the design aspects for lathe and single-point cutting tools. It also includes a discussion on the tool-in-use angles. Machining of different polymer-based products and hard materials is discussed in Chapter 14.

Appendices include a discussion on machine tool monitoring and on-line gauging, as well as an overview of special machining methods with a view to motivate students by exposing them to other related areas, that they may find useful, and thereby help develop their competitiveness and ensure success.

The other notable features of the book is the use of ISO recommended nomenclature and symbols, and SI units. Exercise problems with answers are given at the end of the chapters, wherever required. A comprehensive Bibliography is also included.

The book will be of considerable use in various postgraduate programmes in the areas of metal-cutting, machine tools, and manufacturing, and also for the elective programmes in mechanical engineering at the undergraduate level. Researchers looking for a quick review of relevant topics and updated nomenclature, symbols and units will also find it useful.

I wish to express my gratitude to the Centre for Continuing Education at the Indian Institute of Technology, Madras, India, for its assistance and support, in writing this book.

**Madras** **G. Kuppuswamy**

# List of symbols

| Symbol | Description |
|---|---|
| $\gamma_p$ | Back rake angle |
| $\gamma_f$ | Side rake angle |
| $\psi$ | Side cutting edge angle |
| $k_r$ | Principal cutting edge angle |
| $k_r'$ | End cutting edge angle |
| $\lambda_s$ | Inclination angle |
| $\gamma_o$ | Orthogonal angle |
| $\gamma_n$ | Normal rake angle |
| $\alpha_p$ | Front/end clearance/relief angle |
| $\alpha_f$ | Side clearance/relief angle |
| $\alpha_o$ | Orthogonal clearance angle |
| $\alpha_o'$ | Auxiliary orthogonal clearance angle |
| $\alpha_n$ | Normal clearance angle |
| $\alpha_n'$ | Auxiliary normal clearance angle |
| $r$ | Nose radius |
| $k_\alpha$ | Angle of swivel for tool while grinding principal flank |
| $\alpha_m$ | Angle of tilt for tool while grinding principal flank |
| $k_\gamma$ | Angle of swivel for tool while grinding rake face |
| $\gamma_m$ | Angle of tilt for tool while grinding rake face |
| $\rho_r$ | Chip deviation angle |
| $\gamma_e$ | Effective rake angle |
| $\eta$ | Cutting speed angle |
| $B$ | Setting angle for tool increasing the principal cutting edge angle |
| $C$ | Setting angle for tool increasing the back rake |
| $\gamma_{pm}$ | Changed back rake on introduction of setting angles |
| $\gamma_{fm}$ | Changed side rake on introduction of setting angles |
| $\alpha_{pm}$ | Changed end relief/clearance on introduction of setting angles |
| $\alpha_{fm}$ | Changed side relief/clearance on introduction of setting angles |
| $k_{rm}$ | Changed principal cutting edge angle on introduction of setting angles |
| $\lambda_{sm}$ | Changed inclination angle on introduction of setting angles |

| | |
|---|---|
| $\gamma_{pe}$ | Back rake on considering the effect of feed |
| $\gamma_{fe}$ | Side rake on considering the effect of feed |
| $\alpha_{pe}$ | End relief/clearance on considering the effect of feed |
| $\alpha_{fe}$ | Side relief/clearance on considering the effect of feed |
| $k_{re}$ | Principal cutting edge angle on considering the effect of feed |
| $\lambda_{se}$ | Working or effective inclination angle on considering setting angles and feed |
| $\gamma_{oe}$ | Working or effective orthogonal rake on considering setting angles and feed |
| $\gamma_{ne}$ | Working or effective normal rake on considering setting angles and feed |
| $\alpha_{oe}$ | Working or effective orthogonal clearance on considering setting angles and feed |
| $\alpha_{ne}$ | Working or effective normal clearance on considering setting angles and feed |
| $h_c$ | Thickness of chip, mm |
| $b_c$ | Width of chip, mm |
| $l_c$ | Length of chip, mm |
| $h_D$ | Nominal thickness of uncut layer of cut, mm |
| $b_D$ | Nominal width of uncut layer of cut, mm |
| $l_D$ | Nominal length of uncut layer of cut, mm |
| $f$ | Feed in turning, mm/rev |
| $b$ | Depth of cut in turning, mm |
| $\Lambda_h$ | Chip reduction coefficient or chip thickness compression ratio |
| $\Lambda_l$ | Chip compression ratio based on length measurement |
| $\Lambda_b$ | Chip compression ratio based on width measurement |
| $\Lambda_a$ | Chip compression ratio based on area measurement |
| $r_c$ | Cutting ratio |
| $\phi$ | Shear angle |
| $A_c$ | Area of cross-section of chip, mm$^2$ |
| $A_r$ | Area of uncut layer to be removed, mm$^2$ |
| $\epsilon_s$ | Dynamic shearing strain |
| $F_f$ | Feed or axial force |
| $F_D$ | Thrust or radial force |
| $F_C$ | Cutting or tangential force |
| $F_{CN}$ | Cutting normal force |
| $F_{shN}$ | Normal force on shear plane |
| $F_\gamma$ | Friction force on rake face |
| $F_{\gamma N}$ | Normal force on rake face |
| $\mu$ | Kinetic coefficient of friction |
| $\delta$ | Friction angle |
| $v_c$ | Cutting velocity or the velocity of tool relative to work that is parallel to the machined surface |
| $v_f$ | Chip velocity or the velocity of chip relative to tool that is parallel to the rake face |
| $v_s$ | Shear velocity or the velocity of chip relative to work that is parallel to the shear plane |
| $\tau_s$ | Dynamic shear stress on shear plane |

| | |
|---|---|
| $A_{sh}$ | Area of shear plane |
| $e_c$ | Specific energy of cutting or the total specific energy |
| $e_s$ | Specific energy of shear |
| $e_f$ | Specific energy of friction |
| $W_c$ | Rate of energy consumption during orthogonal cutting |
| $Q$ | Total heat generated in orthogonal cutting |
| $Q_s$ | Heat generated in shear zone |
| $Q_f$ | Heat generated in frictional zone |
| $Q_c$ | Heat conducted to chip |
| $Q_w$ | Heat conducted to workpiece |
| $Q_t$ | Heat conducted to tool |
| $\rho$ | Density of material |
| $C$ | Specific heat of material |
| $\theta_s$ | Temperature rise of the material by shear zone |
| $\theta_f$ | Temperature rise of the material by frictional heat |
| $\theta_t$ | Temperature of chip along the rake face |
| $VB$ | Average width of flank wear-land |
| $VB_{max}$ | Maximum width of flank wear-land |
| $KT$ | Maximum depth of crater wear |
| $t_c$ | Machining time |
| $t_d$ | Tool changing time |
| $t_w$ | Work changing time |
| $X_1$ | Machine and operator cost with overhead |
| $X_2$ | Mean cost of the cutting edge or the tool cost |
| $TC$ | Total cost per part |
| $t_o$ | Tool life for minimum cost |
| $t'_o$ | Tool life for maximum production rate |
| $v_o$ | Cutting speed corresponding to minimum cost criterion |
| $v'_o$ | Cutting speed corresponding to maximum production rate criterion |
| $M_{60}$ | Machinability index based on tool life criterion ($v_{60}$ material/$v_{60}$ standard) |
| $M_o$ | Machinability index based on cost criterion ($TC$ material/$TC$ standard) |
| $R_{max}$ or $R_t$ | Theoretical maximum height or peak to valley roughness |
| $R_a$ | Theoretical arithmetical mean value or centre-line-average of roughness |
| $l_n$ | Chip-breaker distance |
| $h$ | Chip-breaker height |
| $\gamma_{chip}$ | Radius of chip curvature |
| $l_f$ | Contact length between chip and tool |
| $q_n$ | Chip-breaker groove radius |
| $l$ | Tool overhung (distance from the tool nose to the place of critical cross-section) |
| $\sigma_{bp}$ | Permissible bending stress of the shank material |
| $F_{zp}$ | Maximum permissible load based on tool rigidity |
| $E$ | Young's modulus of shank material |
| $I$ | Moment of inertia of shank cross-section |

# 1 Introduction

All metal-cutting operations involve a wedge-shaped tool with a straight cutting edge, having a relative velocity with reference to the workpiece, contributing to chip formation. For analytical purposes, cutting operations are classified as oblique cutting and orthogonal cutting (Fig.1.1).

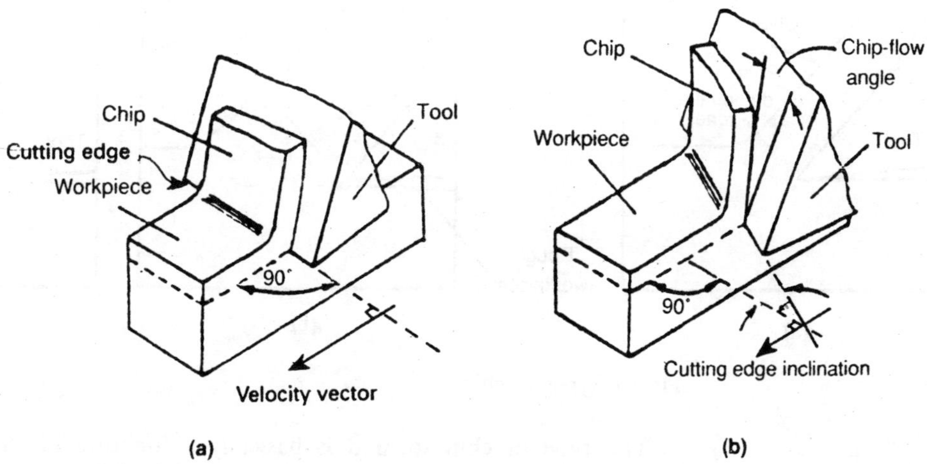


**Fig.1.1** Orthogonal and oblique cutting, (a) orthogonal cutting, (b) oblique cutting

Oblique cutting is the most common type, normally found in several machining operations. The cutting edge is inclined to the normal to cutting velocity vector by an angle called the *inclination angle*. This type of cutting is also called three-dimensional cutting due to forces raised in three directions perpendicular to one another.

Orthogonal cutting is a special kind of cutting where the cutting edge is normal to the cutting velocity vector. Being a two-dimensional problem, in view of forces in two perpendicular directions, where the number of independent variables are reduced, this type of cutting is often used for research purposes.

### *Chip formation*

In a typical metal-cutting operation, chips are separated from the workpiece to impart the required size and shape to the workpiece. This situation requires a tool that is harder than the workpiece and also a set of suitable cutting conditions, like cutting velocity, feed and depth of cut.

The chips are classified according to their behaviour during formation. The general classification is as given below (Fig.1.2):

(a) discontinuous or segmental,

(b) continuous, without built-up edge, and

(c) continuous, with built-up edge,

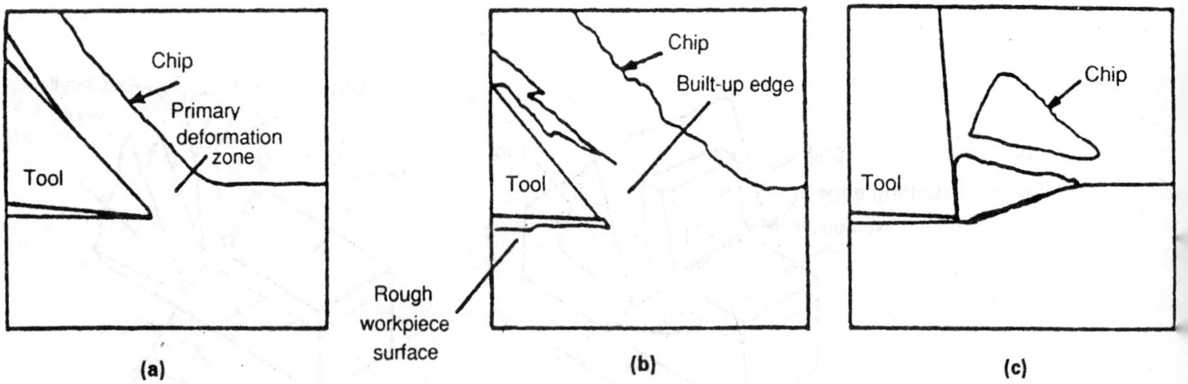


Fig.1.2 Types of chips

The type of chip formed is basically a function of the work material and cutting conditions. The discontinuous chip is typical with more brittle materials such as cast iron. Continuous chips are normally formed with ductile materials such as steel.

The ideal type of continuous chip, though seldom achieved, is associated with high strength materials having low work-hardening capacity, low coefficients of friction, and high cutting speeds.

Sometimes, as the chip passes over the tool face, cutting forces contribute to very high unit pressures, sufficient to form pressure welds between the chip and the tool, particularly at the cutting edge. If the portion of the chip welded to the tool shears off as the chip is displaced, a *built-up edge* is said to have formed. This is a common phenomenon, for example, when machining aluminium and some stainless steels. The edge grows and breaks down at a certain size, partly sticking with the chip and partly with the work surface, leaving the surface rough. However, the built-up edge offers some protection to the cutting edge, reducing wear. Therefore a small amount of built-up edge may be desirable, thus demanding size control, if unavoidable.

Being an introduction to the theory of metal cutting, this work deals mainly with single-point cutting tool and orthogonal cutting, in the area of mechanics of metal cutting. Tool life, machinability analysis and machining economics, surface roughness estimation and chip control are the other areas discussed.

In view of their importance to metal cutting, a general discussion of cutting fluids and tool materials has also been included.

# 2 Tool geometry of single-point cutting tools

## 2.1 Introduction

The geometry of a single-point cutting tool is determined by the following features:

(a) Face or rake surface, which is the surface of the cutting tool along which the chips move.

(b) Flank surfaces that face the workpiece. There are two flank surfaces, namely principal and auxiliary flank surfaces.

(c) Cutting edges that remove material from the workpiece. There are two cutting edges. The principal cutting edge performs the function of major material removal and is formed by the intersecting line of rake face with the principal flank surface. The auxiliary cutting edge, often called as end cutting edge, is formed by the intersection of rake face with the auxiliary flank surface.

(d) Corner or cutting point, which is the meeting point of the principal and auxiliary cutting edges. Often a nose radius is provided to avoid a sharp corner.

The above mentioned features are shown in Fig.2.1.

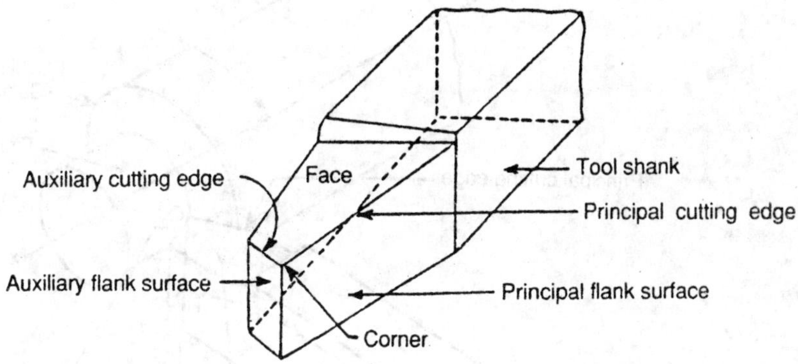


**Fig. 2.1** Features of a single point tool

## 2.2 Tool-point reference systems

To determine the orientation and inclination of the rake face and flank surfaces, a coordinate system is essential, resulting in a set of planes with reference to which the orientations or inclinations can be determined. Two planes are of significance: the first one is called the tool reference plane or principal plane, which is perpendicular to the cutting velocity vector, and the second one is called the cutting plane, which is tangential to the cutting edge and contains the velocity vector. The cutting plane is also perpendicular to the principal plane or the tool reference plane.

There are three different types of coordinate systems that are popular, when it comes to tool nomenclature. They are:

(a) Machine reference system,

(b) Orthogonal tool reference system, and

(c) Oblique or normal tool reference system.

## 2.3 Machine reference system

The machine reference system defines the coordinates with respect to the machine axis. For example, in a lathe, $xx'$ is the spindle or workpiece axis, $yy'$ is the tool axis and $zz'$ is the vertical axis. Figure 2.2 depicts the $x-y-z$ axes and Fig.2.3 shows the principal plane and the cutting plane under this system, along with the reference planes formed by the coordinates.

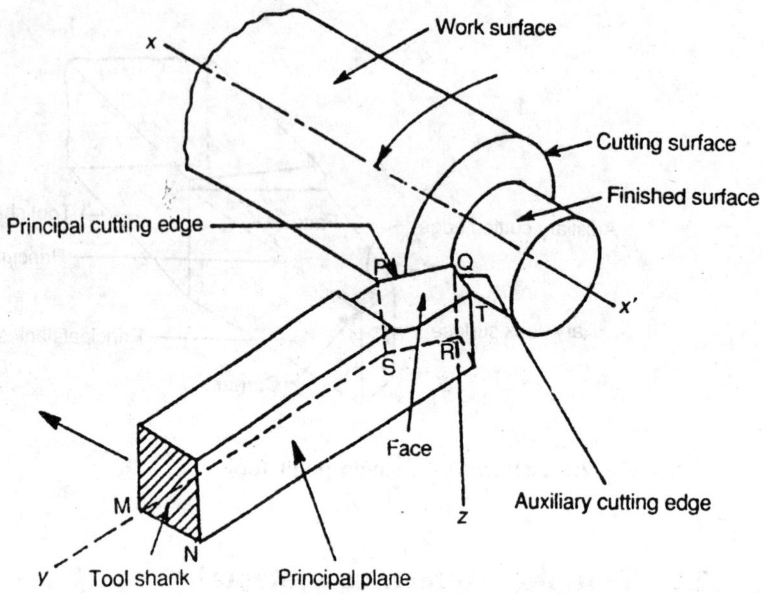


**Fig.2.2 $x$-$y$-$z$ coordinates of machine reference system**

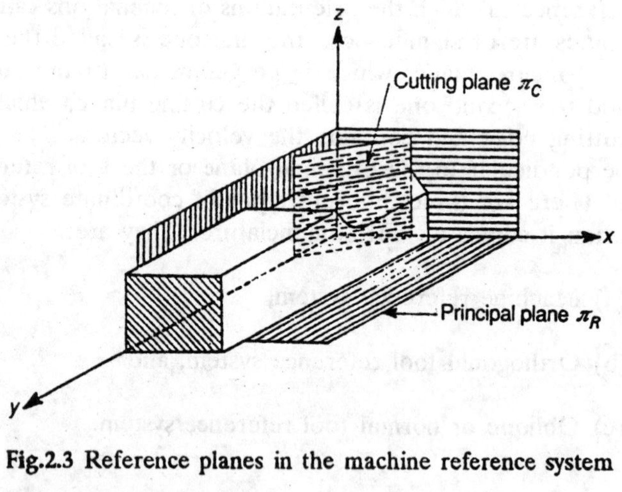


**Fig.2.3 Reference planes in the machine reference system**

**Figure 2.4 shows the orientation of rake face and flank surfaces with respect to the machine reference system along with the tool angles, in symbolic form. The following terminology is applicable to this system of tool nomenclature:**

$\gamma_p$ = **back rake angle**

$\gamma_f$ = **side rake angle**

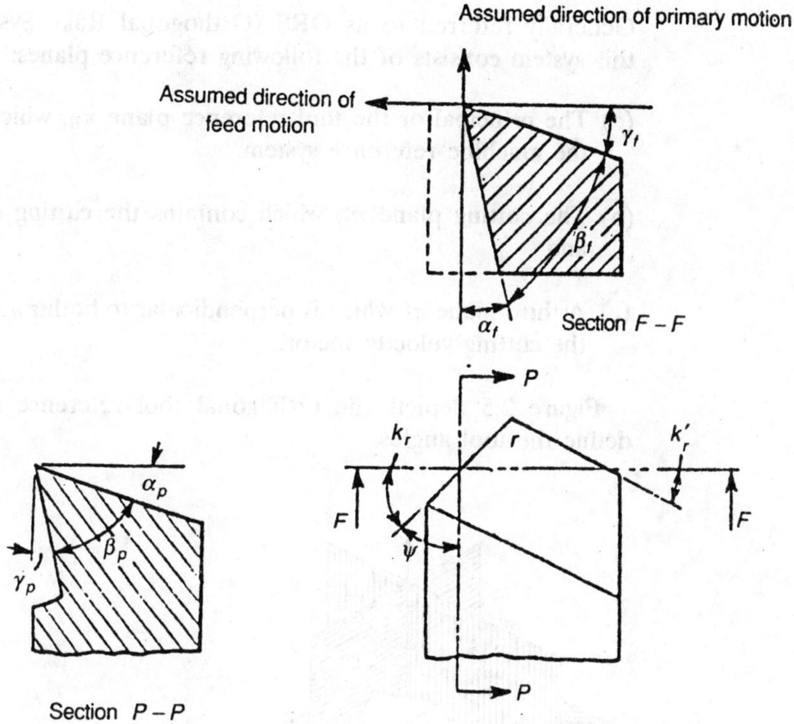


**Fig.2.4** Machine reference system

$\alpha_p$ = front or end clearance or relief angle

$\alpha_f$ = side clearance or relief angle

$k'_r$ = end cutting edge angle

$\psi$ = side cutting edge angle

$r$ = nose radius

The machine reference system of defining angles is sometimes called the old American System of Tool Nomenclature, because of its popularity in earlier times. In its abbreviated form it is referred to as ASA (American Standards Association) system.

The shape of the tool is normally specified in a special sequence, often referred to as tool signature, as shown below:

$$\gamma_p - \gamma_f - \alpha_p - \alpha_f - k'_r - \psi - r \qquad \text{(ASA)}$$

## 2.4 Orthogonal tool reference system

Generally referred to as ORS (Orthogonal Rake System) nomenclature, this system consists of the following reference planes:

(a) The principal or the tool reference plane $\pi_R$, which is the same as for the machine reference system.

(b) The cutting plane $\pi_c$, which contains the cutting edge, normal to $\pi_R$, and

(c) A third plane $\pi_0$ which is perpendicular to both $\pi_R$ and $\pi_C$, and contains the cutting velocity vector.

Figure 2.5 depicts the orthogonal tool reference system of planes to define the tool angles.

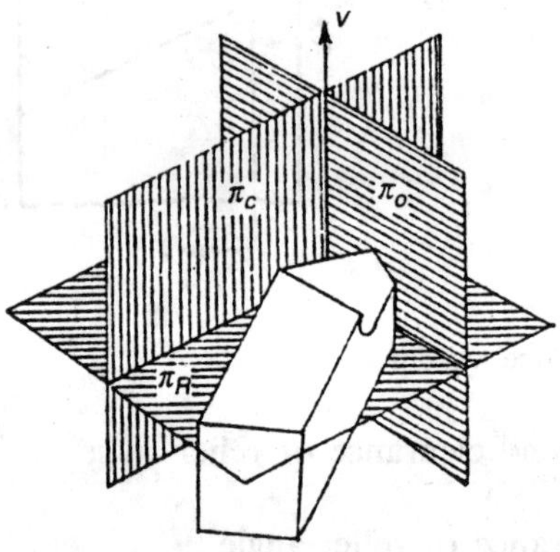


**Fig.2.5** Orthogonal tool reference system of planes

Figure 2.6 shows the orientation of rake face and flank surfaces with respect to the orthogonal tool reference system and the tool angles in symbolic form. The following terminology is applicable to this system of tool nomenclature:

$\lambda_s$ = inclination angle

$\gamma_o$ = orthogonal rake

$\alpha_o$ = orthogonal clearance angle

$\alpha'_o$ = auxiliary clearance angle

$k'_r$ = end cutting edge angle

$k_r$ = principal cutting edge angle

$r$ = nose radius

The shape of the tool is usually specified in a special sequence, called ORS tool signature, as given below:

$$\lambda_s - \gamma_o - \alpha_o - \alpha'_o - k'_r - k_r - r \qquad \text{(ORS)}$$

The ORS features have been incorporated by the new American system as ANSI (American National Standards Institute) nomenclature.

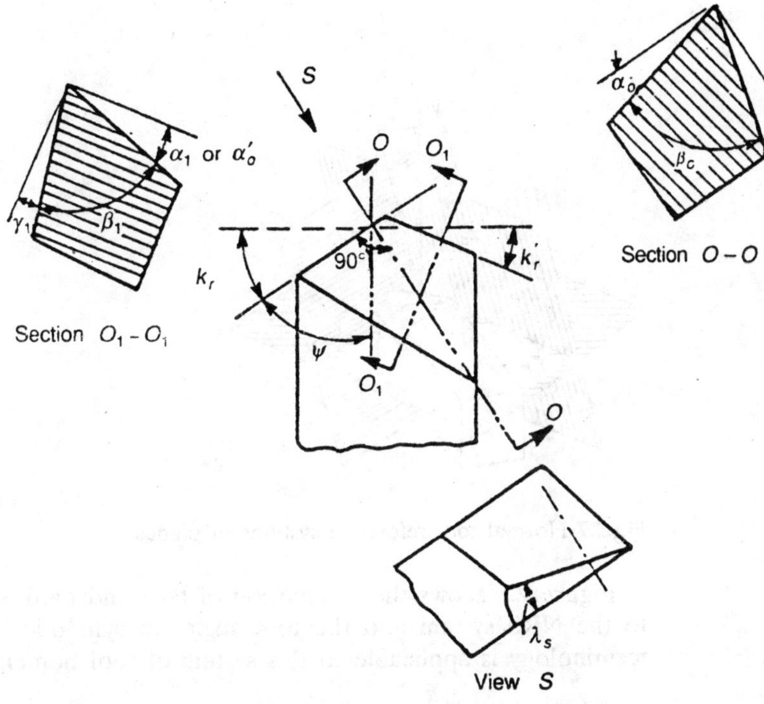


Fig.2.6 Orthogonal rake system (ORS) geometry

## 2.5 Normal tool reference system

Also called the oblique tool reference system, this system consists of the following planes:

(a) The principal or tool reference plane $\pi_R$, which is the same as in the machine reference system and orthogonal tool reference system.

(b) Cutting plane $\pi_c$, which is the same as that of the orthogonal tool reference system, and

(c) The third plane $\pi_n$, which is not perpendicular to the $\pi_R$ plane but is perpendicular to the principal cutting edge. This third plane is known as the 'normal plane' because it is perpendicular to the cutting edge. $\pi_n$ is inclined to the normal to velocity vector by the inclination angle $\lambda_s$.

Figure 2.7 depicts the normal tool reference system (NRS) of planes to define the tool angles, and is generally referred to as NRS (Normal Rake System) nomenclature.

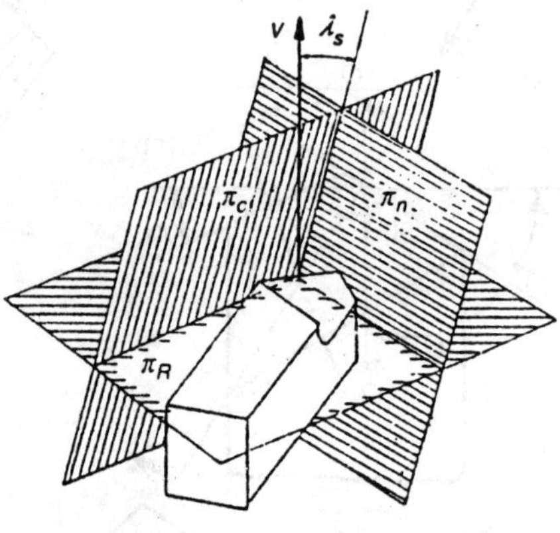


Fig.2.7 Normal tool reference systems of planes

Figure 2.8 shows the orientation of face and flank surfaces with respect to the NRS system and the tool angles in symbolic form. The following terminology is applicable to this system of tool nomenclature:

$\lambda_s$ = inclination angle

$\gamma_n$ = normal rake

$\alpha_n$ = normal clearance angle

$\alpha'_n$ = auxiliary normal clearance angle

$k'_r$ = end cutting edge angle

$k_r$ = principal cutting edge angle

$r$ = nose radius

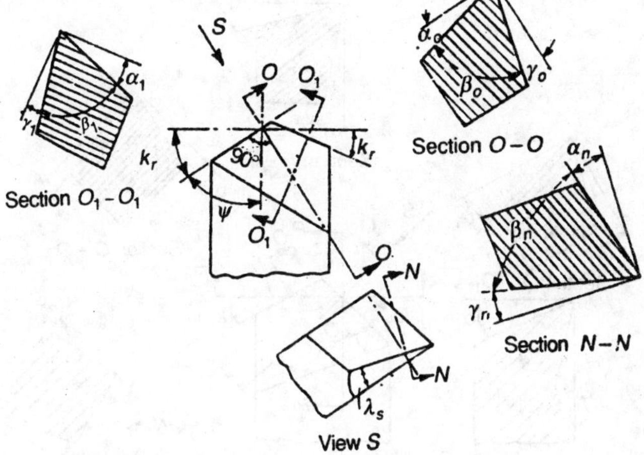


**Fig.2.8** Orthogonal rake system (ORS) and normal rake system (NRS) geometry

The NRS tool signature is given below:

$$\lambda_s - \gamma_n - \alpha_n - \alpha'_n - k'_r - k_r - r \qquad \text{(NRS)}$$

Table 2.1 gives a summary and comparison of the three systems of nomenclature, and Fig.2.9 depicts all three systems.

Tool signatures:

$$\gamma_p - \gamma_f - \alpha_p - \alpha_f - k'_r - \psi - r \qquad \text{(MRS)/(ASA)}$$

$$\lambda_s - \gamma_o - \alpha_o - \alpha'_o - k'_r - k_r - r \qquad \text{(ORS)}$$

$$\lambda_s - \gamma_n - \alpha_n - \alpha'_n - k'_r - k_r - r \qquad \text{(NRS)}$$

**Table 2.1** Tool nomenclature systems

| | | Tool reference system: Orthogonal rake system | Tool reference system: Normal rake system | Machine reference system: (ASA) |
|---|---|---|---|---|
| 1. | Location of cutting edges | $k_r, k'_r$ | $k_r, k'_r$ | $\psi, k'_r$ |
| 2. | Orientation of face | $\gamma_o, \lambda_s$ | $\gamma_n, \lambda_s$ | $\gamma_p, \gamma_f$ |
| 3. | Orientation of principal flank | $\alpha_o$ | $\alpha_n$ | $\alpha_p, \alpha_f$ |
| 4. | Orientation of auxiliary flank | $\alpha'_o$ | $\alpha'_n$ | – |
| 5. | Nose radius | $r$ | $r$ | $r$ |

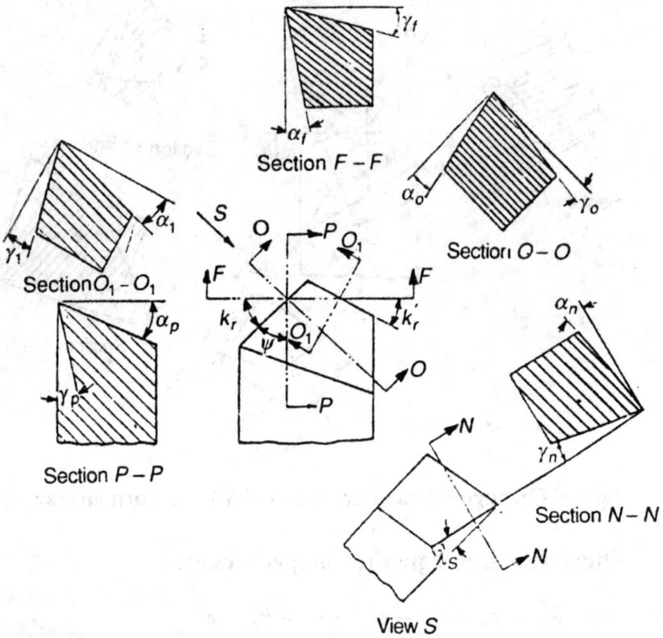


Fig.2.9 Single-point tool geometry

## 2.6 Interrelation between different systems of nomenclature

Interrelations can be established between MRS or ASA and ORS or between ORS and NRS systems, and vice versa.

**Rake face angles**

(1) Given the back rake ($\gamma_p$) and side rake ($\gamma_f$) angles in ASA system, to find inclination angle $\lambda_s$ and orthogonal rake $\gamma_o$ in the ORS system. Assume either $k_r$ or $\psi$ is known.

$$\tan \lambda_s = \tan \gamma_p \sin k_r - \tan \gamma_f \cos k_r$$

*Note*: $k_r$ in the above relation is of the ORS system.

Since $\psi = 90° - k_r$ or $k_r = 90 - \psi$,

$$\tan \lambda_s = \tan \gamma_p \cos \psi - \tan \gamma_f \sin \psi$$

$\lambda_s$ can be calculated from any of the above two equations.

Also,

$$\tan \gamma_o = \tan \gamma_p \cos k_r + \tan \gamma_f \sin k_r, \text{ or}$$

$$\tan \gamma_o = \tan \gamma_p \sin \psi + \tan \gamma_f \cos \psi$$

**Sign conventions**

**(1) Figure 2.10 indicates how positive or negative rake angles are denoted. Similarly, Fig.2.11 indicates how the positive inclination angle is denoted. Note that $\lambda_s$ is negative, if the cutting edge slopes up from the cutting point at the nose.**

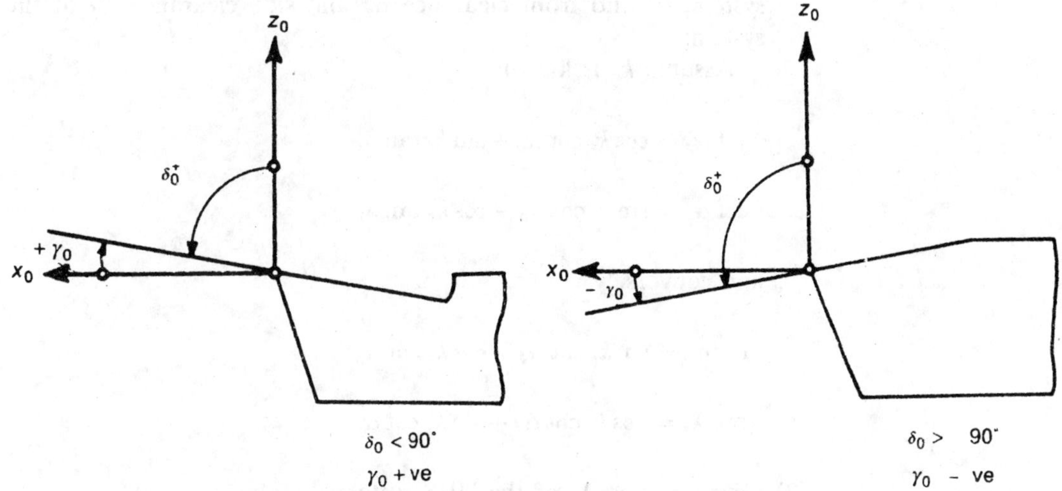


**Fig.2.10** Sign convention for rake angle

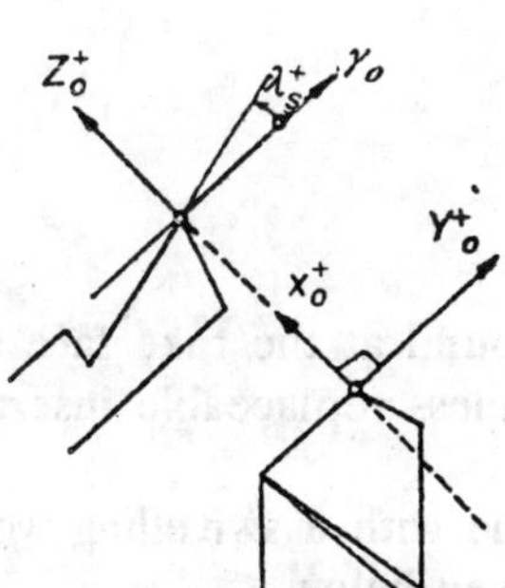


**Fig.2.11** Sign convention for inclination angle

**(2) Given inclination angle ($\lambda_s$) and orthogonal rake ($\gamma_o$) of the ORS system, to find back rake $\gamma_p$ and side rake $\gamma_f$ of the ASA system: Assume $\psi$ is known.**

$$\tan\gamma_p = \tan\lambda_s \cos\psi + \tan\gamma_o \sin\psi,$$

and

$$\tan\gamma_f = \tan\gamma_o \cos\psi - \tan\lambda_s \sin\psi$$

(3) Given $\gamma_o$ and $\lambda_s$ of the ORS system, to find $\gamma_n$ of the NRS system:

$$\tan\gamma_n = \tan\gamma_o \cos\lambda_s$$

**Clearance angles**

(1) Given orthogonal clearance $\alpha_o$ and inclination angle $\lambda_s$ of the ORS system, to find front clearance $\alpha_p$ and side clearance $\alpha_f$ of the ASA system:

Assume $k_r$ is known.

$$\cot\alpha_p = \cos k_r \cot\alpha_o + \sin k_r \tan\lambda_s$$

$$\cot\alpha_f = \sin k_r \cot\alpha_o - \cos k_r \tan\lambda_s$$

and conversely,

$$\cot\alpha_o = \sin k_r \cot\alpha_f + \cos k_r \cot\alpha_p$$

$$\tan\lambda_s = \cos k_r \cot\alpha_f + \sin k_r \cot\alpha_p$$

(2) Given $\alpha_o$ and $\lambda_s$ of the NRS system:

$$\tan\alpha_n = \tan\alpha_o / \cos\lambda_s$$

## 2.7 Grinding tool angle

Generally, cutting tools are ground at the rake face and flank surfaces to impart geometrical features, unless replaceable inserts (also called throw-away tips or inserts) are used.

Assuming a grinding machine with a swivelling work table is used, the procedure for grinding is as given below.

**Grinding principal flank**

The tool is set as shown in Fig.2.12. The first swivel is made through an angle $k_\alpha$ about the I-I axis, and an angle of tilt $\alpha_m$ is then made about the II-II axis.

The following equations are used to compute $k_\alpha$ and $\alpha_m$:

$$\cot \alpha_m = \sqrt{\cot^2 \alpha_o + \tan^2 \lambda_s}$$

$$= \sqrt{\cot^2 \alpha_f + \cot^2 \alpha_p}$$

$$\tan k_{r\alpha} = \tan \alpha_o \tan \lambda_s$$

$$k_\alpha = k_r - k_{r\alpha}$$

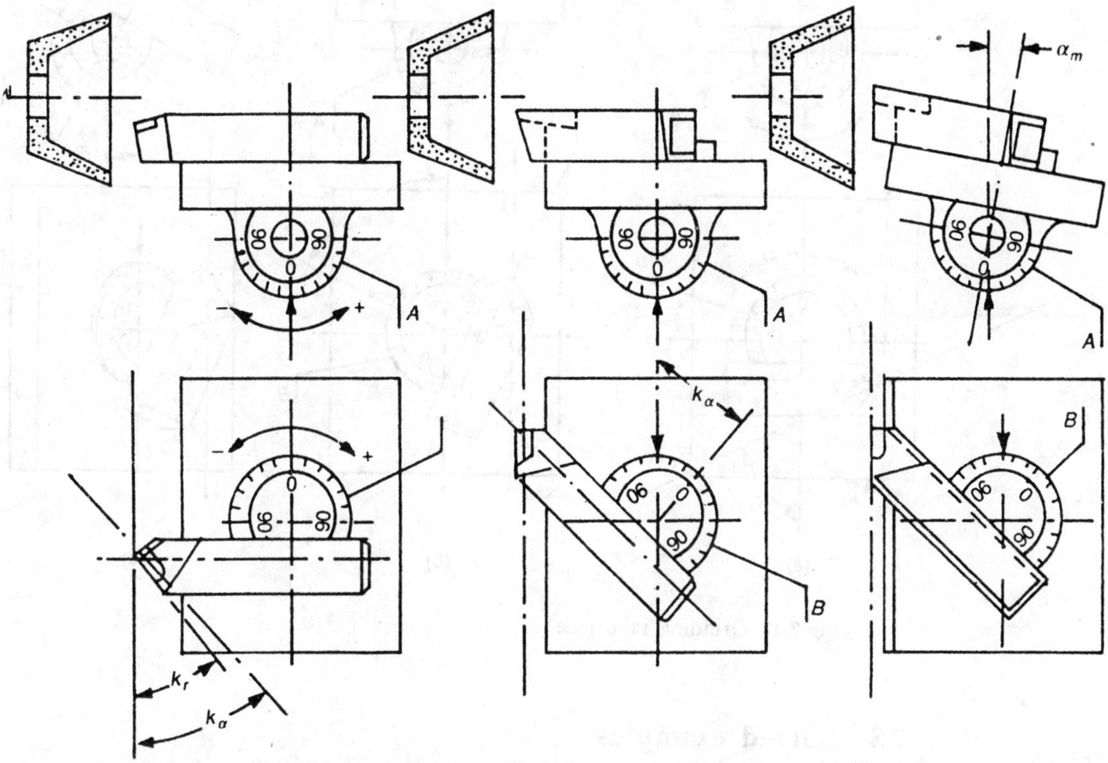


**Fig.2.12** Grinding principal flank or clearance face

## Grinding rake face

The tool is set as shown in Fig.2.13. First, the tool is rotated in a horizontal plane by an angle $k_\gamma$. The amount of tilt is $\gamma_m$. The following equations are used to compute $k_\gamma$ and $\gamma_m$.

$$\tan \gamma_m = \sqrt{\tan^2 \gamma_o + \tan^2 \lambda_s}$$

$$\tan k_{r\gamma} = \frac{\tan \lambda_s}{\tan \gamma_o}$$

$$k_\gamma = k_r - k_{r\gamma}$$

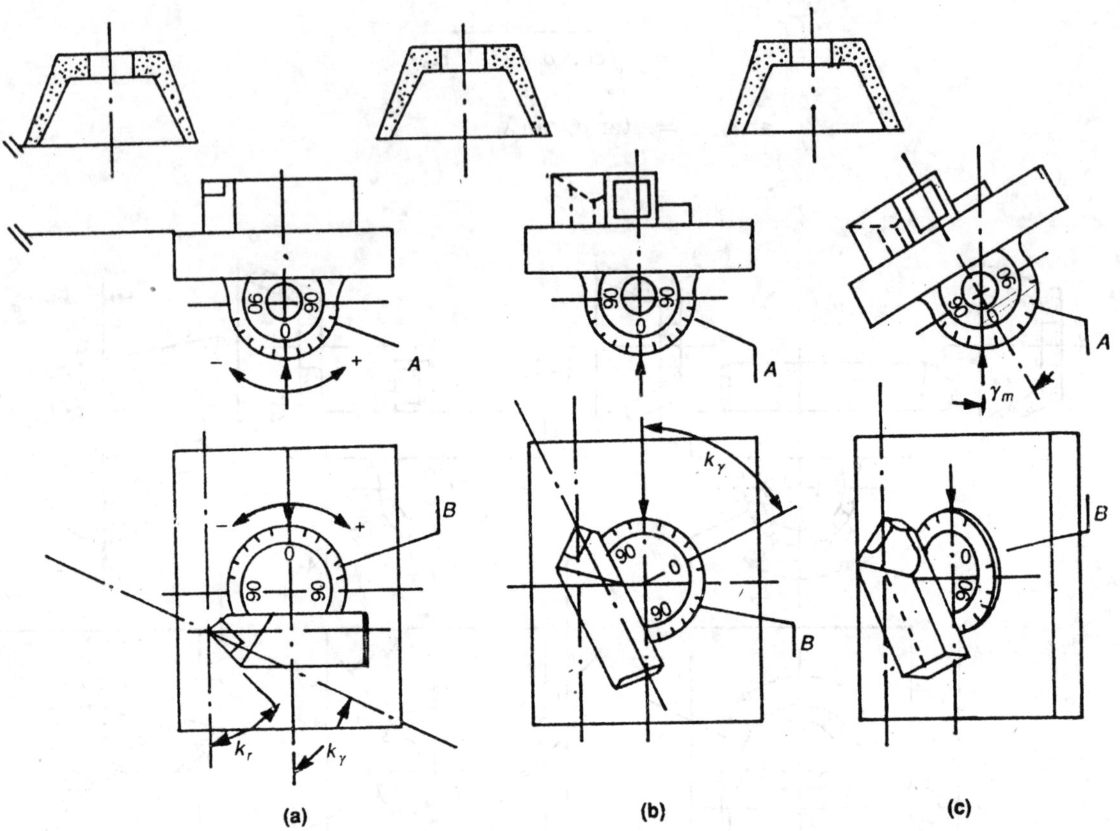


Fig.2.13 Grinding rake face

## 2.8 Solved examples

### *Example 2.1*

During machining of C-40 steel, a double carbide cutting tool of 0° – 10° – 6° – 6° – 8° – 75° – 1mm ORS geometry was used. Calculate back rake, side rake, front and side clearances. Sketch the tool in ORS and ASA geometries, and also the normal rake and normal clearance.

***Solution***

Given,

$$\lambda_s = 0°, \ \gamma_o = 10°, \ k_r = 75°, \ \alpha_o = 6°, \ \psi = 90° - 75° = 15°$$

**Back rake $\gamma_p$**

$$\tan\gamma_p = \tan\lambda_s\cos\psi + \tan\gamma_o\sin\psi$$

$$= \tan 0^\circ\cos 15^\circ + \tan 10^\circ\sin 15^\circ$$

$$= 0 + (0.1763)(0.2588) = 0.0456$$

$$\gamma_p = 2^\circ 36'$$

**Side rake $\gamma_f$**

$$\tan\gamma_f = \tan\gamma_o\cos\psi - \tan\lambda_s\sin\psi$$

$$= \tan 10^\circ\cos 15^\circ - \tan 0^\circ\sin 15^\circ$$

$$= (0.1763)(0.9659) - (0.0)(0.2588) = 0.1703$$

$$\gamma_f = 9^\circ 36'$$

**Front clearance $\alpha_p$**

$$\cot\alpha_p = \cos k_r\cot\alpha_o + \sin k_r\tan\lambda_s$$

$$= \cos 75^\circ\cot 6^\circ + \sin 75^\circ\tan 0^\circ$$

$$= (0.2588)(9.514) + 0 = 2.4622$$

$$\alpha_p = 22^\circ 6'$$

**Side clearance $\alpha_f$**

$$\cot\alpha_f = \sin k_r\cot\alpha_o - \cos k_r\tan\lambda_s$$

$$= \sin 75^\circ\cot 6^\circ - \cos 75^\circ\tan 0^\circ$$

$$= (0.9659)(9.514) - 0 = 9.1896$$

$$\alpha_f = 5^\circ 15'$$

**ORS geometry**

$$0^\circ - 10^\circ - 6^\circ - 6^\circ - 8^\circ - 75^\circ - 1\text{ mm}$$

$$\lambda_s - \gamma_o - \alpha_o - \alpha_o' - k_r' - k_r - r \qquad \text{(ORS)}$$

Figure 2.14(a) shows the tool, in ORS geometry.

**ASA geometry**

$$\gamma_p - \gamma_f - \alpha_p - \alpha_f - k_r' - \psi - r \qquad \text{(ASA)}$$

$$2°36' - 9°36' - 22°6' - 5°15' - 8° - 15° - 1 \text{ mm} \qquad \text{(ASA)}$$

Figure 2.14(b) gives the sketch of the tool in ASA geometry.

**Normal rake $\gamma_n$**

$$\tan\gamma_n = \tan\gamma_o \cos\lambda_s$$

$$= \tan 10° \cos 0° = 0.1763 \times 1 = 0.1763$$

or $\gamma_n = \gamma_o = 10°$

*Note*: $\lambda_s = 0°$, i.e. orthogonal cutting.

**Normal clearance $\alpha_n$**

$$\tan\alpha_n = \frac{\tan\alpha_o}{\cos\lambda_s} = \frac{\tan 6°}{\cos 0°} = \tan 6°$$

$\alpha_n = \alpha_o = 6°$, since $\lambda_s = 0$, i.e. orthogonal cutting.

The sketches for the normal rake and normal clearance are given in Fig.2.14(c).

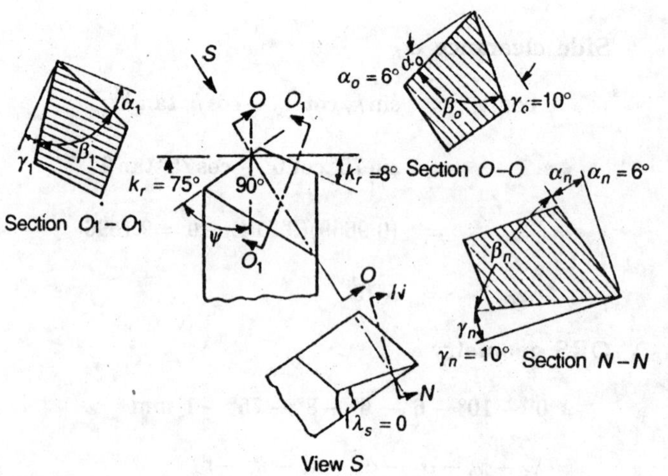


Fig.2.14(a) Orthogonal rake system (ORS) and normal rake system (NRS) geometry

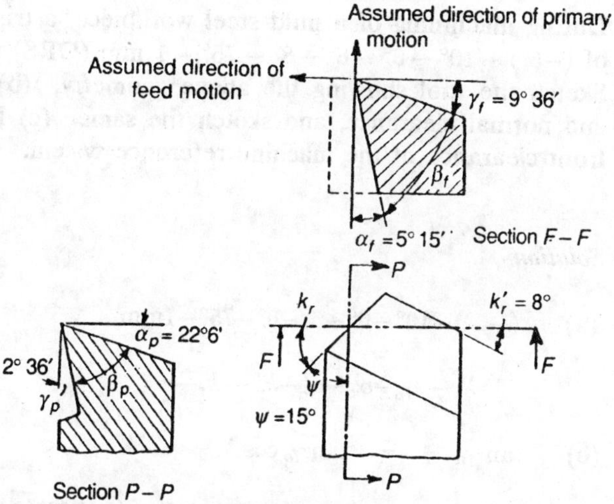


**Fig.2.14(b)** Machine reference system

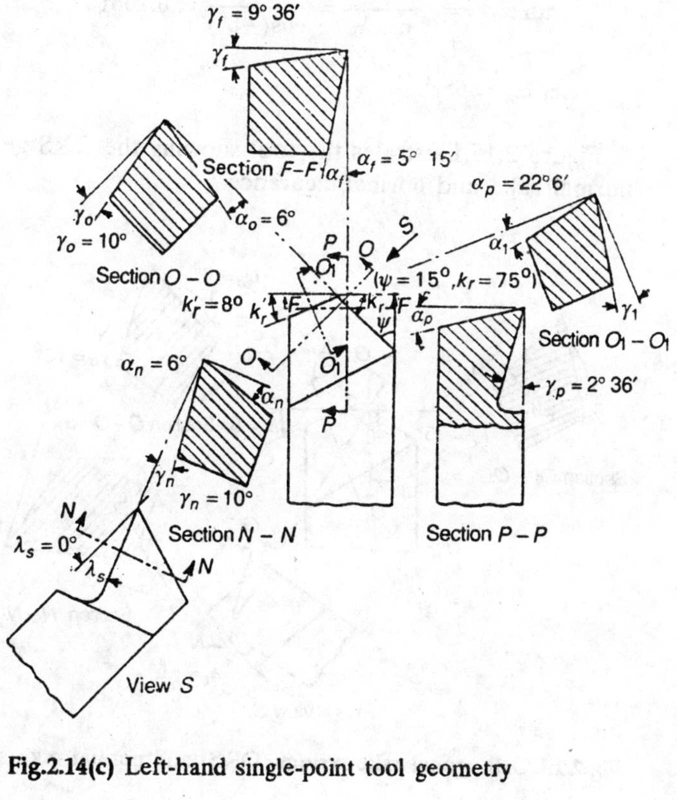


**Fig.2.14(c)** Left-hand single-point tool geometry

*Example 2.2*

During machining of a mild steel workpiece, a triple carbide turning tool of (−5°) − 10° − 6° − 6° − 8° − 75° − 1 mm (ORS) geometry was used. (a) Sketch the tool showing the above geometry. (b) Find the normal rake and normal clearance, and sketch the same. (c) Find the back rake and front clearance of the machine reference system.

***Solution***

(a) (−5°)−10° −6° −6°−0°−75°−1mm (ORS)

$\lambda_s - \gamma_o - \alpha_o - \alpha'_o - k'_r - k_r - r$ (ORS)

(b)
$$\tan\gamma_n = \tan\gamma_o \cos\lambda_s$$

$$= \tan 10° \cos(-5°) = (0.1763)(0.9962) = 0.1756$$

or, $\gamma_n = 9°57'$

$$\tan\alpha_n = \frac{\tan\alpha_o}{\cos\lambda_s} = \frac{\tan 6°}{\cos(-5°)} = 0.1051$$

or, $\alpha_n = 6°2'$.

Figure 2.15 illustrates the tool showing the ORS geometry, and also the normal rake and normal clearance.

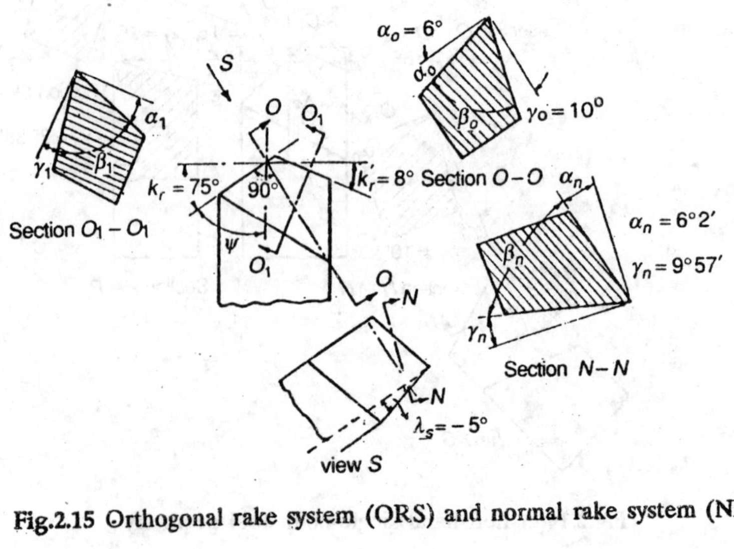


Fig.2.15 Orthogonal rake system (ORS) and normal rake system (NRS) geometry

(c) $\lambda_s = -5°, \gamma_o = 10°$

$\alpha_o = \alpha'_o = 6°, k_r = 75°$

or

$\psi = 90° - 75° = 15°.$

**Back rake $\gamma_p$**

$$\begin{aligned}\tan\gamma_p &= \tan\lambda_s\cos\psi + \tan\gamma_o\sin\psi \\ &= \tan(-5°)\cos 15° + \tan 10°\sin 15° \\ &= (-0.0875)(0.9659) + (0.1763)(0.2588) \\ &= -0.0388\end{aligned}$$

$$\text{or,}\qquad \gamma_p = -2°12'.$$

**Front clearance $\alpha_p$**

$$\begin{aligned}\cot\alpha_p &= \cos k_r\cot\alpha_o + \sin k_r\tan\lambda_s \\ &= \cos 75°\cot 6° + \sin 75°\tan(-5°) \\ &= (0.2588)(9.514) + (0.9659)(-0.0875) \\ &= 2.3777\end{aligned}$$

$$\text{or,}\qquad \alpha_p = 22°54'.$$

*Example 2.3*

(a) Sketch a single-point turning tool of specification 10° – 8° – 6° – 10° – 15° – 45° – 1 mm (ORS). (b) For the same tool indicated above, determine the normal rake and normal clearance and sketch them. (c) Calculate the effective rake.

*Solution*

(a) $10° - 8° - 6° - 10° - 15° - 45° - 1\text{mm}$ (ORS)

$\lambda_s - \gamma_o - \alpha_o - \alpha'_o - k'_r - k_r - r$ (ORS)

**(b) Normal rake $\gamma_n$**

$$\tan\gamma_n = \tan\gamma_o \cos\lambda_s = \tan 8^\circ \cos 10^\circ$$

$$= (0.1405)(0.9348) = 0.1313$$

or, $\gamma_n = 7^\circ 30'$.

**Normal clearance $\alpha_n$**

$$\tan\alpha_n = \frac{\tan\alpha_o}{\cos\lambda_s} = \frac{\tan 6^\circ}{\cos 10^\circ} = \frac{0.1055}{0.9348} = 0.1124$$

or, $\alpha_n = 6^\circ 24'$.

The ORS tool geometry, along with the normal rake and normal clearance are shown in Fig.2.16.

**Effective rake $\gamma_e$**

$$\sin\gamma_e = \cos\lambda_s \cos\rho_r \sin\gamma_n + \sin\lambda_s \sin\rho_r,$$

where $\rho_r$ = chip deviation angle. Assuming unrestricted cutting, $\rho_r = \lambda_s$

$$\sin\gamma_e = \cos^2\lambda_s \sin\gamma_n + \sin^2\lambda_s = \cos^2 10^\circ \sin 7^\circ 30' + \sin^2 10^\circ$$

$$= (0.9348)^2(0.1317) + (0.1763)^2$$

or, $\gamma_e = 8^\circ 24'$.

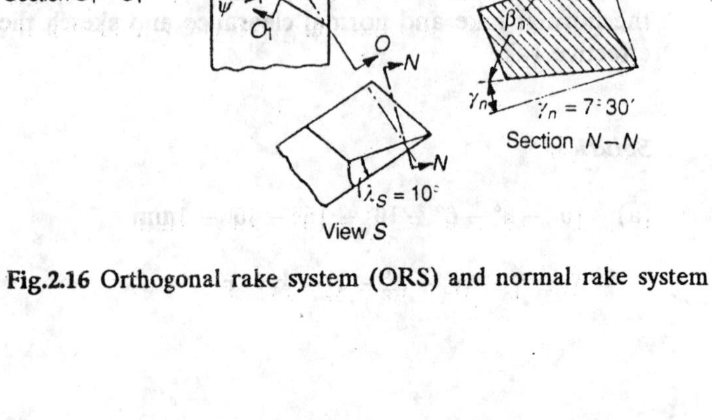


**Fig.2.16** Orthogonal rake system (ORS) and normal rake system (NRS) geometry

*Example 2.4*

A conventional turning tool designated by $8° - 14° - 6° - 6° - 8° - 15° - 1.2$mm (MRS), has to be ground in a swivelling table-type grinder. (a) Sketch the MRS geometry. (b) Calculate the swivelling angles for grinding the clearance and rake surfaces.

*Solution*

$8° - 14° - 6° - 6° - 8° - 15° - 1.2$ mm (ASA)/(MRS)

$\gamma_p - \gamma_f - \alpha_p - \alpha_f - k_r' - \psi - r$ (ASA)/(MRS)

Figure 2.17(a) gives the MRS tool geometry.

Now $\gamma_p = 8°$, $\gamma_f = 14°$, $\psi = 15°$.

First to find $\gamma_o$ and $\lambda_s$, we have

$$\begin{aligned}
\tan\gamma_o &= \tan\gamma_p \sin\psi + \tan\gamma_f \cos\psi \\
&= \tan 8° \sin 15° + \tan 14° \cos 15° \\
&= (0.1405)(0.2588) + (0.2493)(0.9659) \\
&= 0.0364 + 0.2408 \\
&= 0.2772
\end{aligned}$$

or,

$$\gamma_o = 15°30'$$

and
$$\begin{aligned}
\tan\lambda_s &= \tan\gamma_p \cos\psi - \tan\gamma_f \sin\psi \\
&= \tan 8° \cos 15° - \tan 14° \sin 15° \\
&= (0.1405)(0.9659) - (0.2493)(0.2588) \\
&= 0.1357 - 0.0645 = 0.0712
\end{aligned}$$

or, $\lambda_s = 4°6'$.

Assume grinding is to be done on a 2-dimensionally swivelled work table.

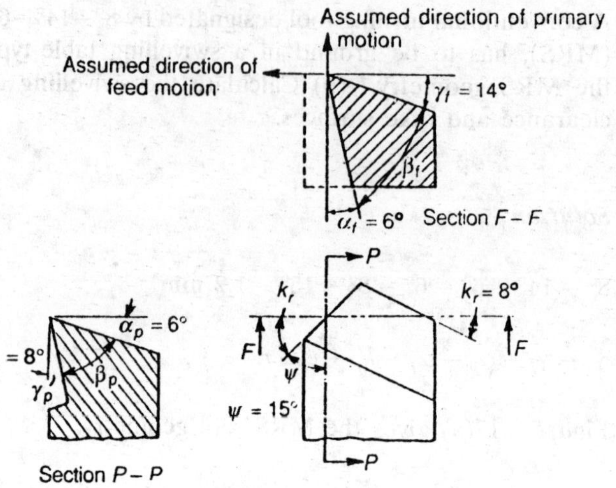


Fig.2.17(a) Machine reference system or ASA system

**For grinding clearance surface**

Given,

$$\alpha_p = 6°, \alpha_f = 6°$$

Let $\alpha_m$ = angle of tilt, $k_\alpha$ or $\pi_\alpha$ = swivelling angle

$$\cot \alpha_m = \sqrt{\cot^2 \alpha_o + \tan^2 \lambda_s}$$

$$= \sqrt{\cot^2 \alpha_f + \cot^2 \alpha_p}$$

$$= \sqrt{\cot^2 6° + \cot^2 6°}$$

$$= \sqrt{2 \times 9.9514^2}$$

$$= 13.455$$

$$\alpha_m = 4°15'$$

$$k_\alpha = k_r - k_{r\alpha}$$

$$\text{where} \quad \tan k_\alpha = \tan \alpha_o \tan \lambda_s$$

$$k_r = 90° - \psi = 90° - 15° = 75°$$

We know, $\cot^2 \alpha_m = \cot^2 \alpha_f + \cot^2 \alpha_p$ or $\cot^2 \alpha_o + \tan^2 \lambda_s$

i.e. $13.455^2 = \cot^2 \alpha_o + \tan^2 4°6'$

or $\cot^2 \alpha_o = 13.455^2 - \tan^2 4°6'$

$= 181.03$

or $\cot \alpha_o = 13.455$,

$\therefore \alpha_o = 4.250 = 4°15'$.

Now

$$\tan k_{r\alpha} = \tan \alpha_o \tan \lambda_s$$

$$= \tan 4°15' \tan 4°6'$$

$$= (0.0740)(0.0712) = 0.0053$$

or, $k_{r\alpha} = 0°18'$

$k_\alpha = k_r - k_{r\alpha} = 75° - 0°18'$

$\therefore$ Swivelling angle $= k_\alpha = 74°62'$ (see Fig.2.17(b)).

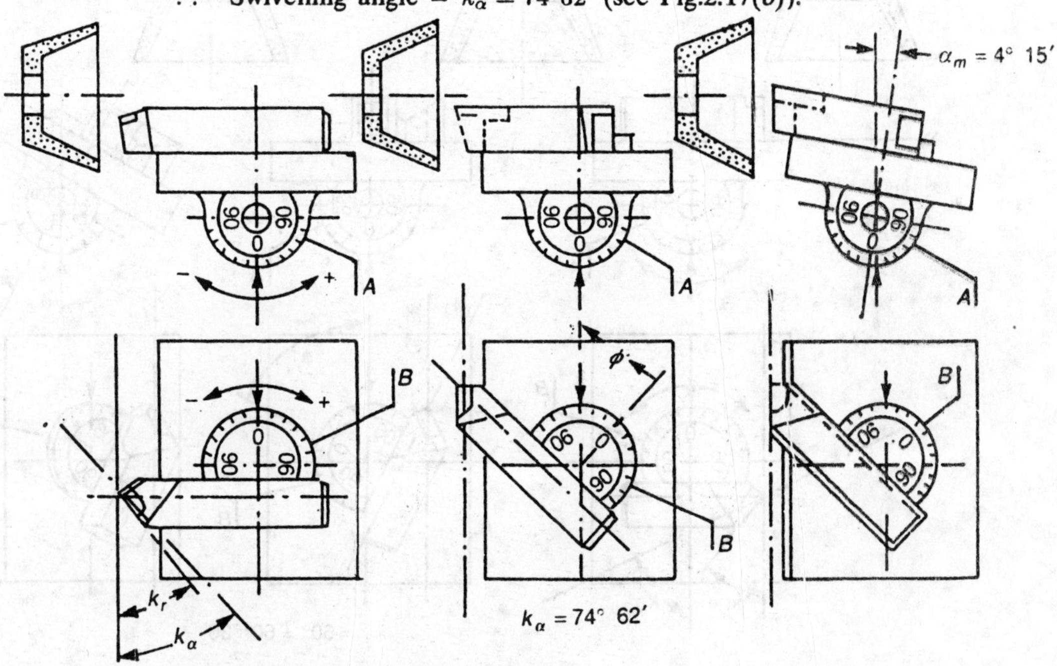


**Fig.2.17(b)** Grinding clearance angles

**For grinding rake surface**

Let, $\gamma_m$ = angle of tilt; $k_\gamma$ or $\phi_\gamma$ = swivelling angle.

$$\tan\gamma_m = \sqrt{\tan^2\gamma_o + \tan^2\lambda_s} = \sqrt{\tan^2 15°30' + \tan^2 4°6'}$$

$$= \sqrt{0.2772^2 + 0.0712^2} = 0.0819$$

or, $\gamma_m = 4°42'$.

Now

$$k_\gamma = k_r - k_{r\gamma}$$

where

$$\tan k_{r\gamma} = (\tan\lambda_s / \tan\gamma_o) = (\tan 4°6' / \tan 15°30')$$

$$= (0.0712/0.2772) = 0.2568, k_{r\gamma} = 14°24'$$

Therefore, swivelling angle $k_\gamma = k_r - k_{r\gamma} = 75° - 14°24' = 60°36'$.

Figure 2.17(c) gives the swivelling angle for grinding the rake surface.

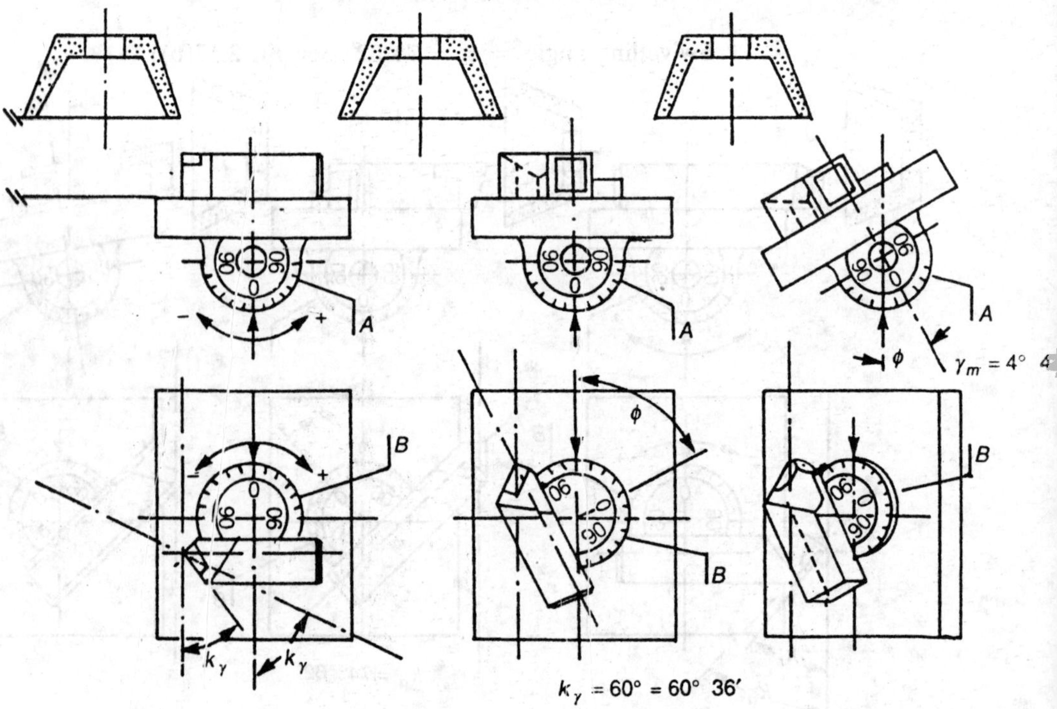


Fig.2.17(c) Grinding rake angle

## 2.9 Exercise problems

2.1 A single-point turning tool to be used for orthogonal cutting has a back rake of 8°, principal cutting edge angle of 75°, auxiliary cutting edge angle of 8°, orthogonal clearance of 6°, auxiliary orthogonal clearance of 6° and nose radius 1 mm. (a) Find the complete tool nomenclature in the ORS system and sketch the geometry. Also calculate normal rake and normal clearance. (b) Sketch the MRS geometry rakes. (c) Compute the setting angles for grinding the rake surface.

2.2 In an orthogonal cutting operation, the orthogonal rake is 10° while the principal cutting edge angle is 60°. (a) Calculate back rake and side rake. (b) If the principal cutting edge angle is made 90°, what will the back and side rakes be?

2.3 Calculate (a) orthogonal rake, (b) inclination angle and (c) normal rake of a cutting tool having side rake of (−10°), back rake of (−5°) and side cutting edge angle of 30°. Sketch the above geometries for the tool.

2.4 Calculate (a) back rake, (b) side rake and (c) normal rake for a cutting tool having an inclination angle of 5° and an orthogonal rake of 12° with a side cutting edge of 15°. Sketch the above geometries for the tool.

2.5 A cutting tool has been ground with a back rake of 8° and side rake of 14°. How much is the orthogonal rake? How much is the inclination angle? Assume principal cutting edge angle as 75°.

2.6 A metal-cutting test result indicates that for a given operation, the optimum normal rake should be 10°. For convenience of chip flow, an inclination angle of 5° is recommended. What is the back rake and side rake of this tool, if the principal cutting edge angle is 60°?

# 3 Chip formation mechanism

## 3.1 Introduction

**In metal cutting operations, chips are formed due to shear deformation. A distinct shear plane is generally assumed for analytical purposes and the assumption is fairly justified in most practical situations. The geometry of chip formation is shown in Fig.3.1.**

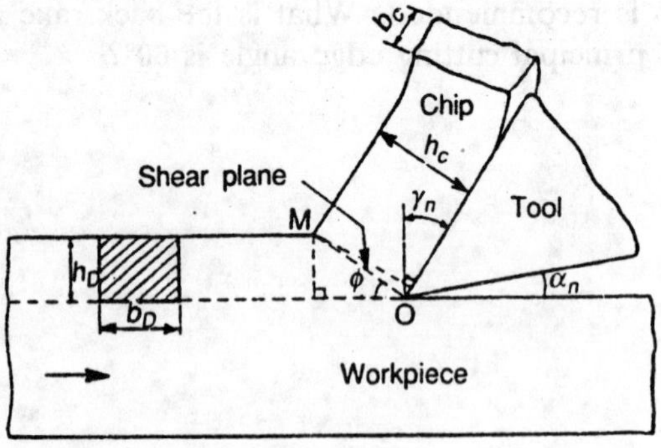


**Fig.3.1 Chip formation**

**Let, $\phi$ = shear angle, degrees**

**$h_c$ = thickness of chip, mm**

$b_c$ = width of chip, mm

$l_c$ = length of chip, mm

$h_D$ = nominal thickness of uncut layer of cut, mm

$b_D$ = nominal width of uncut layer of cut, mm

$l_D$ = nominal length of uncut layer of cut, mm

$f$ = feed in turning, mm/rev

$b$ = depth of cut in turning, mm

$k_r$ = principal or major cutting edge angle

$\gamma_n$ = normal rake

$\Lambda_h$ = chip-reduction coefficient or chip thickness compression ratio

$\Lambda_l$ = chip compression ratio based on length measurement

$\Lambda_b$ = chip compression ratio based on width measurement

$\Lambda_A$ = chip compression ratio based on area measurement

$r_c$ = cutting ratio

$\Lambda_h = 1/r_c$

*Note*: $\Lambda_h$ is an index of the extent of deformation during chip formation, with an increase in thickness of cut layer and a decrease in length. Hence $\Lambda_h$ is always greater than unity.

## 3.2 Orthogonal cutting

Since $\lambda_s = 0, \gamma_n = \gamma_o$

$$\Lambda_h = h_c/h_D$$

From the geometry of Fig.3.1,

$$h_D/OM = \sin\phi \text{ and } h_c/OM = \cos(\phi - \gamma_o)$$

Therefore

$$h_c/h_D = \Lambda_h = \cos(\phi - \gamma_o)/\sin\phi$$

Rearranging,

$$\tan\phi = \cos\gamma_o/(\Lambda_h - \sin\gamma_o)$$

Shear angle can be calculated from the above equation.

The chip compression ratio can also be calculated based on chip length measurements:

$$\Lambda_l = l_D/l_c$$

For the same volume removal

$$\Lambda_l = h_c b_c/h_D b_D = A_c/A_r = \Lambda_A$$

where $A_c$ = area of cross-section of chip, ($mm^2$), $A_r$ = area of uncut layer to be removed, ($mm^2$). If no side flow of chips is assumed,

$$b_c = b_D$$

Then

$$\Lambda_l = \Lambda_A = \Lambda_h$$

If there is side flow,

$$\Lambda_l = h_c b_c/h_D b_D = \Lambda_h \Lambda_b$$

with $\Lambda_h \neq \Lambda_b$

*Calculation of h for turning process* The uncut layer thickness in turning is given by (refer Fig.3.2)

$$h_D = f \sin k_r$$

Similarly, $h_D = b/\sin\phi$. Hence for orthogonal turning,

$$\Lambda_h = h_c/(f \sin\phi)$$

*Note*: 'Restricted cutting' in the present discussion indicates that both the major cutting edge and the auxiliary or minor cutting edge are effective, especially when the minor cutting edge angle $k_r'$ is small. This contributes to deviation of chip flow from the normal plane. If $k_r'$ is sufficiently large, the deviation is almost zero and the situation approximates to unrestricted cutting.

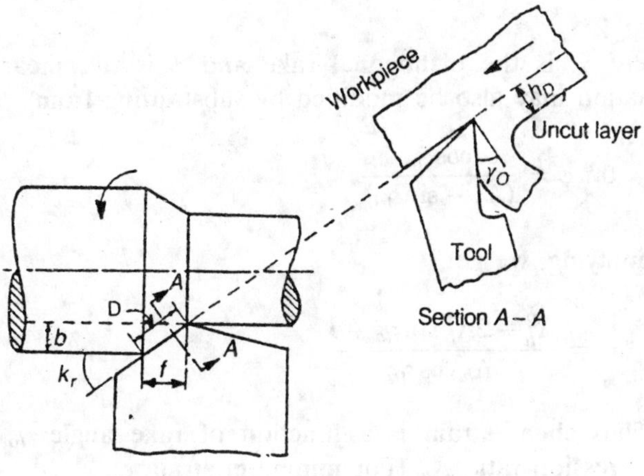


**Fig.3.2** Restricted orthogonal turning

When $k_r$ and $k_r'$ are both effective, the chip deviation angle $\rho_r$ due to the restriction effect is given by

$$\tan \rho_r = \frac{\sin(k_r + k_r')}{(2b/f \sin k_r) + \cos(k_r + k_r')}$$

**Dynamic shearing strain $\epsilon_s$**
Figure 3.3 gives an illustration of shearing process.

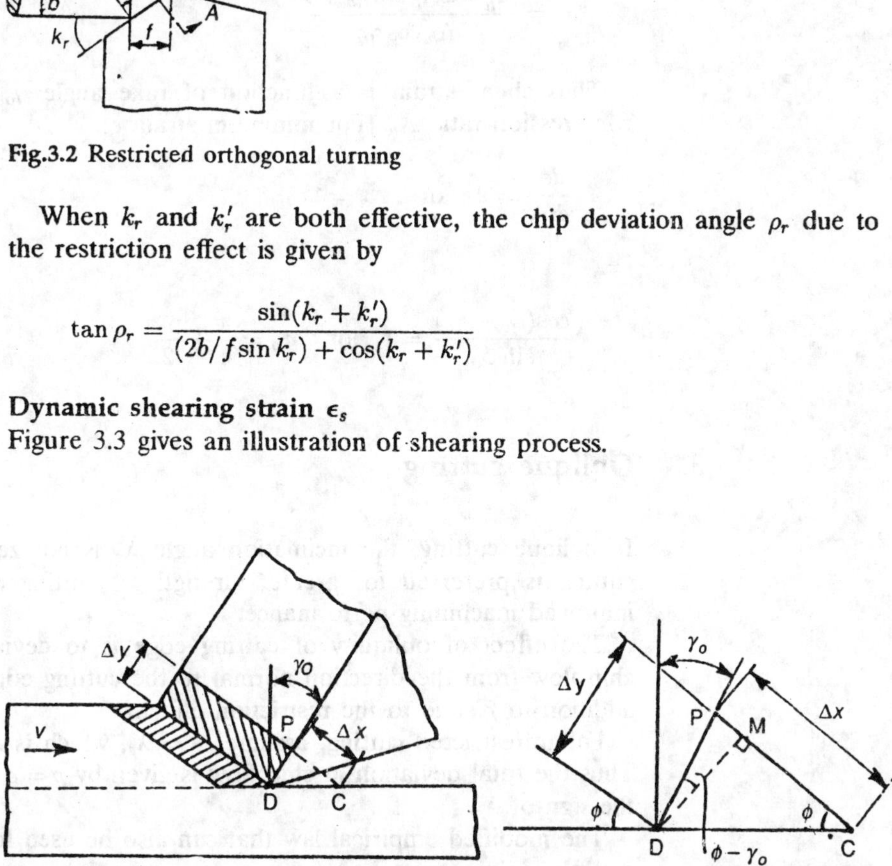


**Fig.3.3** Shearing process

From Fig.3.3, we have

$$\epsilon_s = \frac{\Delta x}{\Delta y} = \frac{CP}{DM} = \frac{CM}{DM} + \frac{MP}{DM}$$

or,

$$\epsilon_s = \cot \phi + \tan(\phi - \gamma_o)$$

where $\gamma_o$ is the orthogonal rake and $\phi$ is the shear angle. The above equation may also be modified by substituting from

$$\tan\phi = \frac{\cos\gamma_o}{(\Lambda_h - \sin\gamma_o)}$$

Simplifying, we get

$$\epsilon_s = \frac{\Lambda_h^2 - 2\Lambda_h \sin\gamma_o + 1}{\Lambda_h \cos\gamma_o}$$

Thus shear strain is a function of rake angle $\gamma_o$ and chip thickness compression ratio $\Lambda_h$. For minimum strain $\epsilon_s$,

$$\frac{d\epsilon_s}{d\Lambda_h} = 0 \quad \text{or} \quad \Lambda_h = 1$$

i.e.

$$\frac{\cos(\phi_o - \gamma_o)}{\sin\phi_o} = 1 \quad \text{or} \quad \phi_o = \frac{\pi}{4} + \frac{\gamma_o}{2}.$$

## 3.3 Oblique cutting

In oblique cutting, the inclination angle $\lambda_s$ is not zero. Often, oblique cutting is preferred for greater strength of cutting edge as well as for improved machining performance.

The effect of obliquity of cutting edge is to deviate the direction of chip flow from the direction normal to the cutting edge by an angle $\rho_o$ in addition to $\rho_r$ due to the restriction effect.

For unrestricted cutting, assume $\rho_0 = \lambda_s$, which is called *Stabler's Law*. Thus the total deviation in chip flow is given by $\rho = \rho_r \pm \lambda_s$, depending on the sign of $\lambda_s$.

The modified empirical law that can also be used for restricted oblique cutting is given by

$$\rho = m\lambda_s.$$

where the factor $m$ lies between 0.8 and 0.9.

**Effect on chip reduction coefficient or chip compression ratio**

Let $\Lambda_h$ = normal chip reduction coefficient or normal chip compression ratio. For oblique cutting,

$$\Lambda_h = \cos\lambda_s / \cos\rho$$

If $\Lambda_A$ is determined from experiments, $\Lambda_h$ can be calculated. For unrestricted free cutting, i.e., if $\rho = \lambda_s$, $\Lambda_h = \Lambda_A$. If $\gamma_n$ = normal rake angle, and $\phi_n$ = normal shear angle, then

$$\tan \phi_n = \cos \gamma_n / (\Lambda_h - \sin \gamma_n)$$

From the above equation shear angle $\phi_n$ can be calculated.

## 3.4 Solved examples

*Example 3.1*

During orthogonal turning of mild steel at a feed of 0.25 mm/rev. and cutting speed of 25 m/min, it was observed that the average thickness of chip was 0.5 mm. Determine the chip reduction coefficient, shear angle and shear strain along the shear plane.

The tool had the following geometry:

| | | |
|---|---|---|
| inclination angle | = | 0° |
| orthogonal rake | = | 10° |
| principal cutting edge angle | = | 75° |
| auxiliary cutting edge angle | = | 8° |
| orthogonal clearance | = | 6° |
| nose radius | = | 1 mm |

Also sketch the tool geometry.

*Solution*

Given that

$$\lambda_s = 0° \quad \gamma_o = 10° \quad k_r = 75° \quad f = 0.25 \text{ mm/rev}, \ h_c = 0.5 \text{ mm},$$

$$h_D = f \sin k_r = (0.25) \sin 75° = (0.25)(0.9659)$$

$$= 0.2415$$

**(a) Chip reduction coefficient or chip thickness compression ratio, $\Lambda_h$**

$$\Lambda_h = (h_c/h_D) = 0.5/0.2415 = 2.07$$

**(b) Shear angle, $\phi$**

$$\tan \phi = \frac{\cos 10°}{2.07 - \sin 10°} = 0.5193$$

or, $\phi = 27°27'$

**(c) Shear strain, $\epsilon_s$**

$$\epsilon_s = \cot\phi + \tan(\phi - \gamma_o)$$

$$= \cot 27°27' + \tan(27°27' - 10°)$$

$$= 1.9251 + 0.3112 = 2.2363$$

or, $\epsilon_s = 2.2363$

**(d) ORS geometry**

Assume $\alpha_o' = 6°$.

$$\lambda_s - \gamma_o - \alpha_o - \alpha_o' - k_r' - k_r - r \text{ (ORS)}$$

$$0° - 10° - 6° - 6° - 8° - 75° - 1 \text{ mm (ORS)}$$

Figure 3.4 gives the sketch of tool geometry.

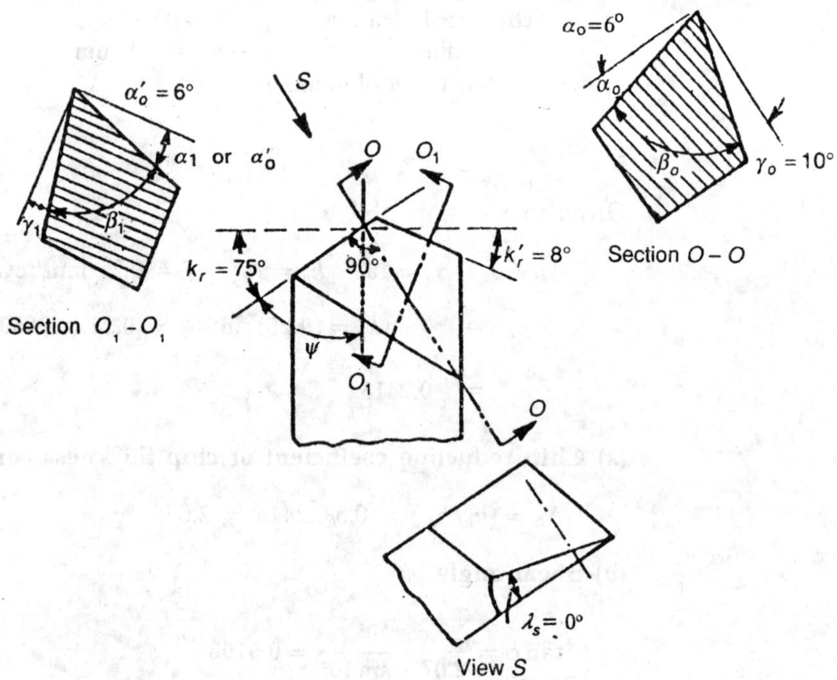


**Fig.3.4** Orthogonal rake system (ORS) geometry

*Example 3.2*

During machining of carbon steel having carbon 0.2%, with a triple carbide cutting tool of 0° – 10° – 6° – 6° – 8° – 75° – 1 mm, ORS shape using a feed of 0.2 mm/rev. and a depth of cut of 2 mm at a cutting speed of 140 m/min, a chip thickness of 0.36 mm has been obtained. Calculate (a) the chip reduction coefficient or chip thickness compression ratio, and (b) the shear angle. Sketch the tool showing ORS geometries.

***Solution***

Given:

$$\lambda_s = 0^\circ$$

$$\gamma_o = 10^\circ$$

$$k_r = 75^\circ$$

$$\text{Feed } f = 0.2 \text{ mm/rev.,}$$

Chip thickness $h_c = 0.36$mm.

Nominal thickness of cut, or the depth of uncut layer

$$\begin{aligned} h_D &= f \sin k_r \\ &= 0.2 \sin 75^\circ = (0.2)\ (0.9659) \\ &= 0.1932 \text{ mm.} \end{aligned}$$

**(a) Chip thickness compression ratio $\Lambda_h$**

$$\Lambda_h = h_c/h_D = 0.36/0.1932$$

or,

$$\Lambda_h = 1.8633$$

**(b) Shear angle $\phi$**

$$\tan \phi = \frac{\cos 10^\circ}{1.8633 - \sin 10^\circ} = 0.5828$$

or, $\phi = 30^\circ 14'$

## ORS geometry

$$0° - 10° - 6° - 6° - 8° - 75° - 1\text{mm} \quad \text{(ORS)}$$

$$\lambda_s - \gamma_o - \alpha_o - \alpha_o' - k_r' - k_r - r \quad \text{(ORS)}$$

Figure 3.5 illustrates the ORS geometry of the tool.

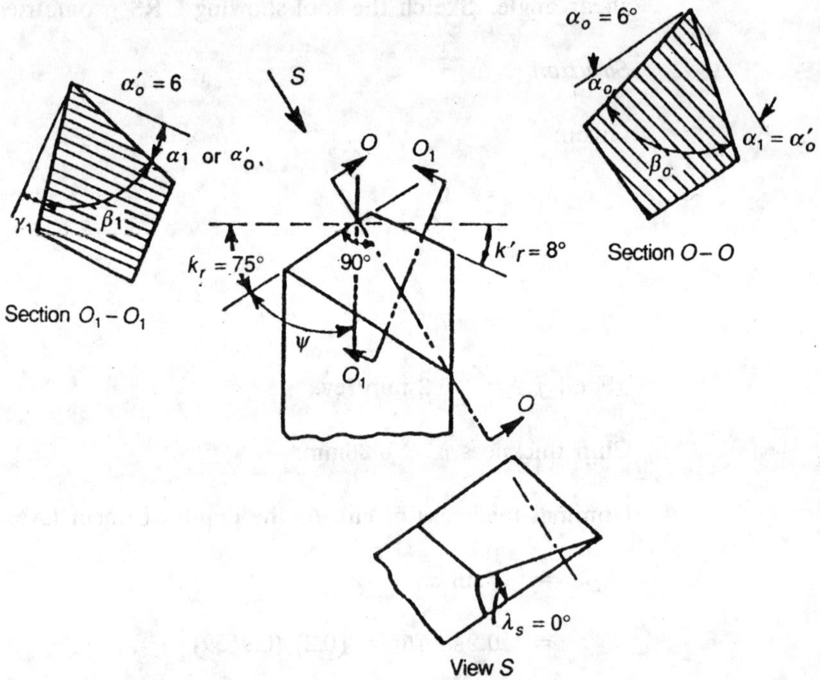


Fig.3.5 Orthogonal rake system (ORS) geometry

### *Example 3.3*

While machining C-20 steel with a P-10 carbide tool at a cutting speed of 200 m/min, under conditions of orthogonal cutting with orthogonal rake of +10°, principal cutting edge angle of 90° and a feed of 0.2 mm/rev., a chip thickness of 0.38 mm has been observed. Calculate (a) shear angle and (b) dynamic shear strain. What will be the effect if rake angle is changed to 20°, other parameters remaining same?

### *Solution*

Given that

$$\gamma_o = 10°$$

$k_r = 90°$

$f = 0.2$mm/rev.

$h_c = 0.38$mm

$h_D = f \sin k_r = 0.2 \sin 90° = 0.2$mm

$\Lambda_h = (h_c/h_D) = (0.38/0.2) = 1.9$

**(a) Shear angle $\phi$**

$$\tan\phi = \frac{\cos\gamma_o}{\Lambda_h - \sin\gamma_o}$$

$$= \frac{\cos 10°}{1.9 - \sin 10°} = \frac{0.9848}{1.9 - 0.1736}$$

$$= 0.5704$$

$$\text{or } \phi = 29°42'$$

**(b) Dynamic shear strain $\epsilon_s$**

$$\epsilon_s = \cot\phi + \tan(\phi - \gamma_o)$$

$$= \cot 29°42' + \tan(29°42' - 10°)$$

$$= 1.7532 + 0.3581 = 2.1113$$

$$\text{or } \epsilon_s = 2.1$$

**$\phi$ and $\epsilon_s$ when $\gamma_o = 20°$**

$$\tan\phi = \frac{\cos\gamma_o}{\Lambda_h - \sin\gamma_o} = \frac{\cos 20°}{1.9 - \sin 20°}$$

$$= 0.6031$$

$$\text{or } \phi = 31°6'.$$

$$\epsilon_s = \cot\phi + \tan(\phi - \gamma_o)$$

$$= \cot 31°6' + \tan(31°6' - 20°) = \cot 31°6' + \tan 11°6'$$

$$= 1.6577 + 0.1962 = 1.8539.$$

*Note*: When $\gamma_o$ has been changed from 10° to 20°, shear angle has increased from 29°42′ to 31°6′ and shear strain $\epsilon_s$ has decreased to 1.8539 from 2.1.

## 3.5 Exercise problems

3.1 Given feed = 0.47 mm/rev., chip thickness = 1.198 mm, tool geometry = 0° – (–10°) – 6° – 6° – 8° – 90° – 1 mm ORS, cutting speed = 200 m/min, calculate shear angle and dynamic cutting strain. If the rake angle is +10°, what would be the shear angle and dynamic cutting strain, other conditions being same ?

3.2 During machining of C-20 steel with a 0° – (–5°) – 6° – 6° – 8° – 90° – 1 mm (ORS) cemented carbide cutting tool using a feed of 0.19 mm/rev. and a depth of cut of 2 mm, a chip thickness of 0.4 mm is obtained. Calculate the shear angle and the dynamic shear strain. What will be the change, if the rake angle is +5° for the same chip thickness compression ratio ?

3.3 (a) State the physical significance of the 'chip reduction coefficient' or the 'chip thickness compression ratio' and justify that its value cannot be less than unity in any conventional machining. (b) If the obtained thickness of the chip is 0.6 mm during turning C-20 steel, at a speed of 50 m/min and feed of 0.25 mm/rev. by a turning tool of specification 0° – 0° – 10° – 10° – 15° – 60° – 0.2 mm (ORS), determine the value of the chip-reduction coefficient, shear angle and dynamic cutting strain. What will be the change, if the rake angle is increased to +20°, assuming that other conditions remain same ?

3.4 During machining of C-20 steel with a 0° – (–10°) – 6° – 6° – 8° – 60° – 1 mm (ORS) cemented carbide cutting tool, a chip thickness of 0.38 mm was observed, while the feed was 0.2 mm/rev. Determine chip-reduction coefficient, shear angle and dynamic shearing strain. Assuming that the chip thickness compression ratio remains the same, what will be the change if the rake angle is changed to 0° or +10° ?

3.5 During machining with a 8° – 14° – 6° – 6° – 8° – 15° – 1 mm (MRS) cutting tool at a feed of 0.2 mm/rev. and a depth of cut of 2 mm, a chip thickness of 0.4 mm and a chip width of 2.2 mm is observed. Calculate the normal chip-reduction coefficient and normal shear angle.

4

# Force system in orthogonal cutting

## 4.1 Introduction

The force system in the general case of the traditional turning process is illustrated in Fig.4.1.

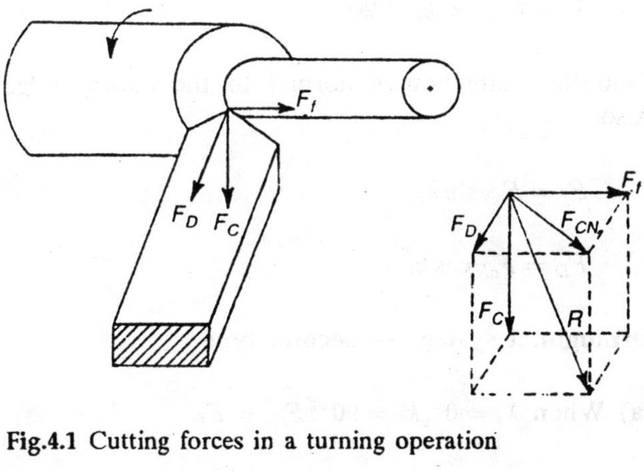


**Fig.4.1** Cutting forces in a turning operation

Let,

$F_f$ = feed or axial force,

$F_D$ = thrust or radial force.

$F_c$ = cutting or tangential force,

$F_{cN}$ = cutting normal force.

The force components, it may be noted, correspond to machine reference axes ($x$, $y$, $z$ axes) and a properly designed dynamometer can measure the forces in any experiment. The resultant force $R$ is given by

$$R = \sqrt{F_f^2 + F_D^2 + F_c^2}$$

For an orthogonal cutting system, which is a two-dimensional force system,

$$F_{cN} = \sqrt{F_f^2 + F_D^2}$$

and

$$R = \sqrt{F_c^2 + F_{cN}^2}$$

This condition is possible under two cases:

**Orthogonal system — first type**

$$\lambda_s = 0°, 0 < k_r < 90°$$

Chip flow direction is normal to the cutting edge (in the plan view). Also

$$F_f = F_{cN} \sin k_r$$

$$F_D = F_{cN} \cos k_r$$

**Orthogonal system — second type**

(a) When $\lambda_s = 0°, k_r = 90°, F_{cN} = F_f$.

(b) For radial turning or facing operation

$$\lambda_s = 0°, k_r = 0°, F_{cN} = F_D.$$

## 4.2 Merchant's circle diagram

For purpose of analysis, a simplified scheme of chip formation is often adopted with assumptions that include a perfectly sharp tool, no side flow of chips, uniform cutting velocity, continuous chip with no built-up-edge , no chip flow deviation, and collinear equal and opposite resultant forces with respect to shear plane and rake face. Let

$F_c$ = cutting or tangential force

$F_{cN}$ = cutting normal force

$F_{sh}$ = shear force along the shear plane

$F_{shN}$ = normal force on shear plane

$F_\gamma$ = friction force on rake face

$F_{\gamma N}$ = normal force on rake face.

Often these forces are represented in a circle, called Merchant's circle diagram of cutting forces as in Fig.4.2.

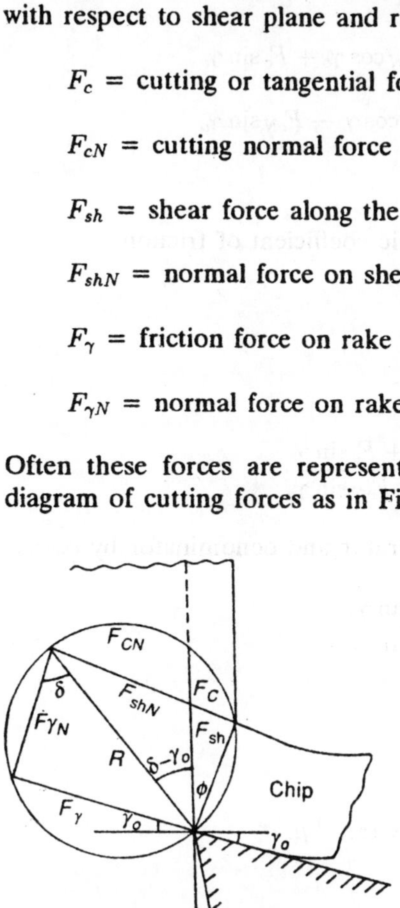


**Fig.4.2** Merchant's circle of forces

The forces $F_c$ and $F_{cN}$ can be experimentally determined. From the values of $\gamma_o$, $\phi$, $F_c$ and $F_{cN}$, the other forces are estimated.

The following relationships can be easily derived based on geometries:

**Forces on shear plane**

$$F_{sh} = F_c \cos\phi - F_{cN} \sin\phi$$

$$F_{shN} = F_c \sin\phi + F_{cN} \cos\phi$$

Also

$$F_{shN} = F_{sh} \tan(\phi + \delta - \gamma_o)$$

**Forces on rake face**

$$F_\gamma = F_{cN} \cos\gamma_o + F_c \sin\gamma_o$$

$$F_{\gamma N} = F_c \cos\gamma_o - F_{cN} \sin\gamma_o$$

Let

$\mu$ = kinetic coefficient of friction

$$\mu = \frac{F_\gamma}{F_{\gamma N}}$$

or,

$$\mu = \frac{F_{cN} \cos\gamma_o + F_c \sin\gamma_o}{F_c \cos\gamma_o - F_{cN} \sin\gamma_o}$$

Dividing both numerator and denominator by $\cos\gamma_o$, we get

$$\mu = \frac{F_{cN} + F_c \tan\gamma_o}{F_c - F_{cN} \tan\gamma_o}$$

Also

$$\mu = \tan\delta$$

or, friction angle $\delta = \tan^{-1}\mu$.

## 4.3 Velocity relations

Let

$v_c$ = cutting velocity or the velocity of tool relative to work that is parallel to the machined surface.

$v_f$ = chip velocity or velocity of chip relative to tool that is parallel to rake face.

$v_s$ = shear velocity or velocity of chip relative to workpiece that is parallel to the shear plane.

It may be noted from the vector diagram shown in Fig.4.3, that

$$\vec{v}_s = \vec{v}_c + \vec{v}_f$$

$v_s$ and $v_f$ can be expressed in terms of $v_c$ by sine rule as below:

$$\frac{v_s}{\sin[90^\circ - \gamma_o]} = \frac{v_c}{\sin[90^\circ - (\phi - \gamma_o)]} = \frac{v_f}{\sin \phi}$$

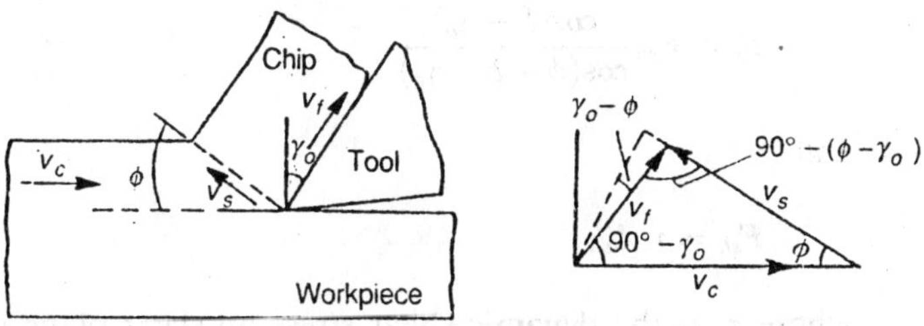


**Fig.4.3** Velocities in metal cutting

Hence,

$$v_s = v_c \frac{\sin(90^\circ - \gamma_o)}{\sin(90^\circ - \phi + \gamma_o)}$$

or

$$v_s = v_c \frac{\cos \gamma_o}{\cos(\phi - \gamma_o)}$$

and

$$v_f = v_c \frac{\sin \phi}{\sin(90^\circ - \phi + \gamma_o)}$$

or

$$v_f = v_c \frac{\sin \phi}{\cos(\phi - \gamma_o)}$$

Also

$$v_f = v_c / \Lambda_h.$$

Since $v_c$ and $\gamma_o$ are known for any machining operation, $v_s$ and $v_f$ can be estimated if shear angle $\phi$ is known.

**Stress in shear plane and cutting forces**
From Merchant's circle of forces,

$$F_c = R\cos(\delta - \gamma_o)$$

and

$$F_{sh} = R\cos(\phi + \delta - \gamma_o)$$

or

$$F_c = F_{sh}\frac{\cos(\delta - \gamma_o)}{\cos(\phi + \delta - \gamma_o)}$$

But

$$F_{sh} = \tau_s A_{sh}$$

where $\tau_s$ is the dynamic shear stress on shear plane of area $A_{sh}$. Also,

$$A_{sh} = (h_D b_D)/\sin\phi$$

Hence,

$$F_c = \tau_s h_D b_D \frac{\cos(\delta - \gamma_o)}{\sin\phi\cos(\phi + \delta - \gamma_o)}$$

Similarly,

$$F_{cN} = \tau_s h_D b_D \frac{\sin(\delta - \gamma_o)}{\sin\phi\cos(\phi + \delta - \gamma_o)}$$

It may be noted that in a turning operation,

$$h_D = f\sin k_r$$

where $f$ = feed mm/rev, $b$ = depth of cut, $k_r$ = principal cutting edge angle and $b_D = b/\sin k_r$.

Hence,

$$h_D b_D = f \cdot b$$

The term $f \cdot b$ can also be used instead of $h_D b_D$ in the above expressions for $F_c$ and $F_{cN}$.

The above expressions can be used for estimating or evaluating $F_c$ and $F_{cN}$ for a given set of cutting conditions and initial properties of work material with known $\tau_s$ ,$\phi$ and $\delta$ values, as will be discussed later.

## 4.4 Specific energies in the cutting process

Normally three types of specific energies can be analysed for the evaluation of cutting process based on forces and velocities.

**(a) Total specific energy or specific energy of cutting, $e_c$**

$$e_c = (F_c v_c)/(A_r v_c)$$

for unit volume of metal removal,

or, $e_c = F_c/A_r$,

where $A_r = h_D b_D$, i.e. area of uncut workpiece material.

**(b) Specific energy of shear, $e_s$**

$$\begin{aligned} e_s &= \frac{(F_{sh} v_s)}{(A_r v_c)} \\ &= \tau_s \frac{v_s}{v_c \sin\phi} \\ &= \tau_s \frac{\cos\gamma_o}{\sin\phi\cos(\phi-\gamma_o)} \\ &= \tau_s \epsilon_s \end{aligned}$$

**(c) Specific energy of friction, $e_f$**

$$e_f = \frac{(F_\gamma V_f)}{(A_r V_c)}$$

*Note*: For energy balance $e_c = e_s + e_f$

## 4.5 Effect of restricted cutting

As mentioned in chapter 3 on 'chip formation' mechanism, restricted cutting is present if the auxiliary cutting edge is also active when $k_r'$ is small, and the chip deviation angle $\rho_r$, due to restricted cutting, is as:

$$\tan\rho_r = \frac{\sin(k_r + k_r')}{[2b/(f\sin k_r) + \cos(k_r + k_r')]}$$

Accordingly, the equations for $F_f$ and $F_D$ are modified as below:

$$F_f = F_{cN}\sin(k_r - \rho_r)$$

and

$$F_D = F_{cN} \cos(k_r - \rho_r)$$

Since,

$$F_{cN} = F_c \tan(\delta - \gamma_o),$$

$$F_f = F_{cN} \tan(\delta - \gamma_o) \sin(k_r - \rho_r)$$

and

$$F_D = F_{cN} \tan(\delta - \gamma_o) \cos(k_r - \rho_r).$$

## 4.6 Theoretical cutting forces

Sometimes it will be necessary to estimate the cutting forces from known physical parameters of the workpiece without any dynamometer.

The tangential cutting force for orthogonal rake system is given by

$$F_c = h_D b_D \tau_s \frac{\cos(\delta - \gamma_o)}{\sin\phi \cos(\phi + \delta - \gamma_o)}$$

where

$h_D$ = thickness of uncut layer

$b_D$ = width of uncut layer

$\tau$ = dynamic shear stress

$\phi$ = shear angle

$\gamma_o$ = orthogonal rake

$\delta$ = friction angle

In the above equation, for any cutting conditions, $h_D$, $b_D$ and $\gamma_o$ are known. Assuming $\tau_s$ is estimated under cutting conditions, the chief problem is one of finding a suitable angle relationship among $\gamma_o$,$\phi$ and $\delta$.

Some of the well-recognised angle relationships are given in Table 4.1.

**Table 4.1** Angle relationships

| Author | Angle relationship |
|---|---|
| Ernst and Merchant | $2\phi + \delta - \gamma_o = (\pi/2)$ |
| Merchant's second solution | $2\phi + \delta - \gamma_o = C_m$ |
| Lee and Shaffer | $\phi + \delta - \gamma_o = (\pi/4)$ |
| Stabler | $\phi + \delta_0 - (\gamma_o/2) = (\pi/4)$ |

The constant $C_m$ in the angle relationship of Merchant's second solution of the above table is called the machining constant, which is affected by microstructure and grain size of work material and is independent of cutting conditions. Some typical values of $C_m$, as suggested by Merchant, are given in Table 4.2. It is to be noted that cold working of material will increase the machining constant.

**Table 4.2** Merchant's machining constants

| Work material (Hot-rolled steel) | $C_m$ degrees |
|---|---|
| AISI - 1010 | 69.8 |
| AISI - 1020 | 69.6 |
| AISI - 1045 | 78.0 |
| AISI - 2340 | 76.22 |
| AISI - 3140 | 70.6 |
| AISI - 4340 | 74.5 |
| Stainless steel - 303 | 92.0 |
| Stainless steel - 304 | 82.0 |

A similar equation for cutting normal force $F_{cN}$ is given below:

$$F_{cN} = h_D b_D \tau_s \left[ \frac{\sin(\delta - \gamma_o)}{\sin\phi \cos(\phi + \delta - \gamma_o)} \right]$$

The feed force $F_f$ and radial force $F_D$ may then be calculated by substituting $F_{cN}$.

## 4.7 Measurement of cutting forces: Dynamometry

The metal cutting dynamometers are measuring devices used for sensing cutting forces during machining. Generally, the constructional feature of a typical dynamometer is based on the principle that force can be measured through its action on a system offering a finite resistance, that is usually pre-calibrated, and the technique is based on the principles of transducer or sensor technology. The measurement system hence, involves (a) a transducer, (b) a signal conditioner to convert the transducer output into a measurable parameter, and (c) an indicator or recorder to register the final results. There is a wide choice for the first element, namely the type of transducer, and the later two are invariably electric and electronic devices, such as carrier-frequency amplifier, level recorders, oscillographs, oscilloscopes, tape recorders, etc.

The chief requirements of a cutting force dynamometer are as follows:

(a) The dynamometer should have sufficient mechanical rigidity to avoid excessive deformation of the cutting edge under the action of cutting forces.

(b) It should have sufficient sensitivity to enable measurement of cutting forces with sufficient accuracy.

(c) It should be of high stiffness and low mass, ensuring 100 per cent transmissibility of force by its very high natural frequency. This feature will also enable the recorded force to be unaffected by the exciting vibration due to machining process itself, e.g., milling, grinding and shaping.

(d) It should be capable of indicating individual force components without any cross effect, while measuring such forces simultaneously.

(e) The measuring system should be stable with reference to time, temperature and humidity, requiring only occasional checking after calibration.

The system consists of a two- or three-dimensional cutting force dynamometer. The type of the dynamometer to be used, is determined by the form of the transducing element, that converts mechanical deformation into electrical signals. Some of the devices that are in use are:
(a) capacitative devices,
(b) piezoelectric devices,
(c) inductance devices, and
(d) strain gauge pick-up oriented devices.
A simple mechanical tool force dynamometer is shown in Fig.4.4.

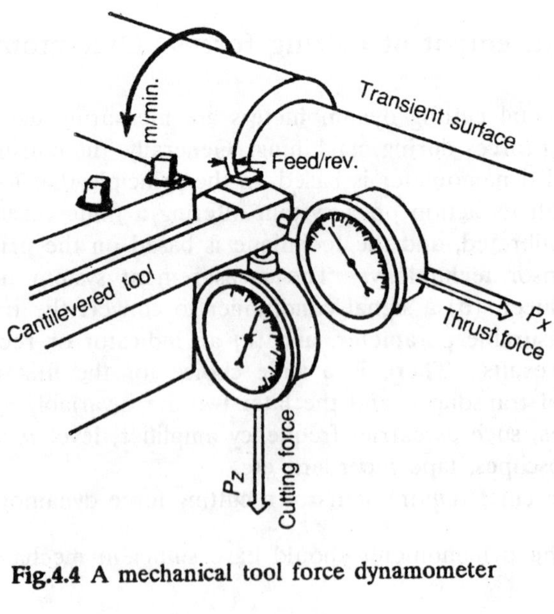


**Fig.4.4 A mechanical tool force dynamometer**

The capacitative pick-up (Fig.4.5) consists of two plates with an intervening air gap. The mechanical deformation causes a change in the air gap, thus changing the capacitative effect.

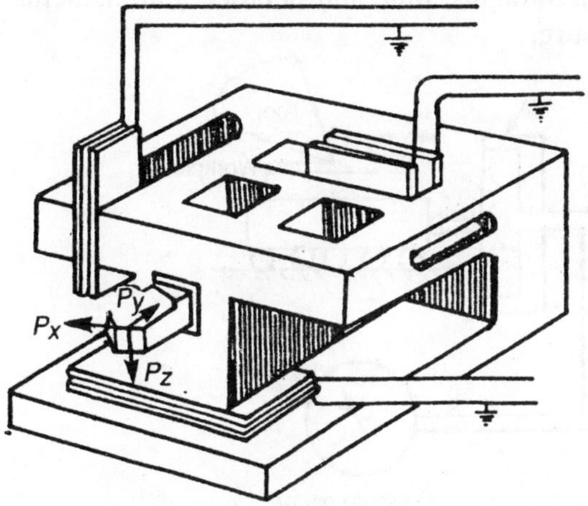


**Fig.4.5** Scheme of a capacitative pick-up dynamometer

Inductance dynamometer (Fig.4.6) employs the unbalancing of circuits due to change in mutual inductance carried by mechanical deformation.

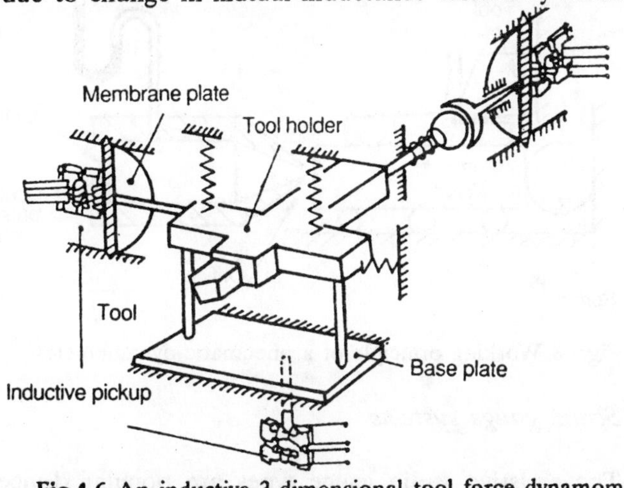


**Fig.4.6** An inductive 3-dimensional tool force dynamometer

The piezoelectric set-up uses quartz crystals for producing an electric charge when deformed.

The cutting forces are measured either by directly gauging the deformation caused by them or by measuring the transformed deformation by a transducer or sensing element. The deformation is magnified by an amplifier to achieve sensitivity.

The capacitative and inductive gauges are normally more rigid than the resistive ones and maintain the calibration over a long period of time.

However, the resistive strain gauges are preferred because of their smallness in size and mass.

Certain systems are of hydraulic or pneumatic type (Figs.4.7 and 4.8), utilising diaphragms, tube and bellows, and elements providing changes in fluid pressure.

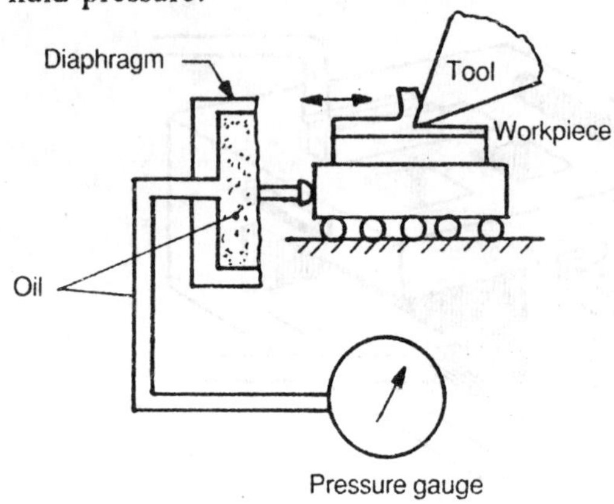


Fig.4.7 Working principle of a hydraulic dynamometer

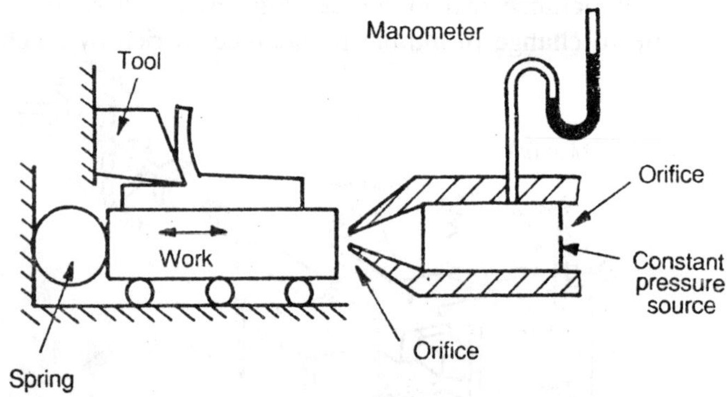


Fig.4.8 Working principle of a pneumatic dynamometer

### 4.7.1 *Strain gauge systems*

The resistive strain gauge types are popular devices used especially for academic or industrial research purposes.

A strain gauge is present in the form of a flat coil cemented between two thin insulating sheets of paper or plastic. The gauge is first cemented to the members to be strained. The bond between the member and the grid should be stronger than the grid itself for satisfactory performance, so as to force on to the grid to follow the strain of the support. Since the area of wires used in gauges is large compared to their volume, the cement medium can easily transmit the force onto the member that is necessary to deform the wire.

The strain gauge dynamometer uses strain rings that are based on the thin ring principle as in Fig.4.9(a). When a thin metal ring of thickness $t$, radius $r$ and width $b$, fixed at the bottom is subjected to radial and tangential forces $F_r$ and $F_t$, the ring deforms into an ellipse. When the radial force $F_r$ alone is applied, the ring deforms into an ellipse as in Fig.4.9(b). Based on the elastic theory of thin rings, the strains at the inner and outer surface of the ring along the horizontal diameter, i.e at point $A$, will be

$$\epsilon_A = \frac{\pm 1.09 F_r \cdot r}{Ebt^2}$$

and the strain at point $B$ (39.6° from the vertical axis) will be zero. Similarly, if the tangential force $F_t$ alone is applied, as in Fig.4.9(c), the strain at $A$ will be zero, while that at $B$ will be

$$\epsilon_B = \frac{\pm 1.09 F_t \cdot r}{Ebt^2}$$

Thus in a thin ring rigidly fixed at a point along its circumference so as to avoid rolling, when a force $F$ of $F_r$ and $F_t$ simultaneously, as in Fig.4.9(a) acts in the plane of the ring at the diametrically opposite point, a system of tensile and compressive stresses that are individually proportional to the component of the forces in the radial and tangential directions is produced.

Therefore, by mounting strain gauges on the inside and outside of the ring at $A - A$ along the opposite arms of a Wheatstone bridge, the force $F_r$ can be monitored precisely. Similar mounting of gauges at points $B - B$ in turn, will provide for the tangential force $F_t$.

The stiffness of the thin ring in the radial, tangential and axial directions, namely, $k_r$, $k_t$ and $k_a$ is given by

$$k_r = Ebt^3/(1.8r^3); \quad k_t = Ebt^3/(3.6r^3); \quad k_a = Ebt/(40r)$$

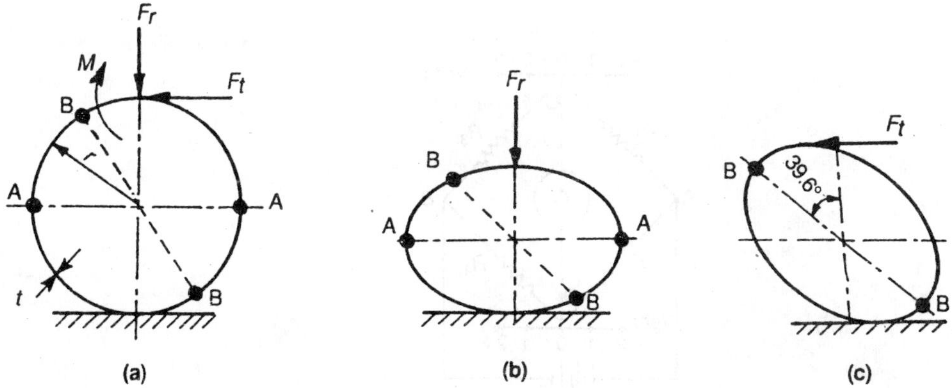


(a) (b) (c)

**Fig.4.9** Circular strain ring showing the type of deformation produced by radial load $F_r$ and by tangential load $F_t$

Normally, an octagonal ring with strain gauges is used to incorporate the above discussed principles (Fig.4.10), and invariably a Wheatstone bridge circuit is used in conjunction. The electrical resistance strain gauges are fixed on the octagonal faces of the dynamometer and are connected into separate or independent bridge circuits for the radial force, feed force or cutting force for a three-dimensional type.

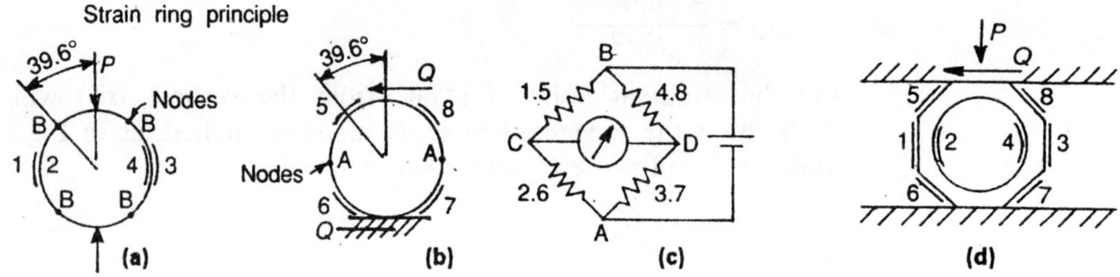


Fig.4.10 Positions and circuitry of strain gauges on an octagonal ring

### 4.7.2 *Principle of strain gauge systems*

Normally, two important information featnres are supplied with every gauge, namely, resistance $R$ and gauge factor $F$. The gauge factor is a measure of the sensitivity of the gauge.

The change in resistance of the bonded wire strain gauge is usually less than 0.5 % and measurements of such an order of magnitude may be made by means of a Wheatstone bridge (Fig.4.11). No current will flow through the galvanometer $G$, if the resistances are such that $(R1/R4) = (R2/R3)$. If $R1$ changes by $+\Delta R$, then point $D$ will have a drop of $+\Delta V$.

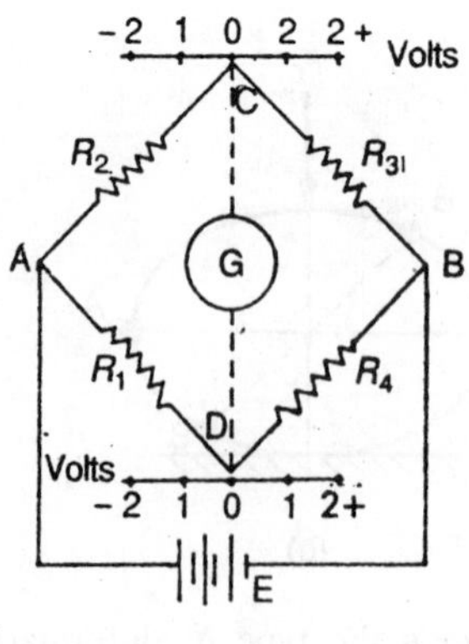


Fig.4.11 Wheatstone bridge principle

If $R4$ changes simultaneously by $-\Delta R$, there will be a further drop of $+\Delta V$, and point $D$ will be at $+2\Delta V$. If at the same time $R2$ changes by $-\Delta R$, and $R3$ changes by $+\Delta R$, then point C moves to $-2\Delta V$. Thus the total voltage difference between $C$ and $D$ will be $4\Delta V$.

Thus for higher sensitivity,two gauges are used for tensile strain, while two others are used for compressive strain, total of which adds up to four gauges.

### 4.7.3 *Three-dimensional lathe dynamometer*

A typical 3-D dynamometer as shown in Fig.4.12, uses a pair of extended octagonal rings connected by a rigid beam. That is, the front portion of the tool holder is suspended on four symmetrically placed elastic elements, each with a semi-circular ring and external octagonal faces. The four octagonal faces are symmetrical with respect to the tool shank. The system is capable of elastically deflecting in the $x,y,z$ directions. The straining element of the tool holder is machined from one piece of steel to provide maximum stiffness for the required sensitivity and ensure freedom from hysteresis effects. The strain gauges are fixed on the octagonal faces and are connected to three independent Wheatstone bridge circuits to measure the cutting force, feed force and radial force separately and concurrently.

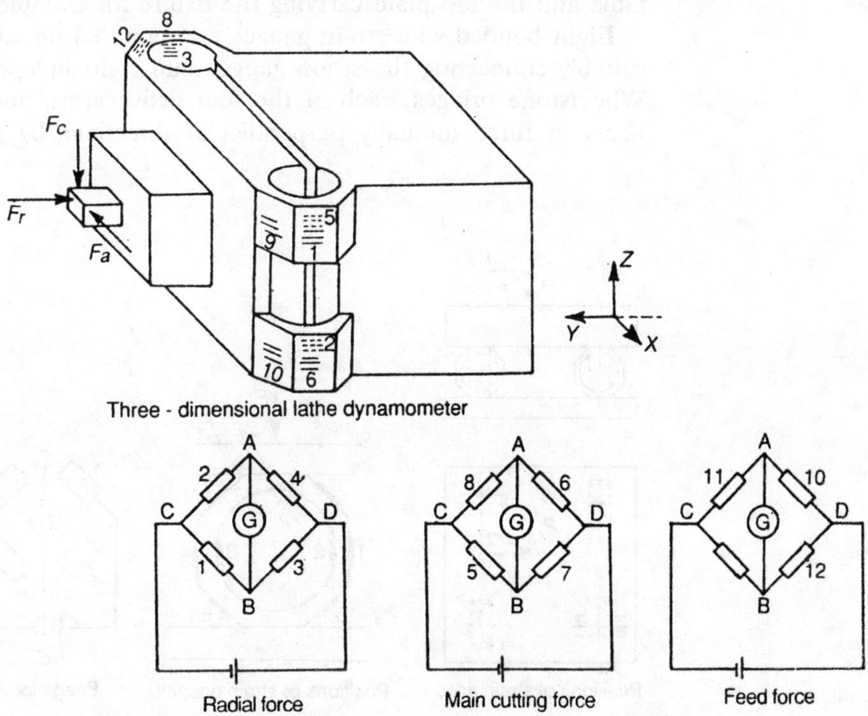


Fig.4.12 Three-dimensional lathe dynamometer

The cutting force will impress a normal tensile strain on the upper pair of elastic elements and a normal compressive strain on the lower pair. Thus gauges 5 and 6 experience tensile strain while gauges 7 and 8 experience compressive strain.

The radial force in $y$-direction induces identical loading on all the four rings, and the gauges on the octagonal faces experience tension while those on the inside of the circular face experience compression. Thus gauges 1 and 4 sense tensile strain and gauges 2 and 3 sense compressive strain.

Similarly, feed force in $x$-direction induces tensile strain in gauges 9 and 10 and compressive strain in gauges 11 and 12.

Also, all the four gauges in each bridge are active gauges, and the bridge fully compensates for temperature induced changes in resistance, if all gauges experience the same temperature changes.

### 4.7.4 *Milling dynamometer*

A typical milling dynamometer is shown in Fig.4.13. The system incorporates higher stiffness of rings and reduced weight of plates above and below, and combines four identical rings as shown, to enable measuring force components in three mutually perpendicular directions. The rings are mounted between two stiff plates, with the base plate clamped to the table and the top plate carrying the fixture for clamping the workpiece.

Eight bonded wire strain gauges are mounted on each of the rings. By suitably connecting the strain gauges into eight independent but identical Wheatstone bridges, each of the four active arms, and the force components in three mutually perpendicular directions by properly connecting

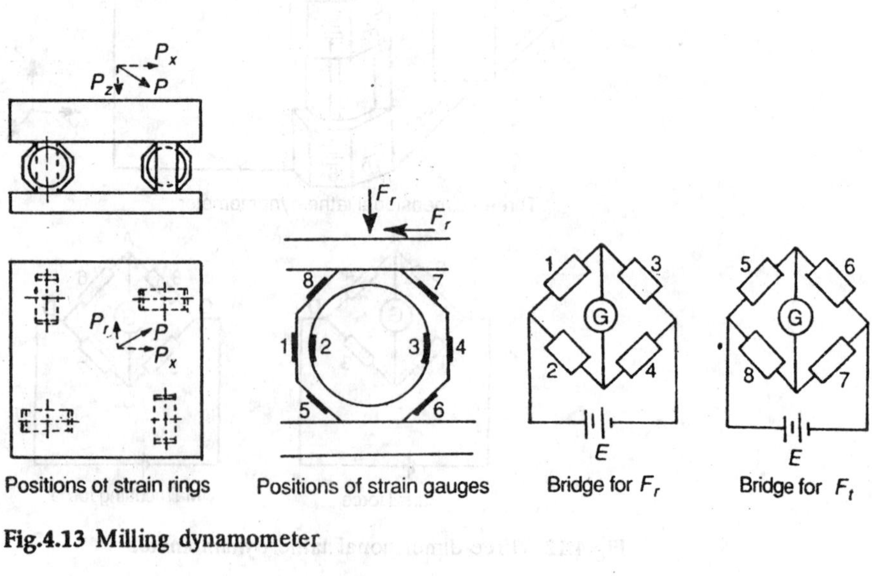


**Fig.4.13 Milling dynamometer**

the outputs together, can be measured independently and without any cross-interference. The gauges in the vertical legs on all the four rings are connected to measure the force component $P_y$ and the gauges in the inclined faces of the two sets, similarly positioned, measure $P_z$ and $P_z$ respectively.

When a straight-tooth cylindrical cutter is used in milling, the resultant cutting force has no component in the direction of spindle axis,and thus the cutter produces only tangential and normal components of forces. However, with a helical cutter, an axial force is also experienced. The vertical force is measured by strain gauges fixed on all the four rings, while each horizontal force is sensed by gauges fixed on two rings only.

### *4.7.5 Drill dynamometer*

In a typical drill dynamometer, forces and torque are measured with the help of strain gauges fixed to the four spokes of a wheel type workpiece fixture as in Fig.4.14. Both thrust and radial forces can be recorded simultaneously.

During the drilling operation, the total cutting load is distributed over the entire contact zone, of tool and workpiece. The total cutting zone, however, is identified by two separate cutting forces $P_{z1}$ and $P_{z2}$, and under ideal conditions the two are equal and symmetrically disposed with respect to the axis of the drill. The forces $P_{z1}$ and $P_{z2}$ can be resolved into (a) $P_{h1}$ and $P_{h2}$ acting opposite to cutting speed, (b) drill thrust $P_{v1}$ and $P_{v2}$ acting opposite to feed, and (c) $P_{r1}$ and $P_{r2}$ acting radially with respect to drill axis.

The four spokes are stressed differently by the drill thrust, torque and radial force. The strain gauges are mounted at points of maximum strain and minimum cross-effects.

Since the radial force is caused by an unbalance in the two lips of the drill, the line of action rotates with the drill.

The measurement of this force is best accomplished by mounting the gauges in the centre as of a pair of opposite gauges. Thus the gauges $V_1$ through $V_8$ form the bridge for thrust force. Also the gauges $M_1$ to $M_8$ form the bridge for torque and $A_1$ through $A_4$ form the bridge for radial loads.

### *4.7.6 Grinding dynamometer*

A simple two-dimensional grinding dynamometer for a surface grinder makes use of an extended octagonal ring as in Fig.4.15. The four gauges mounted on the vertical faces of the octagonal ring constitute the bridge for measuring the vertical component of the grinding force. The horizontal force is measured by a bridge comprising four gauges mounted on the inclined faces of the octagonal rings.

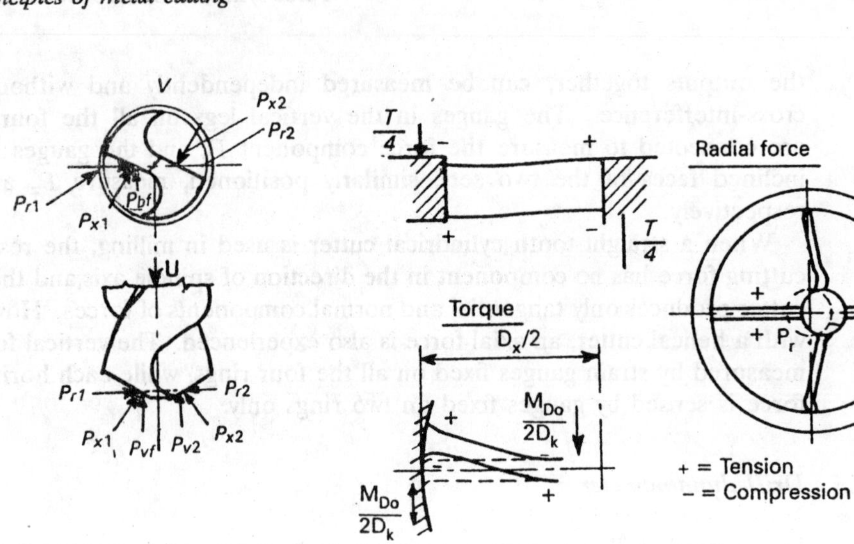


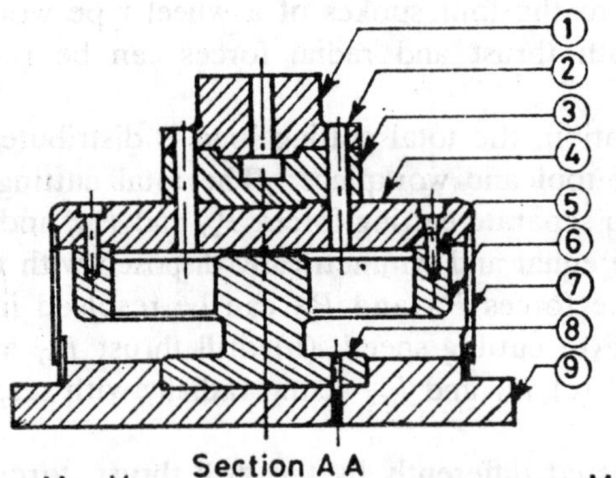


| No. | Qty. | Part | Matl. |
|---|---|---|---|
| 9 | 1 | Base | MS |
| 8 | 1 | Dowl | MS |
| 7 | 2 | Shield | Pers Pex. |
| 6 | 1 | Sporked wheel | MS |
| 5 | 4 | Allen screw | Std. |
| 4 | 1 | Cover plate | Dural |
| 3 | 1 | Mounting block | MS |
| 2 | 2 | Dowel | S Stl. |
| 1 |  | Work piece |  |

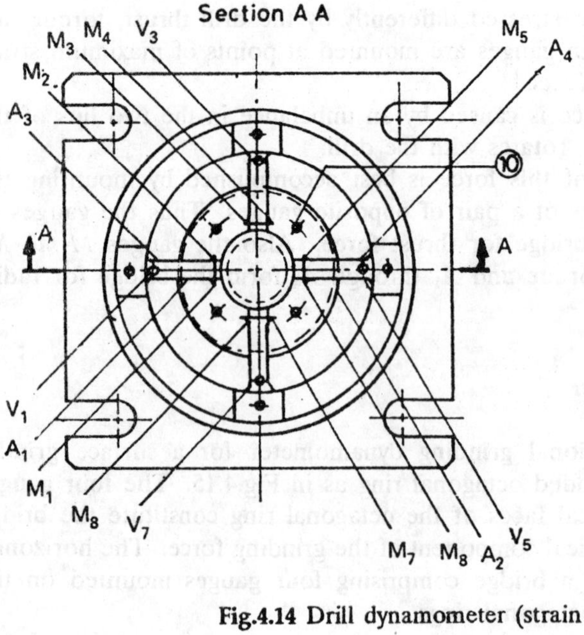


**Fig.4.14 Drill dynamometer (strain gauge type)**

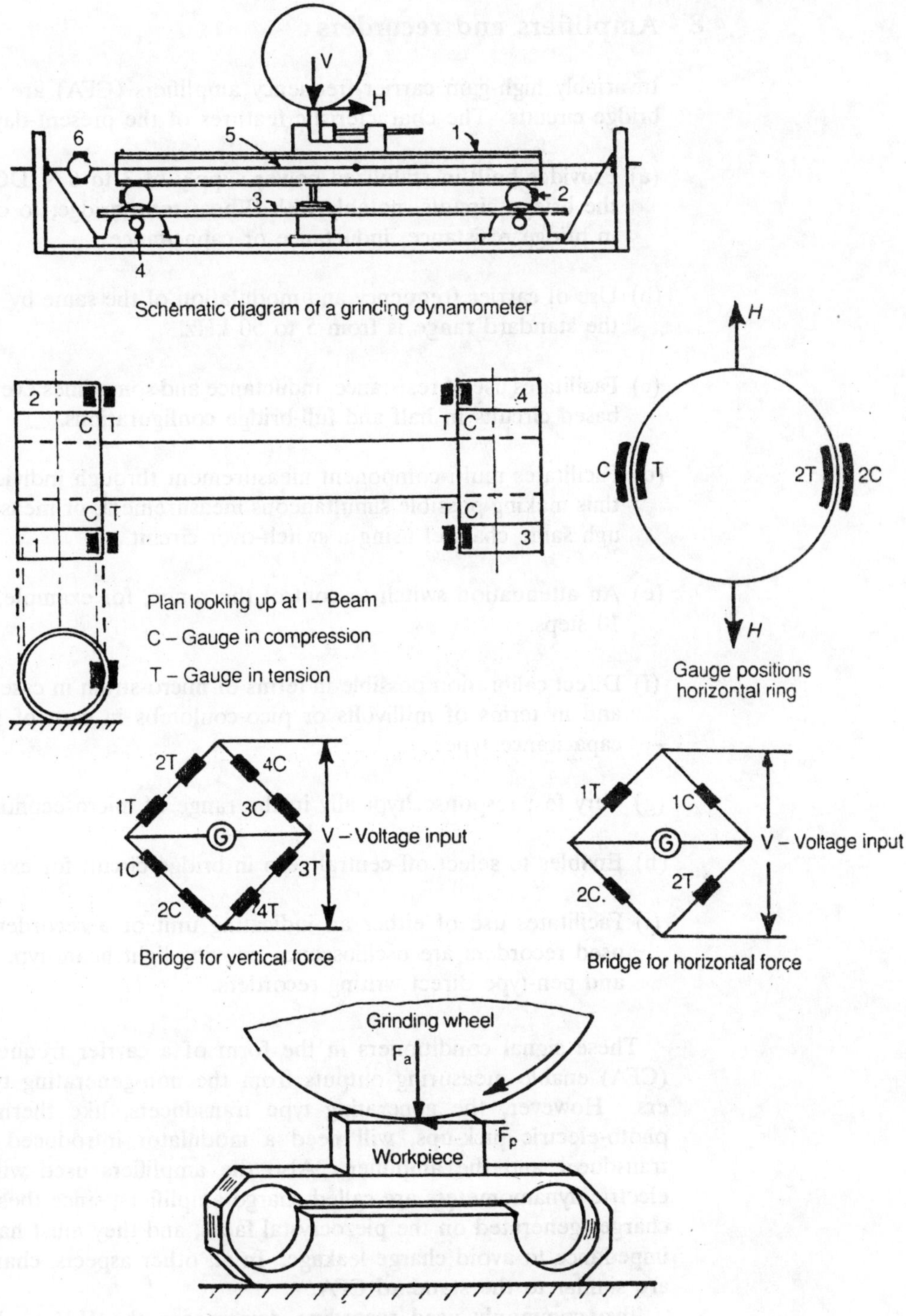


**Fig.4.15 Principles of grinding dynamometer**

## 4.8 Amplifiers and recorders

Invariably high-gain carrier-frequency amplifiers (CFA) are used with the bridge circuits. The characteristic features of the present-day CFA are:

(a) Provides built-in stabilized power supply of 3 to 6 V DC for use with the bridge circuits, notably with Wheatstone bridge, to detect changes in bridge resistance, inductance or capacitance.

(b) Use of carrier frequency and modulation of the same by the signal and the standard range is from 5 to 50 kHz.

(c) Facilitates use of resistance, inductance and sometimes even capacitance-based circuits in half and full-bridge configurations.

(d) Facilitates multi-component measurement through individual channels, thus making possible simultaneous measurement, or measurement through same channel using a switch-over circuit.

(e) An attenuation switch to control the range, for example, 1000 in 5 or 10 steps.

(f) Direct calibration possible in terms of micro-strain in case of resistance, and in terms of millivolts or pico-coulombs in case of inductance or capacitance types.

(g) Very fast response, typically in the range of microseconds.

(h) Enables to select off-central zero in bridge circuit for extending range.

(i) Facilitates use of either an indicating unit or a recorder. Commonly used recorders are oscilloscopes, moving-light beam-type oscillographs and pen-type direct writing recorders.

These signal conditioners in the form of a carrier frequency amplifier (CFA) enable measuring outputs from the non-generating type transducers. However, the generating type transducers, like thermo-electric or photo-electric pick-ups, will need a modulator introduced between the transducer and the amplifier. Also the amplifiers used with the piezo-electric dynamometers are called charge amplifiers, since these amplify the charges generated on the piezocrystal faces, and they must have high input impedance to avoid charge leakage. In all other aspects, charge amplifiers are similar to the standard CFA.

Two commonly used recording devices are the *U-V* or *X-Y* type pen recorders and the light beam oscillographs, suitable for low (0-10 Hz with sensitivity of 1 mV to 10 mV/cm) and medium frequency (0-5 kHz) ranges.

When measuring higher frequencies (above 5 kHz), the poor sensitivity of high-frequency galvanometers is a setback. Thus the sensitivity of miniature galvanometers is reduced significantly for a frequency ratio of 100 to 1000. Hence for high frequency situations, e.g. dynamic chip formation studies of transient higher harmonics, ultra-high-speed machining, explosive forming, etc., it is preferable to use an oscilloscope itself. In addition to the conventional type, storage type oscilloscopes and transient capture units are also available.

For data analysis, digitisation, etc., it is a common practice to record the signal on a magnetic tape, i.e. research type recorders with FM amplifiers. Also in conjunction with the endless spool principle, it is possible to analyse the data repeatedly in the case of the transient type and also spread the time base, i.e. recording at high speeds and replaying at low speeds, during analysis, enabling coverage of very wide frequencies.

## 4.9 Solved examples

*Example 4.1*

During the machining of MS with a cemented carbide tool of $0° - 10° - 6° - 6° - 8° - 75°$–1mm (ORS) geometry using a feed of 0.2 mm/rev., and a depth of cut of 1.9 mm, a chip thickness of 0.46 mm is observed. Estimate the cutting forces assuming no deviation of chip flow, and (a) an angle relationship given by Ernst and Merchant: $2\phi + \delta - \gamma_e = \pi/2$. (b) an angle relationship given by Lee and Shaffer $\phi + \delta - \gamma_e = \pi/4$. For estimating dynamic shear stress, Abuladze's relationship may be used, namely $\lambda = 0.74\sigma_u 6^{0.6\Delta}$ Given that, $\sigma_u = 80$ N/mm², and $\Delta = 0.2$.

*Solution*

$\lambda_s = 0°$, $\gamma_0 = 10°$, $k_r = 75°$, $f = 0.2$ mm/rev. $b_D = 1.9$ mm, $h_c = 0.46$ mm.

**To find $\tau_s$**

$$\tau_s = 0.74\sigma_u 6^{0.6\Delta} = 0.74 \times 80 \times 6^{(0.6\times 0.2)}$$

$$= 59.2 \times 1.237 = 73.24 \text{ N/mm}^2.$$

**Shear angle $\phi$**

$$h_D = f \sin k_r = 0.2 \sin 75° = 0.2 \times 0.9659 = 0.19$$

$$\Lambda_h = (h_c/h_D) = 0.46/0.19 = 2.421$$

$$\tan\phi = \frac{\cos\gamma_0}{\Lambda_h - \sin\gamma_0} = \frac{\cos 10°}{2.421 - \sin 10°}$$

or, $\phi = 23°40'$.

**For orthogonal cutting with no deviation of chip flow,**

$$\gamma_0 = \gamma_n = \gamma_e$$

**or,**

$$\gamma_e = 10°.$$

**(a) Ernst and Merchant**

$$2\phi + \delta - \gamma_e = \pi/2$$

**or,**

$$\delta = (\pi/2 + \gamma_e - 2\phi)$$

$$= 90° + 10° - 2 \times 23°40' = 52°40'.$$

Let

$F_c$ = Cutting force or tangential force

$F_f$ = Feed force or axial force

$F_D$ = Thrust force or radial force

$F_{cN}$ = Cutting normal force

$$F_c = \tau_s f b_D \frac{\cos(\delta - \gamma_0)}{\sin\phi \cos(\phi + \delta - \gamma_0)}$$

**On substitution for $F_c$ and by simplifying, we have**

$$F_c = 127 \text{ N}$$

**Similarly,**

$$F_{cN} = \tau_s f b_D \frac{\sin(\delta - \gamma_0)}{\sin\phi \cos(\phi + \delta - \gamma_0)}$$

$$= 27.832 \frac{\sin 42°40'}{\sin 23°40' \cos 66°20'}$$

$$= 106.8 \text{ N}$$

$$F_f = F_{cN} \sin k_r$$
$$= 106.8 \sin 75°$$
$$= 1106.8 \times 0.9659$$

or, $F_f = 112.82$ N.

$$F_D = F_{cN} \cos k_r = 106.8 \cos 75° = 106.8 \times 0.2588$$

or, $F_D = 30.22$ N.

**(b) Lee and Shaffer**

$$\phi + \delta - \gamma_e = \pi/4$$

or,

$$\delta = \pi/4 + \gamma_e - \phi = 45° + 10° - 47°20' = 7°40'.$$

Proceeding in a similar way as in (a), we get

$$F_c = 97.4 \text{ N} \quad \text{and} \quad F_{cN} = 11.4 \text{ N}$$

$$F_f = F_{cN} \sin k_r = 11.4 \sin 75° = 11.4 \times 0.9659$$

or, $F_f = 11$ N

$$F_D = F_{cN} \cos k_r = 11.4 \cos 75° = 11.4 \times 0.2588$$

or, $F_D = 2.96$ N.

### *Example 4.2*

**While machining C-30 steel with a cemented carbide tool having a tool geometry of 0° – 0° – 6° – 6° – 8° – 90°–l mm (ORS), the tangential force and feed force have been found to be 200N and 120N respectively. Calculate the kinetic coefficient of friction at the interface.**

### *Solution*

Cutting force $F_c = 200$ N;
Feed force $F_f = 120$ N

Now, $F_{cN} = F_f$ since $k_r = 90°$ and $\lambda_s \doteq 0°$.

Let $\mu$ = kinetic coefficient of friction and $\delta$ = mean angle of friction at the rake surface, Then

$$\mu = \frac{(120 + 200 \tan 0°)}{(200 - 120 \tan 0°)} = 0.6$$

$$\tan \delta = \mu = 0.6, \quad \text{or} \quad \delta = 31°.$$

*Example 4.3*

During machining of an alloy steel with a double carbide cutting tool having a geometry of 0° – (–5°) – 6° – 6° – 8° – 75° – 1 mm (ORS), the tangential force and axial force were found by an electromagnetic dynamometer to be 280 N and 130 N respectively. Calculate the radial force, frictional force and the kinetic coefficient of friction at the chip tool interface.

*Solution*

$$\gamma_0 = -5°, \ \lambda_s = 0°, \ k_r = 75°, \ F_c = 280 \text{ N}, \ F_f = 130 \text{ N}$$

(a) Since $0° < k_r < 90°$ and $\lambda_s = 0°$,

$$F_f = F_{cN} \sin k_r \quad \text{and} \quad F_D = F_{cN} \cos k_r$$

Therefore, $F_{cN} = F_f / \sin kr = 130/\sin 75° = 134.58$ N.
And, $F_D = F_{cN} \cos k_r = 134.58 \cos 75° = 34.84$ N.

(b) Let

$$F_\gamma = \text{frictional force}$$

Then,

$$\begin{aligned} F_\gamma &= F_{cN} \cos \gamma_0 + F_c \sin \gamma_0 \\ &= (134.58) \cos(-5°) + 280 \sin(-5°) \\ &= 109.66 \text{ N.} \end{aligned}$$

Let

$$F_{\gamma N} = \text{normal force}$$

$$\begin{aligned} F_{\gamma N} &= 280 \cos(-5°) - 134.58 \sin(-5°) \\ &= 290.68 \text{ N} \end{aligned}$$

$$\mu = \frac{F_\gamma}{F_{\gamma N}}$$

$$= \frac{109.66}{290.68} = 0.377$$

Now $\tan\delta = \mu = 0.377$

or, $\delta = 20°40'$.

Alternatively, coefficient of friction may also be calculated as below:

$$\mu = \frac{F_{cN} + F_c \tan\gamma_0}{F_c - F_{cN}\tan\gamma_0}$$

$$= \frac{134.58 + 280\tan(-5°)}{280 - 134.58\tan(-5°)}$$

$$= 0.377.$$

*Example 4.4*

A pipe 38 mm in diameter is being turned on a lathe with a tool having a rake angle of 33° and a feed of 0.15 mm/rev. The length of chip over one revolution of workpiece is 72 mm. The cutting speed is 12.5 m/min. The tangential force is 410 N and the feed force is 170 N. Calculate: (a) coefficient of friction on the rake force; (b) thickness of chip; (c) angle of shear; (d) velocity of shear; and (e) velocity of chip along the tool face.

*Solution*

Cutting force $F_c$ = 410 N, feed force $F_f$ = 170 N, $\gamma_0 = 33°$, $v_c = 12.5$ m/min. Assume $k_r = 90°$. Then $F_{cN} = F_f = 170$ N.

**(a) Coefficient of friction**

$$\mu = \frac{F_{cN} + F_c \tan\gamma_0}{F_c - F_{cN}\tan\gamma_0}$$

$$= \frac{170 + 410\tan 33°}{410 - 170\tan 33°} = 1.456.$$

**(b) Thickness of chip, $h_c$**

Length of chip/rev. $= l_c = 72$ mm, $f = 0.15$ mm/rev. and $k_r = 90°$.
Length of uncut layer/rev. $= l_D = \pi \times 38 = 119.43$ mm.

$$\Lambda_l = \frac{l_D}{l_c} = \frac{119.43}{72} = 1.66$$

Thickness of uncut layer of chip, $h_D = f \sin k_r = 0.15 \sin 90° = 0.15$ mm. Also taking $\Lambda_h = \Lambda_l$ and $h_c/h_D = \Lambda_h$, we get

$$h_c = \Lambda_h h_D = 1.66 \times 0.15 = 0.25 \text{ mm}$$

or $h_c = 0.25$ mm.

**(c) Shear angle, $\phi$**

$$\tan\phi = \frac{\cos\gamma_0}{\Lambda_h \sin\gamma_0} = \frac{\cos 33°}{1.66 - \sin 33°} = 0.7533$$

or, $\phi = 37°$.

**(d) Velocity of shear, $v_s$**

Cutting velocity = 12.5 m/min.

$$v_s = \frac{v_c \cos\gamma_0}{\cos(\phi - \gamma_0)} = \frac{12.5 \cos 33°}{\cos(37° - 33°)}$$

or, $v_s$ = 10.5 m/min.

**(e) Velocity of chip, $v_f$**

$$v_f = \frac{v_c}{\Lambda_h} = 12.5/1.66$$

or, $v_f = 7.53$ m/min.

*Example 4.5*

During the machining of mild steel with a 0° – 10° – 6° – 6° – 8° – 90° – 1mm ORS shaped triple-carbide cutting tool, the following observations have been obtained:

Depth of cut = 2 mm
Feed = 0.25 mm/rev.
Cutting speed = 200 m/min.
Chip thickness = 0.39 mm
Tangential force = 320 N
Axial force = 170 N

Calculate: (a) shear force and normal force on shear plane; (b) friction force and normal force on rake face; (c) kinetic coefficient of friction; (d) specific energy of cutting; (e) specific energy of shear; and (f) specific energy of friction.

***Solution***

$\lambda_s = 0°$, $\gamma_0 = 10°$, $k_r = 90°$, $f = 0.2\text{mm/rev.}$, $h_c = 0.39\text{mm}$, $F_c = 320$ N and $F_f = 170$ N, $F_{cN} = F_f = 170$ N, since $k_r = 90°$.

**Shear angle, $\phi$**

$$h_D = f \sin k_r = 0.2 \sin 90° = 0.2 \text{ mm}$$

$$\Lambda_h = h_c/h_D = 0.39/0.2 = 1.95$$

$$\tan\phi = \frac{\cos\gamma_0}{\Lambda_h - \sin\gamma_0}$$

$$= \frac{\cos 10°}{1.95 - \sin 10°}$$

$$= 0.5544$$

$$\text{or, } \phi = 29°.$$

**(a) Shear force, $F_{sh}$**

$$F_{sh} = F_c \cos\phi - F_{cN} \sin\phi$$

$$= 320 \cos 29° - 170 \sin 29°$$

$$= 320(0.8746) - 170(0.4848)$$

$$= 187.46 \text{ N}$$

**Normal force on shear plane, $F_{shN}$ is given by**

$$F_{shN} = F_c \sin\phi + F_{cN} \cos\phi$$

$$= 320 \sin 29° + 170 \cos 29°$$

$$= 320(0.4848) + 170(0.8746)$$

$$= 303.82 \text{ N.}$$

**(b) Friction force $F_\gamma$**

$$F_\gamma = F_{cN}\cos\gamma_0 + F_c\sin\gamma_0$$

$$= 170\cos 10° + 320\sin 10°$$

$$= 170(0.9848) + 320(0.1736)$$

$$= 223 \text{ N}.$$

Normal force on rake face, $F_{\gamma N}$

$$F_{\gamma N} = F_c\cos\gamma_0 - F_{cN}\sin\gamma_0$$

$$= 320\cos 10° - 170\sin 10°$$

$$= 320(0.9848) - 170(0.1736)$$

$$= 285.6 \text{ N}.$$

**(c) Coefficient of friction, $\mu$**

$$\mu = (F_\gamma/F_{\gamma N}) = (223/285.6) = 0.78,$$

or $\mu = 0.78$

*Angle of friction, $\delta$:*

$$\tan\delta = \mu = 0.78$$

or, $\delta = 38°$.

**(d) Specific energy of cutting, $e_c$**

$h_D = 0.2$ mm, $b_D = 2$ mm, $v_c = 200$ m/min,

$$e_c = (F_c v_c)/(A_r v_c)$$

$$= F_c/A_r = F_c/(h_D b_D)$$

$$= 320/(0.2 \times 2) = 800 \text{ N/mm}^2.$$

**(e) Specific energy of shear, $e_s$**

$$v_s = v_c\frac{\cos\gamma_0}{\cos(\phi - \gamma_0)} = \frac{200 \times \cos 10°}{\cos(29° - 10°)} = 208.3 \text{ m/min}.$$

$$e_s = \frac{F_{sh}v_s}{h_D b_D v_c} = \frac{187.46 \times 208.3}{0.2 \times 2 \times 200} = 514 \text{ N/mm}^2.$$

**(f) Specific energy of friction, $e_f$**

$$v_f = v_c/\Lambda_h \quad = (200/1.95) = 102.56 \text{ m/min.}$$

or,

$$e_f = \frac{F_\gamma v_f}{h_c b_D v_c} = \frac{223 \times 102.56}{0.2 \times 2 \times 200} = 285.8 \text{ N/mm}^2.$$

## 4.10 Exercise problems

4.1 A seamless tubing of 40 mm outside diameter is turned on a lathe. The following data were obtained: Rake angle = 35°, cutting speed = 15 m/min, feed = 0.10 mm/rev., length of continuous chip in one revolution = 50 mm, tangential force = 400 N, feed force = 160 N. Calculate the coefficient of friction, shear plane angle, velocity of chip along tool face and chip thickness.

4.2 A tool shape with 8° back rake and 45° side cutting edge angle has to be used under an orthogonal cutting condition. The tangential force is 480 N and the force normal to the tangential force is 340 N. The cutting velocity is 100 m/min. Calculate: (a) the required side rake so that cutting is orthogonal, (b) kinetic coefficient of friction, and (c) energy consumed in friction per unit volume of metal removal if the chip reduction coefficient is 2.75.

4.3 During machining of C-20 steel with a 0° – 10° – 6° – 6° – 8° – 90° – 1 mm ORS shaped triple carbide cutting tool, the observations were: depth of cut = 2 mm, feed = 0.25 mm/rev., cutting speed = 200 m/min., chip thickness = 0.39 mm, tangential force = 400 N, axial force = 200 N. Calculate: (a) shear force and normal force on shear plane, (b) friction force and normal force on rake face, (c) kinetic coefficient of friction, (d) specific energy of cutting, (e) specific energy of shear, and (f) specific energy of friction.

4.4 During turning of mild steel by a stellite of specification 0° – 10° – 5° – 6° – 10° – 60° – 1mm (ORS) at a feed of 0.2 mm/rev., depth cut of 2 mm and cutting speed of 40 m/min, a chip thickness of 1 mm was observed. Assuming the coefficient of friction of chip–tool interface as 1.2, find the forces and specific energies.

# 5 Thermal aspects in machining

## 5.1 Heat generation in metal cutting

According to the first law of thermodynamics, when work is transformed into heat, the quantity of heat produced is equivalent to the quantity of work. Heat is generated, through the conversion of mechanical energy. The three distinct sources of heat in metal cutting (Fig.5.1) are given below:

(a) the shear zone, 1, where the primary plastic or shear deformation takes place,

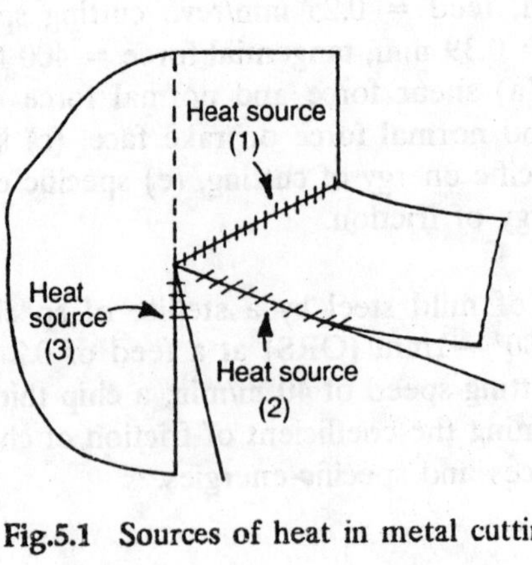


Fig.5.1 Sources of heat in metal cutting

(b) the chip–tool interface, 2, where secondary plastic deformation due to friction between the heated chip and tool takes place, and

(c) the work–tool interface, 3, at flanks where frictional rubbing occurs.

For example, in a typical study of machining mild steel at 30 m/min. at about 750°C of cutting temperature at tool–chip interface, the distribution of total energy developed at the shear plane is as follows:

| | |
|---|---|
| Energy to chip | 60 per cent, |
| Energy to workpiece | 30 per cent, and |
| Energy to tool | 10 per cent |

The rate of energy consumption during orthogonal cutting is given by

$$W_c = F_c V_c \text{ N-m/min.}$$

where

$F_c$ = cutting force, N

$V_c$ = cutting speed, m/min.

When a material is deformed elastically, the energy used is stored in the material as strain energy and no heat is generated. However, when a material is deformed plastically almost all the energy used is converted into heat. In metal cutting, the material is subjected to extremely high strains and elastic deformation forms a very small proportion of the total deformation, hence all the energy is assumed to be converted into heat. Thus,

$$Q = W_c / J = F_c V_c / J$$

where

$Q$ = total heat generated, and

$J$ = mechanical equivalent of heat

The cutting energy is converted into heat in two principal regions of plastic deformation: (i) the shear zone or primary deformation zone AB, and (ii) the secondary deformation zone BC (Fig.5.2). If, as is common in most practical situation, the cutting tool is not perfectly sharp, a third heat source BD would be present due to friction between the tool and the newly machined workpiece surface. However, unless the tool is severely worn, the heat generated at this source will be small and hence could be neglected.

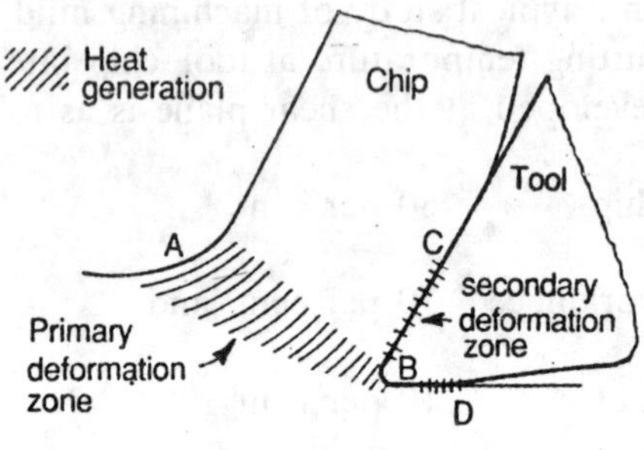


**Fig.5.2** Generation of heat in orthogonal cutting

Thus,

$$Q = Q_s + Q_f$$

where $Q_s$ is heat generated in primary deformation zone, i.e. shearing heat, and $Q_f$ is the heat generated in secondary deformation zone, i.e. frictional heat. Also

$$Q_f = Fv_f/J$$

where

$F$ = frictional force on tool face and

$v_f$ = velocity of chip flow, $(v_c/\Lambda_h)$.

The temperature distribution in the workpiece, in this instance the chip zone, as seen in a typical experimental study, is given in Fig.5.3. As point $X$ in the material moves towards the cutting tool, it approaches and passes through the primary deformation zone, and is heated till it leaves the zone, being carried away within the chip. However point $Y$ passes through both deformation zones and continues to get heated till it leaves the region of secondary deformation. It is then cooled as the heat is conducted into the body of the chip, and eventually the chip achieves a uniform temperature throughout. The maximum temperature thus occurs along the tool face some distance from the cutting edge. The point $Z$, that remains in the workpiece, is heated as it passes below the tool cutting edge, by conduction of heat from the primary deformation zone. Some heat is removed from the secondary deformation zone by conduction into the body of the tool.

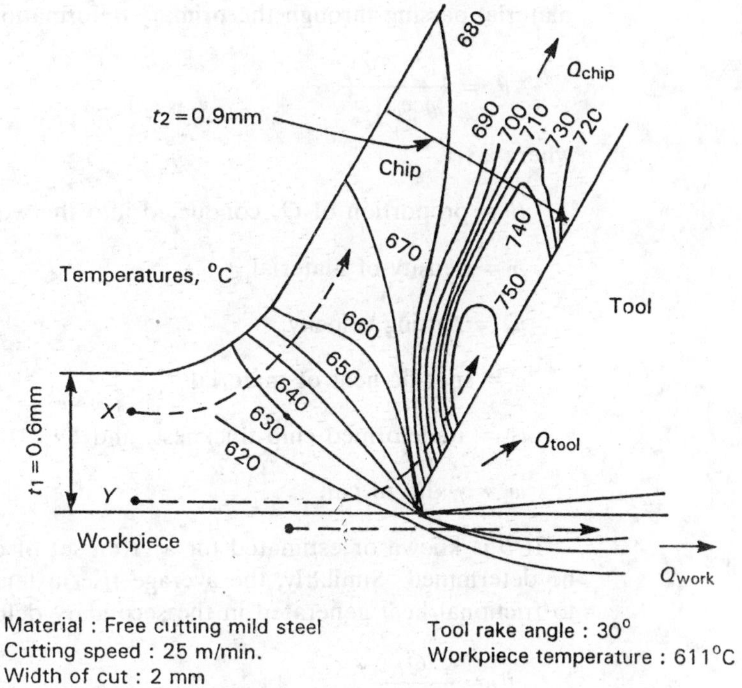


Fig.5.3 Temperature distribution in work and chip during orthogonal cutting

Thus,

$$Q = Q_c + Q_w + Q_t$$

where

$Q$ = total heat generated,

$Q_c$ = heat conducted to chip,

$Q_w$ = heat conducted to workpiece, and

$Q_t$ = heat conducted to tool.

Since the chip material near the tool face is flowing rapidly, it possesses a much greater capacity for heat removal than the tool. Hence $Q_t$ usually forms a very small proportion of $Q$, except at very low cutting speeds.

**Temperatures in the zones**

The heat generated in the primary deformation zone is $Q_s$ and a fraction $\beta$ of this heat is conducted into the workpiece while the remainder, $(1-\beta)Q_s$

is transported into the chip. Thus the average rise in temperature of the material passing through the primary deformation zone is given by

$$\theta_s = \frac{(1-\beta)Q_s}{\rho c v_c t_1 w}$$

where

$\beta$ = proportion of $Q_s$ conducted into the workpiece,

$\rho$ = density of material,

$v_c$ = cutting velocity,

$c$ = specific heat of material,

$t_1$ = undeformed chip thickness, and

$w$ = width of cut.

If $\beta$ is known or estimated for a given set of cutting conditions, $\theta_s$ may be determined. Similarly, the average rise in temperature of the chip due to frictional heat generated in the secondary deformation zone is given by

$$\theta_f = \frac{Q_f}{\rho c v_c t_1 w}$$

And the mean temperature of chip along the tool face $\theta_t$ may be obtained from the shear and friction induced temperatures as follows :

$$\theta_t = \theta_s + \theta_f$$

## 5.2 Tool wear and temperature

Cutting or machining temperatures significantly affect tool wear, tool failure and hence tool life. It is appropriate to briefly discuss here first tool failure and tool wear characteristics, and then the role of temperature. Other aspects of tool wear are discussed in a different section later.

**Tool failure and wear**

A cutting tool can be regarded to have failed if any one of the following processes occur:

(a) *The process of plastic deformation*, whereby the form of the tool is lost. A tool is normally hard; but under cutting conditions when the temperature and stresses are high, plastic deformation may cause loss of form-stability, i.e. cutting capability of the tool;

(b) *The process of mechanical breakage*, if the cutting force is very large, or by the development of fatigue cracks under chatter conditions;

(c) *The process of gradual wear*, which is the result of interaction between the work and tool material. Usually, wear is the predominant cause by which the cutting tool fails, when *form-stability* is achieved, because processes (a) and (b) above can be avoided by proper selection of machinery parameters.

During the process of cutting, a tool penetrates into the workpiece and removes a relatively thin layer known as chip. Thus, new surfaces are constantly being exposed to the environment. This environment consists of the ambient atmosphere, any cutting fluid which may be in use, and the chip and clearance surfaces of the tool. This exposed working material is quite unique in that its surfaces are entirely unaffected by foreign media and this is an active condition for rapid chemical reaction, diffusion and molecular association. Additionally, as a consequence of the relative movement between the tool and workpiece, a sliding contact is set up between the clearance surface of the tool and the newly cut surface of the workpiece and between the chip surfaces of the tool and the newly formed surface of the chip. The surface pressures on the respective surfaces are not uniformly distributed, and also the average values of surface temperature in the contact zones vary widely.

Under normal cutting conditions, when the form-stability of the cutting edge has been achieved, wears due to interaction between the chip and tool and between the workpiece and the tool are the main processes by which a cutting tool fails. After the tool has been in use for sometime, 'wearland' will appear at the flank of the tool below the cutting edge extending approximately parallel to the cutting edge. The wear will also appear on the tool face or rake surface forming a characteristic cavity known as a *crater*, beginning at a certain distance off the cutting edge. The useful life of a tool is limited by the extent of tool wear.

Wear, which can be described as total loss of weight or mass of the sliding members accompanying friction, is classified based on its basic causes or mechanisms, namely abrasion, adhesion, diffusion and chemical wear. These are briefly discussed below:

(a) *Abrasion wear* Abrasion wear is due to ploughing by hard constituents including fragments of built-up edge as they are swept over the tool surface. Such wear occurs predominantly in cases where the prevailing strain rate results in hard spots traversing through asperities in the point contact zone of the interfaces. The process is most nearly comparable to forms of stock removal such as honing or lapping. The peaks of the surface profile are sheared off, and new rupture surfaces with sharp edges and corners are produced. These provide new points of attack at which the stress will again exceed the shear strength.

Also in metal cutting, particles of the built-up edge are carried away with the chip, or escape to the space between the tool and the finished surface. These particles are hard because of the severe strain hardening during the formation of the built-up edge on the cutting face of the tool. When the particles pass by the cutting point to the space between the tool and chip, most of them become embedded in the chip or the newly finished surface since these are softer than the tool. The embedded particles are relatively hard, and thereby will wear the tool. This makes the tool rough, which, in turn, increases friction. The temperature of the tool thus increases and it may lose hardness, which will accelerate abrasion wear. Simultaneously higher tool temperature contributes to more diffusion between contacting asperities and increases metal transfer from the tool.

(b) *Adhesion wear* When metallic surfaces are brought into intimate contact under moderate loads, a metallic bond between adjoining materials takes place. The strength of the bonding at the points of adhesion is often so great that while attempting to free the surfaces, separation takes place not along the interface but in one of the materials itself, transferring and removing materials along with the sliding member of the pair. The main factors which affect metal transfer include the hardness of the two surfaces, their surface finish, and the normal pressure between the parts and conditions of lubrication. The temperature of the surfaces affects the wear, since the hardness of the material depends on its temperature.

(c) *Diffusion wear* Solid state diffusion is a process whereby atoms in a metallic crystal shift from one lattice point to another, causing a transfer of the element in the direction of the concentration gradient. Diffusion is a process which depends on time and temperature, the bonding affinity of the pair and the degree of atomic agitation.

(d) *Chemical wear* Chemical wear occurs due to interaction between tool and work material in an active cutting fluid environment. Related to chemical wear is electrolytic wear, which occurs due to possible galvanic corrosion between the tool and work materials. For example, high-speed steel is anodic to stainless alloys such as 15-25-6, and other high temperature alloys.

## 5.3 Significance of cutting temperatures

Cutting temperature refers to the temperature at the tool–chip interfaces. It consists of the temperature rise $\theta_s$, in the body of the chip due to shear, the further rise $\theta_f$, at the interface as the hot chip rubs on the tool face and affected by the workpiece temperature as discussed earlier. The tool–

chip interface temperature is not uniformly distributed along the path of the chip contact with the tool face. The pattern of temperature distribution is illustrated in Fig.5.4.

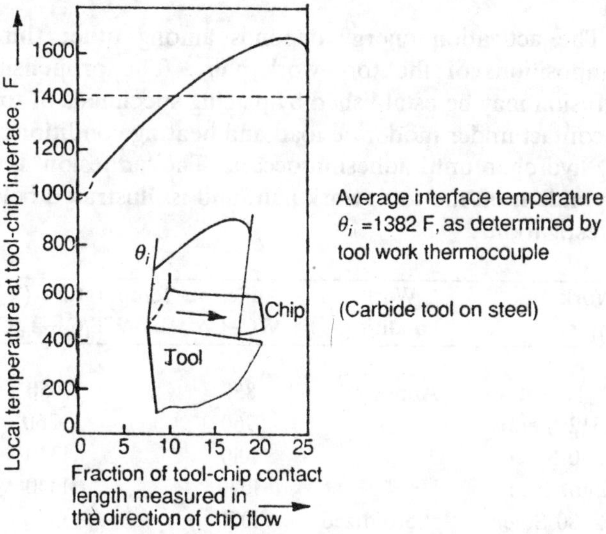


**Fig.5.4** Tool–chip interface temperature distribution

The temperatures attained in metal cutting are important only so far as they affect the thermally activated mass transport phenomenon at the tool–work contacts in the interface. These may involve interfacial diffusion and alloy formation or self-diffusion, resulting in creep and/or softening of tool material. The mutual diffusion of materials at the tool–chip contact is a significant cause for formation of crater wear. Such wear is essentially an exponential function of the average tool–chip interface temperature, provided the temperature is sufficient to cause interfacial diffusion (as illustrated in Fig.5.5), for two tool materials in the machining of mild steel.

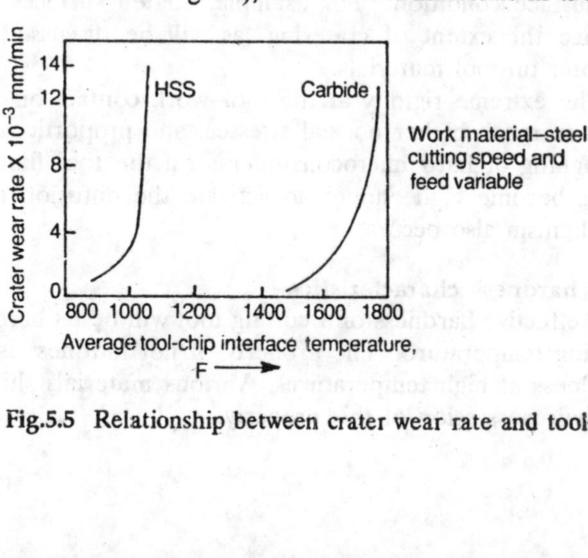


**Fig.5.5** Relationship between crater wear rate and tool–chip interface temperature

Wear, $W$ by such a process is governed by the activation energy $E_a$ and local absolute temperature $T$ according to a relationship of the form,

$$W \propto e^{-E_a/T}$$

The activation energy depends among other things on the chemical compositions of the tool–work pair. The propensity toward interfacial diffusion may be established by placing specimens of tool and work material in contact under moderate load and heating conditions, in an atmosphere of dry hydrogen until adhesion occurs. The 'adhesion' temperature is strongly dependent on the tool–work pair, and is illustrated below as per one typical investigation:

| Work material | Work condition | Adhesion Temperature (+10° F)* WC–Co | $WT_iC_2–T_aC–C$ |
|---|---|---|---|
| 'A' Nickel | Annealed | 850 | 1050 |
| 2512 Steel | " | 960 | 1260 |
| 2340 Steel | " | 1010 | 1310 |
| Ingot Iron | " | 1070 | 1340 |
| 52100 Steel | Spheroidized | 1070 | 1425 |
| 52100 Steel | Quenched and tempered | 1190 | 1425 |

It becomes evident that the significance of the tool–chip interface temperature is largely dependent upon the tool–work pair in contact.

The peak temperature on the tool flank surface has been found to be about two-thirds that on the crater surface. However the contact conditions are quite different. The ribbon-like chip, already heated by shear and heated further by rubbing, exerts moderate stresses at the tool-chip contact. The high temperatures accentuate diffusion, and wear by this mechanism is normally predominant. However, much depends on the tool material and its surface condition. For example, coated surfaces on the rake surface reduce the extent of cratering, as will be discussed later in a separate chapter on tool materials.

The extreme rigidity at the tool–work contact on the flank surface results in much higher normal stresses, and proportionately greater wear by ploughing of hard microconstituents on the tool flank. If local temperatures become high enough to activate the diffusion process, wear by this mechanism also occurs.

### Hot hardness characteristics

The effective hardness of a cutting too! will be its hardness when it is at its cutting temperature. The property of hot hardness is the ability to retain hardness at high temperatures. Various materials show marked variations in their possession of this property.

For example, at 800°F, plain carbon steel loses 70 per cent of its room temperature hardness value, while a high-speed steel loses only 17 per cent as illustrated in Fig.5.6. The general pattern is that the hardness decreases, as the temperature increases.

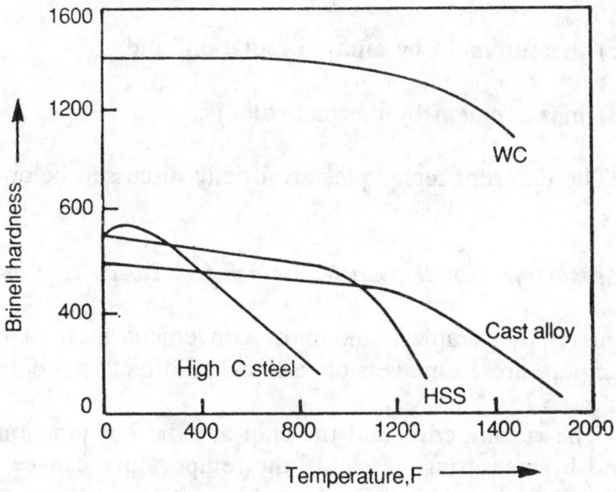


**Fig.5.6** Variation of hardness with temperature

With high-speed steel tools, at 1025°F, even a small temperature increase causes a sharp increase in the rate of crater wear. This is referred to as the temperature-sensitive range of high-speed steel, and varies slightly with the type and composition of the tool material. The crater wear rate is low or negligible at temperatures below this range and excessive above it. Thus, for example, in single-point turning of steel with high-speed steel tools, the cutting temperature is a predominant factor in determining tool life. The tools normally fail due to concentrated wear at flank/rake regions of the active cutting edge. Except at low speeds (and low cutting temperatures), the wear is due, principally, to local temperature and its effect on the softening and flow of the tool material at or near the cutting edge. This action increases edge rubbing and further raises the local temperature.

Sintered carbide tool materials also exhibit a temperature sensitive range in the vicinity of 1700°F. As with high-speed steel tools, the crater wear rate with carbides becomes rapid, when the cutting temperature is above the temperature sensitive range.

## 5.4 Measuring temperatures in metal cutting

Attempts have been made to measure temperatures in metal cutting since 1925 and different strategies have been developed. The general principles of measuring cutting temperature are as follows :

(a) measurement of thermoelectric e.m.f. between tool and workpiece,

(b) measurement by thermocouples inserted into the tool,

(c) measurement by emitted radiation, and

(d) measurement by thermal colours.

The different techniques are briefly discussed below:

### 5.4.1 *Measurement of thermoelectric e.m.f. between tool and workpiece*

This is the simplest and most convenient method of measuring cutting temperatures. One version, also called direct one-tool method, is illustrated in Fig.5.7.

The cutting edge and the chip are the hot junctions of a thermocouple and by measuring its e.m.f., the temperature can be determined. It is to be noted that A and B, the cold junctions, remain at room temperature. The mercury contact is used to make electrical contact with the rotating member. The wires C and D are ordinary copper wires. Since both ends are at the same temperature, they have no influence on the e.m.f. generated as measured with the potentiometer. The tool holder and the work material are insulated from the tool post and the chuck respectively.

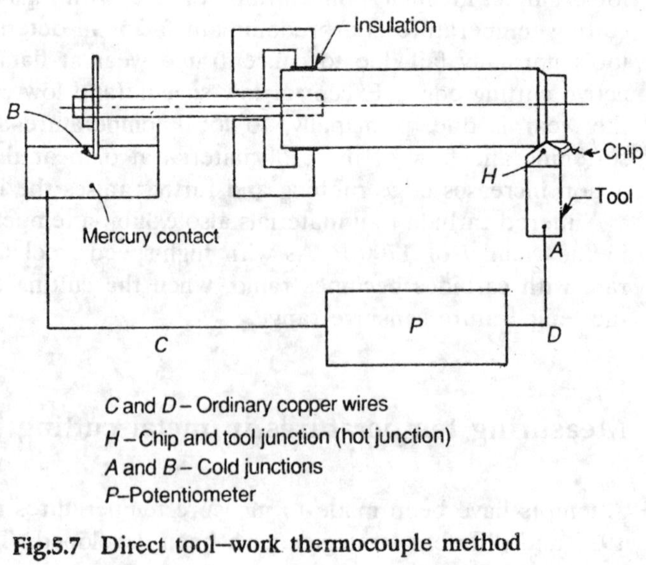


**Fig.5.7** Direct tool–work thermocouple method

The laws of thermoelectric circuits that are applicable to metal cutting may be summarised as follows:

(a) the e.m.f. in the thermoelectric circuit depends only on the difference in temperature between the hot and cold junctions, and is independent of the gradients in the parts making up the system;

(b) the e.m.f. generated is independent of the size and resistance of the conductors; and

(c) if the junctions of the two metals have a uniform temperature, the e.m.f. generated is not affected if a third metal which is at the same temperature is used to make the junction between the first two.

A device like a potentiometer can be used to measure the e.m.f. generated by the thermocouple. To calibrate the thermocouple, an artificial one of a smaller size is made, say by spot welding, and then dipped in a bath of metals of known melting points like tin, zinc or aluminium. The e.m.f. generated can be measured for each of them and the calibration curves can be prepared as in Fig.5.8 for HSS and mild steel combinations.

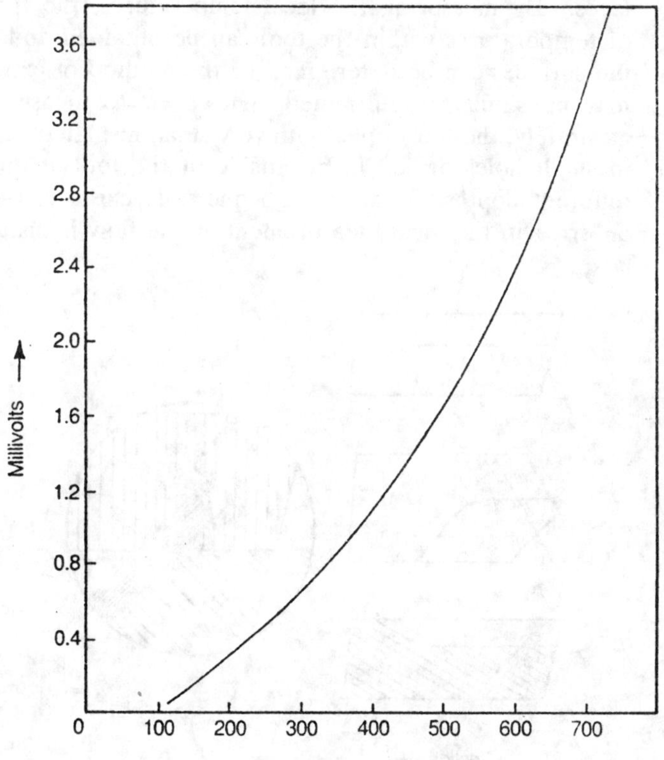


**Fig.5.8** Calibration curve

The chief setback of this method is that the measured temperature is not accurately defined and, in practice, the figures indicated are in terms of a mean value representing the temperatures occurring in the contact zone between tool, workpiece and chip. A reliable thermocouple is formed, only if throughout the hot junction the temperature is constant. The hot junction between the chip and the cutting surface of the tool, and the chip and clearance surface, are extended areas within which large gradients of temperature exist, and these surfaces by no means meet this condition. Further errors may result from unequal temperatures at the junctions of both conductors of the thermocouple leading to the voltmeter. Another important objection is that the e.m.f. is influenced by pressure and friction, and hence no longer corresponds to the calibrated e.m.f., being influenced more by friction.

### 5.4.2 *Measurements by thermocouples in the tool*

In the built-in-thermocouple method (given in Fig.5.9) commercially available separate standard thermocouples, are incorporated in the tool. Thermocouples, for example platinum wire based, are inserted at different places in the interior of the tool, some of them as near as possible to the surfaces. By measuring the local temperatures, the three-dimensional field of temperatures within the tool can be obtained and the temperatures on the surfaces can be determined by the method of extrapolation. Isotherms may be similarly determined. However, to measure local temperatures accurately, thermocouples with very small insulated wires have to be placed in small holes drilled from outside of the tool at different places and to different depths. If more than one hole exists in the tool, there will be an error in the local measurement as the flow is disturbed. It is therefore

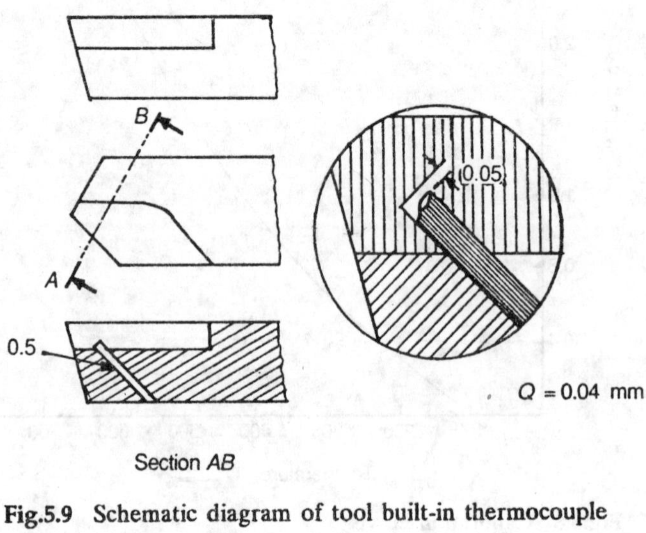


**Fig.5.9** Schematic diagram of tool built-in thermocouple

necessary to prepare as many tools or plates, each with only one hole, as the number of different local temperatures to be measured.

With this method, it is possible to study the temperature distribution on the surface of the tool in relation to various cutting speeds and feeds, by varying the position of the thermocouples and by feeding the results into a computer. However, the chief objection to this method is that it is extremely complicated and tiresome and that it takes a great deal of time and work to establish the field of temperatures just for a single combination of materials and cutting conditions.

Thermocouples could also be placed on the surface of the tool. For example, a thermocouple with two conductors may be placed in a small bowl on the cutting surfaces in such a way that the chip touches it without shearing it. Thus the temperatures on the lower side of the gliding chip is measured. However, the main objection is that it is too tiresome a way of measuring and also that the thermocouple is under friction.

Yet another method involves the use of a thermocouple with one conductor in special cases. For example, when using a ceramic tool, a similar method can be used, inserting only one platinum wire without an insulating cover into the plate. It penetrates the cutting face and is hence rubbed by the chip, and thus a thermocouple is formed by the chip and the wire. The main objection to this method is that it is restricted to ceramics, where it can be inserted when sintering the plate. Moreover, this method is also complicated and the thermocouple is under friction.

### 5.4.3 *Emitted radiation method*

This method is based on the measurement of the radiation emitted by the chip running on the tool through a hole drilled in the tool itself. It requires a special tool holder with a built-in-pyrometer as in Fig.5.10. The pyrometer components, as in Fig.5.11, are quartz lenses, a diaphragm, a photodiode and circuitry to indicating instrument. By varying the position of the hole it is possible to explore the temperature distribution on the tool. The importance of this method lies in the fact that it can be regarded as an absolute method which will be useful for reference purposes, when other methods of measuring the cutting temperatures are under study.

Another modified method measures the temperature in the workpiece–tool contact zone directly. Here, the radiation emitted by the zone of contact between the tool and workpiece is measured through a hole drilled in the wall of a tube in orthogonal cutting (Fig.5.12). The main difference of this method from the above one is that the temperature is mesured directly on the tool instead of on the chip. Furthermore, as there is no limiting minimum distance to the cutting edge, it is possible to measure the temperature on the cutting edge itself. When a built-up edge or layer is present, the temperature can be measured on its upperside. This method of measuring cutting temperatures is not limited to orthogonal cutting, but is also applicable to normal cutting, for which a small key seat is provided instead of the hole in the workpiece.

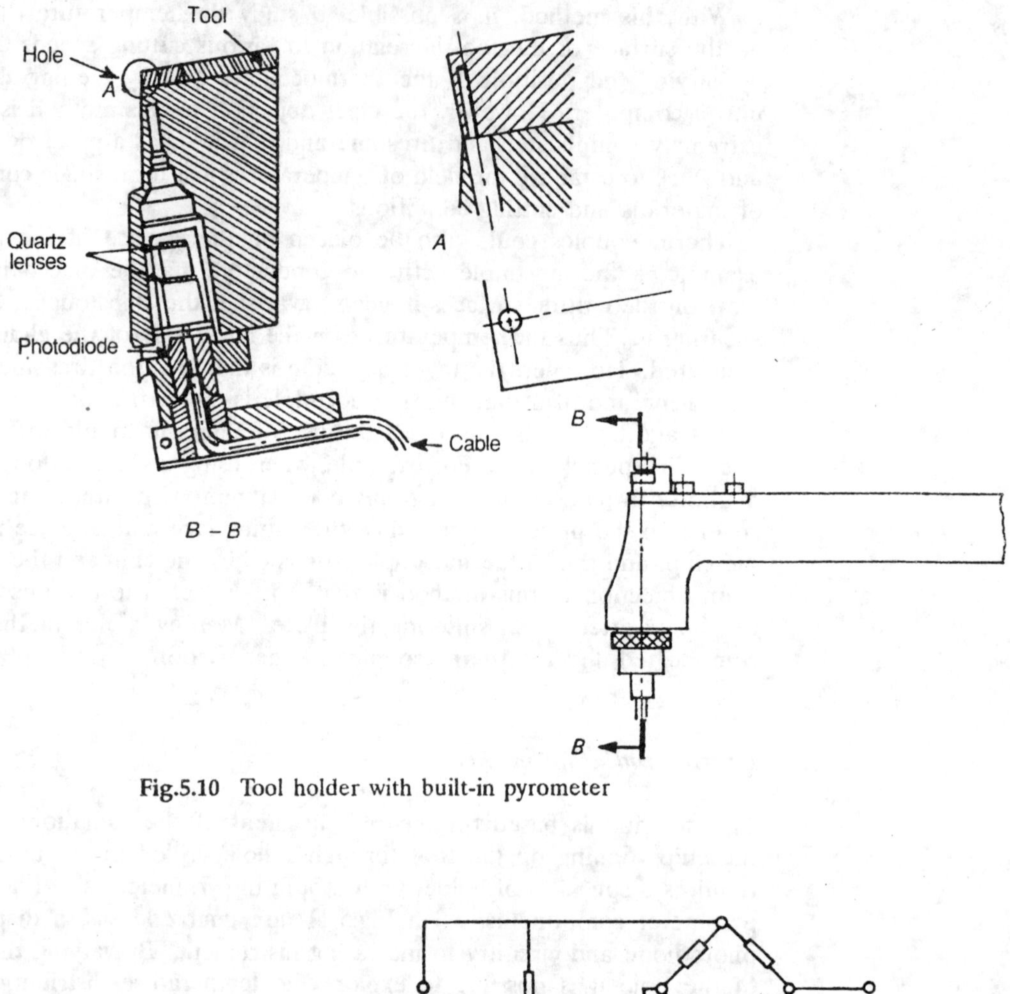


Fig.5.10 Tool holder with built-in pyrometer

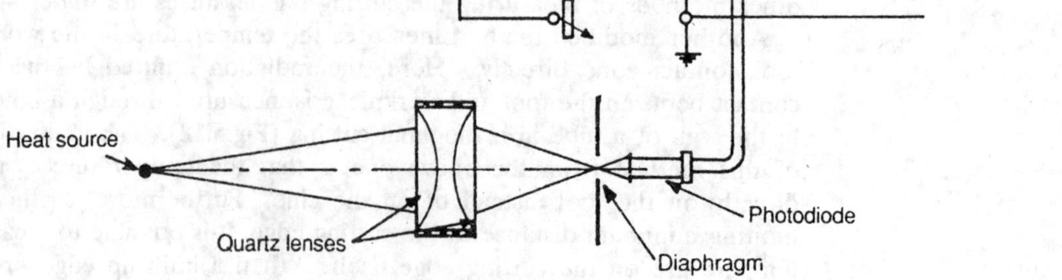


Fig.5.11 Schematic view of the pyrometer

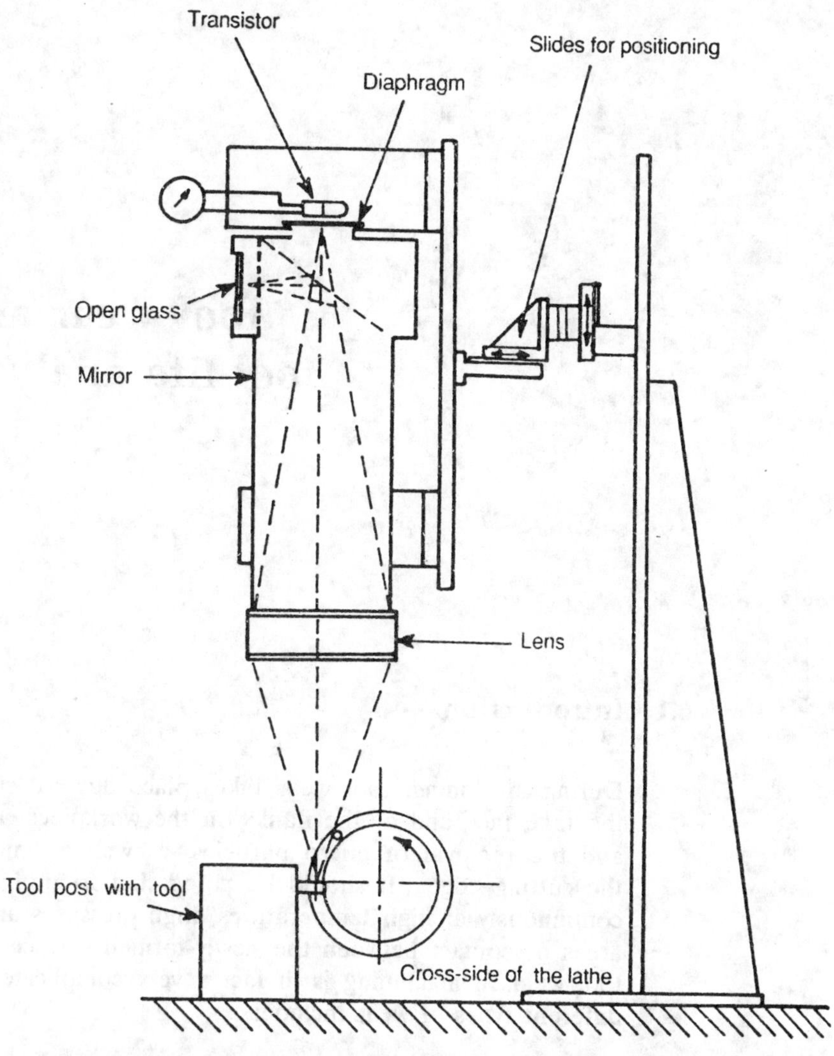


**Fig.5.12** Schematic diagram of temperature measuring device by tool radiation method

### 5.4.4 *Measurement by thermocolour*

Thermocolour materials are colouring agents which, at certain temperatures, change their original colour. The change of colour is very distinct and easily recognisable. There are thermocolours with one or single colour change and others with multiple colour change. With thermocolours, the distribution of temperatures over any heated object can be determined without recourse to measuring appliances or conductors. The measuring range is from 40°C to 1350°C.

# 6 Tool wear and tool-life analysis

## 6.1 Introduction

During machining, tool wear takes place due to friction of the chip on the rake face and of the flanks on the workpiece, and involves abrasion and the removal of micro particles, as well as microscopic chipping of the cutting edge. It should be noted that friction, causing wear, occurs continuously at high temperatures, high pressures and on relatively small areas of contact between the newly-formed surfaces. The mechanism of tool wear in machining is in fact a very complicated phenomenon. The different types of wear include:

(a) *Abrasion wear*. The removal of micro particles of the tool material by the hard constituents of the work material, e.g. casting-skin or forging-scale.

(b) *Adhesive(molecular)* Wear due to forces of molecular adhesion pick-up or sticking between tool and chip, with the sliding chip tearing away minute particles from the tool surface.

(c) *Diffusion wear* Wear due to mutual dissolution of the reacting materials or elements at high surface temperatures.

This features have already been discussed as thermally dependent phenomena, in detail, in Chapter 5.

Tool wear depends on several factors such as:

(i) physico-mechanical properties of the tool material and workpiece material,

(ii) conditions of the cutting edges and surfaces of the tool,

(iii) type of cutting fluid and its physico-chemical properties,

(iv) machining parameters and tool geometry, and

(v) rigidity of the machine tool, rigidity of the machine-fixture-tool-workpiece complex, and other factors.

## 6.2 Types of tool failure

The typical tool failure mechanisms for cutting tools/inserts are: (a) flank wear, (b) crater wear, (c) chipping, (d) thermal cracking, (e) deformation, (f) notching, (g) fracture and (h) built-up edge. However, flank wear and cratering are very important and are discussed below.

### *6.2.1 Flank wear*

Flank wear is noted by a wearland on the flank face of the tool or insert, just adjacent to the rake face (see Fig.6.1). It occurs mainly due to abrasive

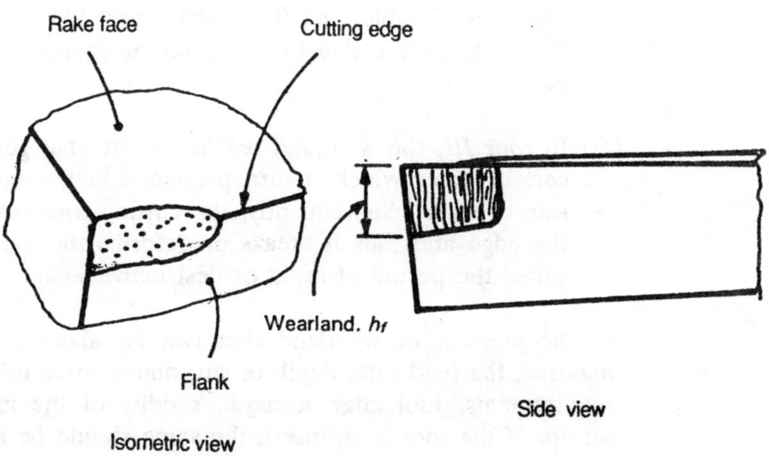


Fig.6.1 Flank wearland

action of the workpiece against the cutting edge at lower speeds, and the chemical reaction (diffusion) between tool and workpiece at higher speeds. The development of wearland usually follows a S-shaped pattern, as in Fig.6.2 with three distinct phases or zones.

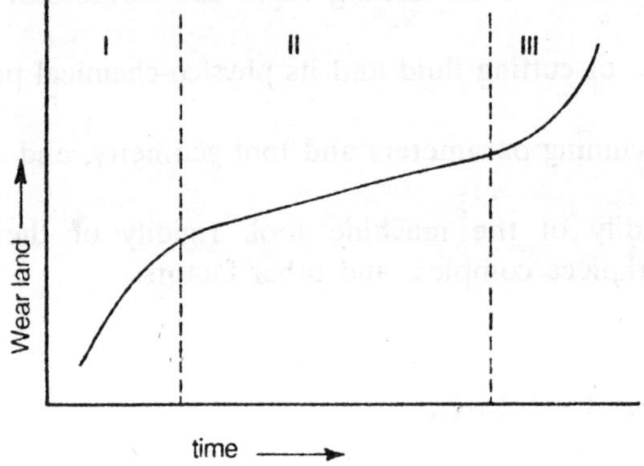


Fig.6.2 Development of wearland

(i) *Zone I* indicates the break-in period — the time of rapid wear. The small workpiece contact area rapidly generates a measurable wearland on removal of small quantities of tool material. The rate of wear in this zone can be minimized by proper honing or lapping of the cutting edge.

(ii) In *zone II*, wear proceeds at a constant rate. Also this zone forms the largest part of a tool's life. Hence flank wear is the most predictable failure mode. Generally flank wear is considered as the most desirable cause of tool failure, since a tool failing by flank wear must have (a) a highly predictable, and (b) a better tool life than it would have if the failure had been due to any other mechanism at the same operating parameters.

(iii) In *zone III*, the wearland reaches a size that generates high heat and certain forces, which, in turn, produce a higher and constantly increasing rate of wear. Subsequently, the cutting force exceeds the strength of the edge and thus it breaks or deforms the tool. This period is also called the period of rapid or destructive wear.

The amount of wearland that can be allowed depends on the tool material, the feed rate, depth of cut, dimensional tolerances, surface finish requirements, tool edge strength, rigidity of the machine tool, and the set-up. If the tool is an insert, the same should be indexed when the rate of wear begins to accelerate, i.e. at the end of zone II. It may be noted that, in practice, the number of parts that are to be machined to generate this wearland is first determined, and then the insert is indexed after it had produced that many number of parts.

### 6.2.2 *Cratering*

Cratering is a comparatively smooth and regular depression or 'pit' on the rake face of the tool or insert (Fig.6.3). This erosion, if not controlled or unchecked, will continue to the point, where it causes a breakthrough at the cutting edge.

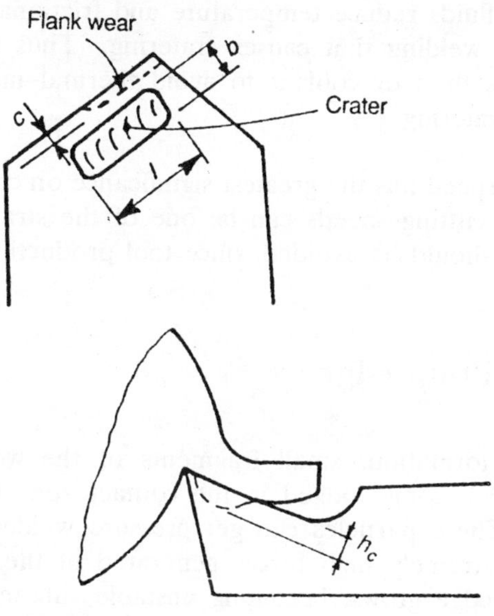


**Fig.6.3** Crater wear

Also called 'face wear', it is characterized by mainly the depth '$h_c$', width '$b$' of the wear crater; the change in length '$l$' of the crater is negligible.

During machining, both crater and flank wears increase, reducing the land width '$c$' behind the cutting edge. When the cratering reaches the cutting edge, tool failure occurs due to crumbling of the cutting edge. The tool has to be reground; or indexing is to be done if an insert is used as the tool.

Cratering is caused by a combined action of galling and welding between the chip and the rake face of the insert. For example, small particles of carbide are pulled out by the chip. Complete elimination of cratering may not always be possible. However, crater growth can be limited such that maximum allowable flank wear is first reached before crater breakthrough occurs. A suggested list of methods is given below:

(a) While using uncoated tungsten carbide tools or inserts, the selected grade should contain titanium carbide. These grades have greater resistance to cratering than the other carbide grades.

(b) It is also advisable to use tools or inserts coated with titanium carbide or aluminium oxide (a ceramic). These grades offer excellent crater resistance because of extreme hardness and anti-welding characteristics of both titanium carbide and ceramic coatings. Also these grades allow greater speeds. These aspects are discussed in detail in chapter 9 on tool materials.

(c) Cutting fluids reduce temperature and frictional forces, and also the pressure welding that causes cratering. Thus application of an appropriate fluid or coolant to avoid thermal–mechanical failure may retard cratering.

(d) Cutting speed has the greatest significance on cratering. At the worst, reduced cutting speeds can be one of the strategies. However, this method should be avoided, since tool productivity will be reduced.

## 6.3 Role of built-up edge

During chip formation, small fragments of the workpiece escape from the chip, and become lodged in the contact zone between the tool and workpiece. These particles can get pressure welded to the cutting edge due to the extremely high forces generated in the zone. Consequently, this built-up edge grows, becoming unstable subsequently, and when the particles break-off the cutting edge, carbide particles are pulled along with them causing rapid tool wear.

The built-up edge is seen as deposits of workpiece material on the rake face of the insert. These deposits periodically break free and leave irregularly shaped depressions along the cutting edge, extending to the crater area and cause generally smooth depression. Methods to cope with the problem of built-up edge are given below:

(a) Cutting speed can be increased, allowing less time for the formation of pressure welds, with other merits such as improved productivity and surface finish.

(b) Coolant application may prevent pressure welding.

(c) Certain chip groove geometries like positive rake tooling will reduce built-up edge with less cutting pressure and hence welding.

(d) Coated tools with either ceramic or titanium carbide coatings resist formation of built-up edge by their hardness and anti-welding characteristics, and possibly also because of their lower coefficient of friction. Further these tools can be used at increased cutting speeds.

## 6.4 Other notable aspects

Flank wear and cratering are the normal wear patterns. Certain other factors have to be considered if the working zone is to be restricted to these two types. These are briefly described.

**Catastrophic failure**
Chipping can occur when the cutting edge is broken off in small fragments without just being worn away. It takes place when the mechanical load exceeds the strength of the small sections of cutting edge, particularly in operations having variable shock loads.

Chipping represents catastrophic failure at increased forces and temperatures. Preventive actions include: (a) minimising deflection of any element in the operation, e.g. chuck, fixturing, tool blocks, turrets or the part itself, that can introduce shock loads on the cutting edge; (b) using honed or lapped insert where the cutting edge's sharp section has been rounded off; (c) selecting stronger geometry; and (d) selecting shock-resistant carbide grade.

**Thermal cracking**
Thermal cracks are caused by very high and rapid temperature changes at the cutting edge, especially if carbides are used. Being a poor conductor of heat, carbide has heat concentrated at the chip contact zone with the rest of the insert remaining relatively cool. Cracks are thus generated by the resulting stress, and isolated at small areas near the cutting edge, making vulnerable for getting dislodged by cutting forces.

Thermal cracks are highly probable in interrupted cutting, or when machining hardened parts with intermittent coolant application. These cracks manifest themselves on the rake surface and are usually perpendicular to the cutting edge. They form in the crater area, migrating forward to the cutting edge. Sometimes the cracks form parallel to the cutting edge or in a random direction. Remedial measures include that of applying a coolant correctly or otherwise removing it from the operation, and of selecting an appropriate shock-resistant carbide grade.

**Edge deformation**
Here the cutting edge is plastically deformed, generally with a part of the rake face depressed and the flanked nose mushroomed out. This phenomenon is common for severe operations, when machining hardened materials and generates intense heat. If the temperature of the chip–tool

interface rises to the point where the cobalt binder gives way, the softened edge is deformed by the cutting force. The countering actions include: (a) applying coolant to reduce temperatures, (b) using grades of higher wear resistance, (c) reducing cutting speed, and (d) reducing feed rate.

**Edge notching**

Edge notching refers to a very high degree of localised wear on both the rake face and the flank at the depth of the cut line, and is especially common while machining high temperature alloys. It is generally caused by a combination of mechanical and chemical factors. For example, the portion of the cutting edge in contact with the workpiece is in compression with the position just outside the cut in tension, thus causing minute chipping in the depth-of-cut zone. Alternatively if the material has a hard outer layer, caused by casting, forging, heat treating or a previous operation on a work-hardening material, this layer can accelerate abrasive wear at the depth-of-cut. Oxidation of the tool material at the machining temperatures, say above 800 °C, can also cause edge notching, wherein the hot carbide exposed to the air at the depth-of-cut time reacts with it to form a soft and unstable material that wears away rapidly. The remedial measures are: (a) selecting a tool geometry with larger lead angles of 30 to 45°, which provide a large portion of the edge in contact with the workpiece to enable uniform distribution of forces over a wider portion; (b) additional honing to strengthen the cutting edge and improve resistance to the abrasive action of the scale; and (c) as a last resort, reducing the feed rate.

**Fracture**

When a section of the tool/insert breaks off, fracture occurs. The broken section is large enough to cause immediate failure of the cutting edge. Fracture is caused by the cutting forces overcoming the bulk mechanical strength of the tool. Such wear should always be avoided since it could be dangerous to the operator. It may damage the machine tool, tool holder or workpiece, or it could prevent the use of other edges if inserts are used. The preventive measures could be that of: (a) selecting a more shock resistant grade, (b) selecting stronger insert geometries or thicker inserts, and reducing the operating parameters such as feed rate and/or depth-of-cut, and (c) indexing the insert with carefully chosen maximum flank wear criterion. Care should be taken to ensure flank wear as the guiding limit.

## 6.5 Cutting parameters on tool life

The metal removal in any machining operation is equal to the product of the operating parameters, namely, cutting speed, $v_c$, feed rate, $f$ and depth-of-cut, $b$. Hence an equal change in any of the three operating conditions will equally affect the metal removal and the tool life as well. Increase in any of the operating parameters in any degree will reduce tool life, and the extent of loss in tool life depends on which specific parameter has been increased.

Figure 6.4 depicts the effect of the parameters on tool life. The slope of the curve is highest for cutting speed, that for feed rate intermediate, and that for depth-of-cut the least. That is, in general, tool life is less affected by changes in depth-of-cut than by changes in either of the other two operating conditions, and that the effect of changes in feed rate is greater than that for change in depth-of-cut. Finally, cutting speed/velocity has a greater effect on tool life than either depth-of-cut or feed rate.

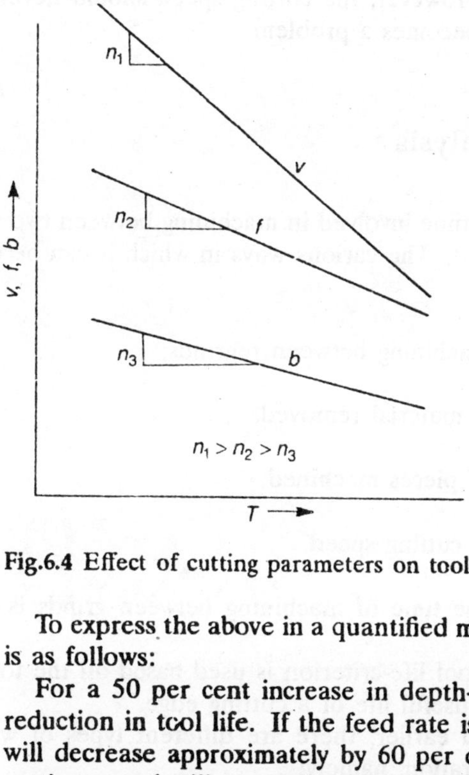


**Fig.6.4** Effect of cutting parameters on tool life

To express the above in a quantified manner, the comparative significance is as follows:

For a 50 per cent increase in depth-of-cut, there is only a 15 per cent reduction in tool life. If the feed rate is increased by 50 per cent, tool life will decrease approximately by 60 per cent, and a 50 per cent increase in cutting speed will generally reduce tool life by about 90 per cent.

Hence, as a general strategy to obtain the best compromise between tool life, and metal-removal rate, depth-of-cut should be maximum. Similarly, for optimizing trade-off between machining time and tool life, feed rate should be at the highest level possible. Finally, the determination of cutting velocity is most critical for establishing operating conditions.

However, there are certain limitations. The surface finish requirement may limit the feed rate, or the strength of the insert to withstand cutting forces may also limit feed rate. Similarly, the capability of the machine tool, part, cutting tool and fixturing to resist cutting forces may limit feed rate and depth-of-cut. Again, the amount of stock that needs to be removed from the part may limit depth-of-cut.

The cutting force is dependent on several factors besides the feed rate. Unit force on the cutting edge is best indicated by the maximum undeformed chip thickness. Increase in feed rate will increase, undeformed chip thickness, which is also affected by changes in lead angle. If lead angle is increased, feed can be increased, which is limited by the strength of the cutting edge.

Additionally, available machine horsepower often limits the metal-removal rate. On limited horsepower applications, depth-of-cut and feed rate should be maximised, and the cutting speed so set that the horsepower drawn is within limits. However, the cutting speed should never be set so low that built-up edge becomes a problem.

## 6.6 Tool-life analysis

Tool life is the time involved in machining between two successive grindings of a cutting tool. The various ways in which it can be expressed are given below:

(a) Time of machining between regrinds;

(b) Volume of material removed;

(c) Number of pieces machined;

(d) Equivalent cutting speed.

However, the time of machining between grinds is a popular measure of tool life.

Often, the tool life-criterion is used based on the tool wear measure to determine the useful life of a cutting edge.

As discussed earlier, there are different types of wear associated in a machining operation, namely:

(a) Attritious (small particle) wear associated with adhesion, shear plane ends,etc.,

(b) Abrasive wear, due to the cutting action of hard particles,

(c) Erosive wear, due to cutting action of particles in a fluid,

(d) Diffusion wear at high surface temperatures,

(e) Corrosive wear, due to chemical attack of a surface, and

(f) Fracture wear, which is chipping of a brittle surface.

The above wear mechanisms manifest themselves in progressive wear of the cutting tool in two forms (refer to Fig.6.5): (i) Crater wear, and (ii) Flank wear.

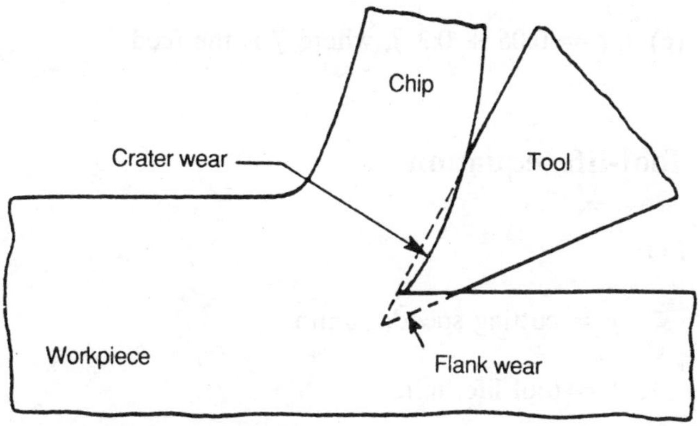


**Fig.6.5** Wear in metal cutting

**Crater wear**
Wear on the tool face characterized by the formation of a crater land resulting from the action of the chip flowing along the face.

**Flank wear**
Wear on the flank, where a wearland is formed from the rubbing action of the newly generated workpiece surface.

The criteria recommended for tool life testing are summarised below: Let

$VB$ = average flank wearland width,

$VB_{max}$ = maximum wearland width,

$KT$ = maximum crater depth,

$f$ = feed.

The criteria recommended to define the effective tool life for high-speed steel tools or ceramic tools are:

(a) catastrophic failure, or

(b) $VB = 0.3$ mm, if the flank is regularly worn, or

(c) $VB_{max} = 0.6$ mm, if the flank is irregularly worn.

For sintered carbide tools, one of the following criteria is recommended:

(a) $VB = 0.3$ mm, or

(b) $VB_{max} = 0.6$ mm, if the flank is irregularly worn, or

(c) $KT = 0.06 + 0.3\ f$, where $f$ is the feed.

## 6.7 Tool-life equation

Let

$v$ = cutting speed, m/min.

$t$ = tool life, min.

The tool-life equation is given by,

$$vt^n = C$$

where $n$ and $C$ are constants for a given work and tool material as well as machining conditions other than cutting speed (feed, depth of cut, fluid, tool geometry, etc.). This is called the Taylor's equation, after F. W. Taylor (1907), who first used to analyse the performance of HSS tools. The constant $C$ gives the cutting speed for one-minute tool life, since $t$ is normally expressed in minutes.

Some of the suggested values of $n$ for different tool materials are given below (refer to Fig.6.6):

| Tool material | $n$ |
|---|---|
| High speed steel | 0.1 |
| Tungsten Carbide | 0.2 |
| Ceramic | 0.4 |

Sometimes the tool-life equation is expressed as below:

$v_{60}$ = cutting speed at $t = 60$ min.

$v_{90}$ = cutting speed at $t = 90$ min.

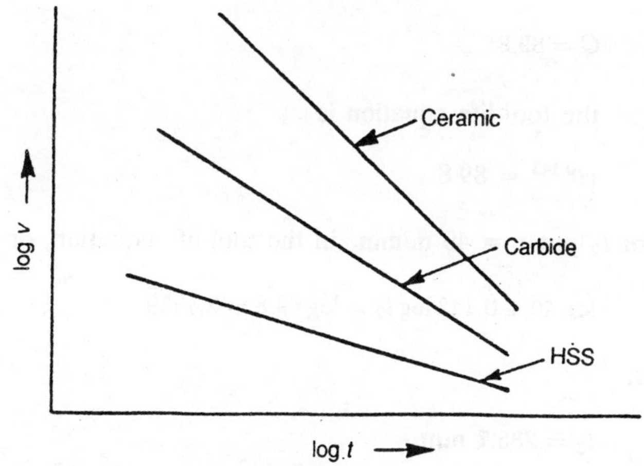


**Fig.6.6** Typical tool-life pattern

## 6.8 Solved examples

*Example 6.1*

While machining carbon steel by a tungsten–cobalt steel tool it was observed that the tool life was 60 minutes for a cutting speed of 50 m/min. Determine the tool life for a cutting speed of 40 m/min., using Taylor's tool-life equation, taking the index $n$ as 0.143.

***Solution***

At $v_1 = 50$ m/min., $t_1 = 60$ min., $v_2 = 40$ m/min., $n = 0.143$, $t_2 = ?$

**Tool-life equation:**

$$vt^n = C$$

or $\log v + n \log t = \log C$

Since $v_1 = 50$ m/min., $t_1 = 60$ min.

$$\log 50 + 0.143 \log 60 = \log C,$$

i.e.

$$\log C = 1.6990 + 0.143 \times 1.7782 = 1.9533$$

or,

$$C = 89.8$$

$\therefore$ the tool-life equation is

$$vt^{0.143} = 89.8$$

For $t_2$ put $v = 40$ m/min. in the tool-life equation, or

$$\log 40 + 0.143 \log t_2 = \log 89.8 = 2.4559$$

or,

$$t_2 = 285.7 \text{ min.}$$

*Example 6.2*

During the machining of low carbon steel with HSS cutting tool, the following observations were made:

| | | |
|---|---|---|
| Cutting speed, m/min. | 40 | 50 |
| Tool life, minutes | 40 | 10 |

Derive the $v - t$ relationship.

***Solution***

At $v_1 = 40$ m/min., $t_1 = 40$ min., $v_2 = 50$ m/min., $t_2 = 10$ min., the tool-life equation is given by

$$vt^n = C$$

or $\log v + n \log t = \log C.$

For $v_1$ and $t_1$

$$\log 40 + n \log 40 = \log C$$

$$1.6021 + 1.6021n = \log C \qquad \text{(i)}$$

For $v_2$ and $t_2$,

$$\log 50 + n \log 10 = \log C$$

$$1.6990 + n = \log C \tag{ii}$$

(i) − (ii) gives

$$(1.6021 - 1.6990) + (1.6021 - 1)n = 0$$

or, $n = 0.16$.

Substituting the value of $n$ in (ii), we get

$$\log C = 1.6990 + 0.16 = 1.859$$

or, $C = 72.28$

∴ The tool-life equation is $vt^{0.16} = 72.28$.

*Example 6.3*

Either cemented carbide or ceramic (oxide) may be used as tool materials while machining medium carbon steel. The Taylor tool-life equations are: (i) for carbide $vt^{0.25} = 800$, (ii) for oxide $vt^{1.25} = 8000$. Calculate the break-even speed above which oxide will give better tool life.

*Solution*

The tool-life equation is given by

$$vt^n = C$$

or

$$\log v + n \log t = \log C.$$

For carbide,

$$\log v + 0.25 \log t = \log 800 \tag{i}$$

For oxide,

$$\log v + 1.25 \log t = \log 8000 \tag{ii}$$

Multiplying (i) by 1.25 and (ii) by 0.25 and subtracting the latter, we get

$$v > \frac{800^{1.25}}{8000^{0.25}}$$

or, $v > 450$ m/min. (refer Fig.6.7).

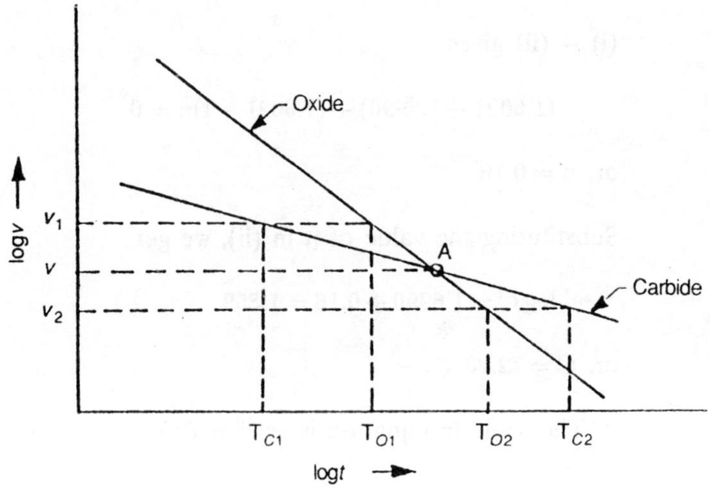


**Fig.6.7** Break-even speed

Point A in the graph gives the break-even speed where the tool life is the same for both carbide and oxide tool materials.

***Example 6.4***

A tool wear test was carried out by turning at two speeds, 60 m/min. and 80 m/min. all other conditions being held constant. The flank-land wear was measured at 5-minute intervals, giving the following values

| Time (min.) | Flank-land wear 60 m/min. (mm) | Flank-land wear 80 m/min. (mm) |
|---|---|---|
| Start | 0 | 0 |
| 5 | 0.375 | 0.575 |
| 10 | 0.525 | 0.775 |
| 15 | 0.650 | 1.05 |
| 20 | 0.800 | 1.30 |

If 0.75 mm wearland is taken as the criterion of failure, estimate the tool life at a speed of 72 m/min. for the same cutting conditions.

***Solution***

First, find the tool life, where wearland = 0.75.

$$v_1 = 60 \text{ m/min.}, \; v_2 = 80 \text{ m/min.}$$

Interpolating from the data,

$$t_1 = 18.33 \text{ min.}, \; t_2 = 9.375 \text{ min.}$$

Next establish tool-life equation at

$$v_1 = 60 \text{ m/min.}, \; t_1 = 18.33 \text{ min.}, \; v_2 = 80 \text{ m/min.}, \; t_2 = 9.375 \text{ min.}$$

The general tool-life equation is given by,

$$vt^n = C$$

$$\log v + n \log t = \log C$$

For $v_1$ and $t_1$,

$$\log 60 + n \log 18.33 = \log C$$

$$1.7782 + 1.2632n = \log C \qquad \text{(i)}$$

For $v_2$ and $t_2$,

$$\log 80 + n \log 9.375 = \log C$$

$$1.9031 + 0.9719 = \log C \qquad \text{(ii)}$$

(i) – (ii) gives

$$(1.7782 - 1.9031) + (1.2632 - 0.9719)n = 0$$

or,

$$n = 0.43.$$

Substituting $n$ in (i)

$$1.7782 + 1.2632 \times 0.43 = \log C$$

i.e. $\log C = 1.7782 + 0.5432 = 2.3214$

or,

$$C = 209.6.$$

Tool-life equation is

$$vt^{0.43} = 209.6$$

To find $t_3$ when $v_3 = 72$ m/min.

Tool-life equation is,

$$\log v_3 + 0.43 \log t_3 = 209.6$$

$$\log 72 + 0.43 \log t_3 = \log 209.6$$

$$1.8573 + 0.43 \log t_3 = 2.3214$$

$$\log t_3 = (2.3214 - 1.8573)/0.43 = 1.0793$$

or, $t_3$ = 12 min.

## 6.9 Exercise problems

6.1 If the life of a turning tool is 40 minutes and 25 minutes when used at speeds 80 m/min. and 100 m/min. respectively, what would be its life at 150 m/min. ?

6.2 The life of a turning tool while turning C-20 steel at 20 m/min. and 40 m/min. was observed to be 40 minutes and 10 minutes respectively. Establish the tool-life equation, and estimate the tool life if the cutting speed employed is 60 m/min.

6.3 When a 50 mm diameter rod of MS is turned in a lathe at 280 rpm, failure occurs in 10 minutes. When the speed is reduced to 180 rpm, the tool fails after 90 minutes of cutting time. Find out the cutting speed to be employed for a 45-minute tool-life. Assume a straight line relationship.

# 7 Machinability and machining economics

## 7.1 Machinability

The term 'machinability' chiefly refers to the evaluation of work materials with reference to machining. A material is said to have good machinability if tool wear is low or tool life is long, the surface finish produced is good and the cutting forces are low. Further, ease of chip disposal and good dimensional accuracy are also important factors. Also numerous variables such as tool material and geometry, and cutting conditions affect the above parameters in assessing machinability. Hence the term 'machinability' is a difficult concept to reduce to quantitative terms. However, some measure of machinability is necessary and useful for proper selection and manufacture of work materials for machining purposes.

Though machinability has various facets, it is common to express it in terms of the cutting speed for a given tool life in minutes, that is commonly taken for the purpose of comparing and ranking materials with reference to a standard one.

The machinability of any other material may be compared to this standard by determining the $v_{60}$ or $v_{90}$ and taking the ratio $v_{60}$ material/$v_{60}$ standard and expressing it as a percentage. This ratio is termed relative machinability. This implies that a material with a comparatively higher cutting speed for a 60 min. tool life will be considered to have a high machinability, which is desirable.

A better assessment of machinability will be to get on different machining operations and tool materials. The machinability rating, in this case, is based on the amount of metal removed per minute, representing average performance of the workpiece materials in different machining operations, i.e. average amount of metal removed per minute in all operations tested.

## 7.2 Solved examples

*Example 7.1*

In assessing machinability of different workpiece materials, the following data were obtained by tests on turning:

| Work material and hardness | Tool life min. | Cutting speed m/min. |
|---|---|---|
| 8640 steel 200 BHN | 30 | 120 |
| | 12 | 180 |
| 1020 steel 115 BHN | 44 | 210 |
| | 20 | 270 |
| 4340 steel 400 BHN | 40 | 60 |
| | 20 | 90 |

Estimate relative machinability considering 8640 steel 200 BHN as standard and, (a) $v_{60}$ as the criterion, (b) $v_{90}$ as the criterion, (c) $v_{40}$ as the criterion.

*Solution*

**8640 Steel 200 BHN**

$$vt^n = C$$

$$\log v + n \log t = \log C$$

At $v_1 = 120$ m/min., $t_1 = 30$ min.

$$\log 120 + n \log 30 = \log C$$

$$2.0792 + 1.4771n = \log C \qquad \text{(i)}$$

At $v_2 = 180$ m/min., $t_2 = 12$ min.

$$\log 180 + n \log 12 = \log C$$

$$2.2553 + 1.0792n = \log C \qquad \text{(ii)}$$

Subtracting (ii) from (i) gives,

$$(2.0792 - 2.2553) + (1.4771 - 1.0792)n = 0$$

or $n = 0.4$.

Substituting the value of $n$ in (i), we get

$$\log C = 2.0792 + 1.4771 \times 0.4$$

$$= 2.6700$$

$$\text{or} \quad C = 467.7.$$

$\therefore$ the tool-life equation is $vt^{0.4} = 467.7$.

*To find* $v_{60}$ *when* $t = 60$ *min.:*

$$\log v_{60} + 0.4 \log v = \log 467.7$$

$$\log v_{60} + 0.4 \log 60 = \log 467.7$$

or $\log v_{60} = 2.6700 - 0.4 \times 1.7782 = 2.6700 - 0.7113 = 1.9587$

Therefore,

$$v_{60} = 90.93 \text{ m/min.}$$

*To find* $v_{90}$ *when* $t = 90$ *min.:*

$$\log v_{90} + 0.4 \log 90 = \log 467.7$$

$$\log v_{90} + 0.4 \times 1.9542 = 2.6700$$

$$\log v_{90} = 2.6700 - 0.7817 = 1.8883$$

Therefore,

$$v_{90} = 77.32 \text{ m/min.}$$

*To find* $v_{40}$, *when* $t = 40$ *min.:*

$$\log v_{40} + 0.4 \log 40 = \log 467.7$$

$$\log v_{40} + 0.4 \times 1.6021 = 2.6700$$

$$\log v_{40} = 2.6700 - 0.6408 = 2.0292$$

Therefore $v_{40} = 106.9$ m/min.

**1020 Steel 115 BHN**

$$vt^n = C$$

$$\log v + n \log t = \log C$$

At $v_1 = 210$ m/min., $t_1 = 44$ min.,

$$\log 210 + n \log 44 = \log C$$

$$2.3222 + 1.6435n = \log C$$

At $v_2 = 270$ m/min., $t_2 = 20$ min.,

$$\log 270 + n \log 20 = \log C$$

$$2.4314 + 1.3010n = \log C$$

Subtracting (ii) from (i) gives

$$(2.3222 - 2.4314) + (1.6435 - 1.3010)n = 0$$

or $n = 0.32$

Substituting the value of $n$ in (i), we get

$$\log C = 2.3222 + 1.6435 \times 0.32 = 2.8481$$

or $C = 704.9$

Hence the tool-life equation $vt^{0.32} = 704.9$.

*To find $v_{60}$, when $t = 60$ min.:*

$$\log v_{60} + 0.32 \times 1.7782 = 2.8481$$

$$\log v_{60} = 2.8481 - 0.5690 = 2.2791$$

Therefore $v_{60} = 190.1$ m/min.

*To find $v_{90}$, when $t = 90$ min.:*

$$\log v_{90} + 0.32 \log 90 = \log 704.9$$

$$\log v_{90} = 2.8481 - 0.32 \times 1.9542 = 2.2228$$

Therefore $v_{90} = 167$ m/min.

*To find $v_{40}$, when $t = 40$ min.:*

$$\log v_{40} + 0.32 \log 40 = \log 704.9$$

$$\log v_{40} = 2.8481 - 0.32 \times 1.6021 = 2.3354$$

Therefore $v_{40} = 216.5$ m/min.

**4340 steel 400 BHN**

$$vt^n = C$$

$$\log v + n \log t = \log C$$

At $v_1 = 60$ m/min., $t_1 = 40$ min.,

$$\log 60 + n \log 40 = \log C$$

$$1.7782 + 1.6021n = \log C \qquad \text{(i)}$$

At $v_2 = 90$ m/min., $t_2 = 20$ min.,

$$\log 90 + n \log 20 = \log C$$

$$1.9542 + 1.3010n = \log C \qquad \text{(ii)}$$

Subtracting (ii) from (i) results in

$$(1.7782 - 1.9542) + (1.6021 - 1.3010)n = 0$$

or, $n = 0.58$.

Substituting the value of $n$ in (i), we get

$$\log C = 1.7782 + 1.6021 \times 0.58 = 2.7074$$

or, $C = 509.8$.

Hence, the tool-life equation is $vt^{0.58} = 509.8$.

*To find $v_{60}$, when $t = 60$ min.:*

$$\log v_{60} + 0.58 \log 60 = \log 509.8$$

$$\log v_{60} = 2.7074 - 0.58 \times 1.7782 = 1.676.$$

Therefore $v_{60} = 47.42$ m/min.

*To find $v_{90}$, when $t = 90$ min.:*

$$\log v_{90} + 0.58 \log 90 = \log 509.8$$

$$\log v_{90} = 2.7074 - 0.58 \times 1.9542 = 1.574$$

Therefore $v_{90} = 37.5$ m/min.

Given from data, $v_{40} = 60$ m/min.

The calculations are summarised as below:

| Work material | Cutting speed m/min. | | |
|---|---|---|---|
| | $v_{60}$ | $v_{90}$ | $v_{40}$ |
| 8640 steel 200 BHN | 90.93 | 77.32 | 106.9 |
| 1020 steel 115 BHN | 190.1 | 167.00 | 216.5 |
| 4340 steel 400 BHN | 47.42 | 37.5 | 60.0 |

**For 1020 steel 115 BHN**

(a) $v_{60}$ *as the criterion:*

$$\text{Relative machinability} = \frac{v_{60}\ \text{material}}{V_{60}\ \text{standard}}$$

$$= 190.1/90.93 = 2.09 \quad \text{or} \quad 209 \text{ per cent.}$$

Similarly,

(b) $v_{90}$ *as the criterion:*

Relative machinability = 167/77.32 = 2.16 or 216 per cent.

(c) $v_{40}$ *as the criterion:*

Relative machinability = 216.5/106.9 = 2.03 or 203 per cent.

**For 4340 steel 400 BHN**

(a) $v_{60}$ *as the criterion:*

Relative machinability = 47.42/90.93 = 0.5215 = 52.15 per cent.

(b) $v_{90}$ *as the criterion:*

Relative machinability = 37.5/77.32 = 0.485 = 48.5 per cent.

(c) $v_{40}$ *as the criterion:*

Relative machinability = 60/106.9 = 0.5613 = 56.13 per cent.

*Example 7.2*

In a machinability test, twelve specific machining operations were done on four workpiece materials. The following table provides the data:.

| | Machining operation | Removal rate for 4130 steel | % relative to 4130 steel | | |
|---|---|---|---|---|---|
| | | | 4340 steel | Inconel | HS-25 |
| | | $R$ | $R_1$ | $R_2$ | $R_3$ |
| (a) | Face milling | 43.76 | 5.9 | 4.5 | 2.6 |
| (b) | End milling | 72.12 | 3.05 | 11.4 | 10.2 |
| (c) | Straddle milling | 79.82 | 6.8 | 11.6 | 9.6 |
| (d) | Turning | 188.49 | 5.4 | 15.2 | 23.2 |
| (e) | Threading, CD | 4.87 | 55.2 | 83.0 | 96.0 |
| (f) | Band sawing | 33.87 | 5.1 | 22.8 | 19.0 |
| (g) | Drilling 6.25 mm dia. | 9.67 | 5.1 | 10.6 | 12.0 |
| (h) | Drilling 12.5 mm dia. | 23.60 | 7.1 | 9.3 | 9.4 |
| (i) | Reaming 6.25 mm dia. | 0.344 | 6.9 | 7.2 | 15.0 |
| (j) | Reaming 12.5 mm dia. | 0.66 | 6.6 | 10.0 | 16.7 |
| (k) | Tapping 6.25 mm dia. | 1.51 | 3.9 | 18.9 | 7.4 |
| (l) | Tapping 12.5 mm dia. | 2.89 | 3.7 | 13.9 | 14.1 |

Calculate the relative machinability of the three workpiece materials, arbitrarily taking the machinability of 4130 steel as 100 per cent.

***Solution***

**To find the cumulative removal rate:**

**Note:** Unit area for band sawing is assumed.

**4130 steel**

$$
\begin{aligned}
\text{Total removal rate, } R &= \sum R_x \\
&= [43.76 + 72.12 + 79.82 + 188.49 \\
&\quad +4.87 + 33.87 + 9.67 + 23.60 \\
&\quad +0.344 + 0.66 + 1.51 + 2.89] \\
&= 461.6 \text{ cm}^3/\text{min.} \\
\text{Average removal} &= 461.6/12 \\
&= 38.47 \text{ cm}^3/\text{min.}
\end{aligned}
$$

**4340 steel**

$$
\begin{aligned}
\text{Total removal rate, } R_1 &= [43.76 \times 0.059 + 72.12 \times 0.0305 \\
&\quad +79.82 \times 0.068 + 188.49 \times 0.054 \\
&\quad +4.87 \times 0.552 + 33.87 \times 0.051 \\
&\quad +9.67 \times 0.051 + 23.60 \times 0.071 \\
&\quad +0.344 \times 0.069 + 0.66 \times 0.066 \\
&\quad +1.51 \times 0.039 + 2.89 \times 0.037] \\
&= [2.58 + 2.20 + 5.43 + 10.18 \\
&\quad +2.69 + 1.73 + 0.49 + 1.68 \\
&\quad +0.02 + 0.004 + 0.06 + 0.11] \\
&= 27.174 \text{ cm}^3/\text{min.} \\
\text{Average removal} &= 27.174/12 = 2.26 \text{ cm}^3/\text{min.}
\end{aligned}
$$

**Inconel**

$$
\begin{aligned}
\text{Total removal rate, } R_2 &= [43.76 \times 0.045 + 72.12 \times 0.114 \\
&\quad +79.82 \times 0.116 + 188.49 \times 0.152 \\
&\quad +4.87 \times 0.83 + 33.87 \times 0.228 \\
&\quad +9.67 \times 0.106 + 23.6 \times 0.093 \\
&\quad +0.344 \times 0.072 + 0.66 \times 0.10 \\
&\quad +1.51 \times 0.189 + 2.89 \times 0.139] \\
&= [1.97 + 8.22 + 9.26 + 28.65 \\
&\quad +4.04 + 7.72 + 1.03 + 2.19 \\
&\quad +0.025 + 0.066 + 0.285 + 0.402] \\
&= 63.86 \text{ cm}^3\text{/min.} \\
\text{Average removal} &= 63.86/12 = 5.32 \text{ cm}^3\text{/min.}
\end{aligned}
$$

**HS-25**

$$
\begin{aligned}
\text{Total removal rate, } R_3 &= [43.76 \times 0.026 + 72.12 \times 0.102 \\
&\quad +79.82 \times 0.096 + 188.49 \times 0.232 \\
&\quad +4.87 \times 0.96 + 33.87 \times 0.19 \\
&\quad +9.67 \times 0.12 + 23.60 \times 0.094 \\
&\quad +0.344 \times 0.157 + 0.66 \times 0.167 \\
&\quad +1.51 \times 0.074 + 2.89 \times 0.141] \\
&= [1.14 + 7.356 + 7.66 + 43.73 \\
&\quad +4.675 + 6.435 + 1.16 + 2.218 \\
&\quad +0.054 + 0.11 + 0.112 + 0.407] \\
&= 75.06 \text{ cm}^3\text{/ min.} \\
\text{Average removal} &= 75.06/12 = 6.255 \text{ cm}^3\text{ /min.}
\end{aligned}
$$

To summarize:

Cumulative removal rates for

(1) 4130 Steel = 461.6 $cm^3$ /min.

(2) 4340 Steel = 27.174 $cm^3$ /min.

(3) Inconel = 63.86 $cm^3$ /min.

(4) HS - 25 = 75.06 $cm^3$ /min.

Taking machinability of 4130 steel as 100 per cent(standard),

Relative machinability of 4340 steel = 27.174/461.6 = 0.059 = 5.9 per cent

Relative machinability of Inconel = 63.86/461.6 =0.138 = 13.8 per cent

Relative machinability of HS-25 = 75.06/461.6 = 0.163 = 16.3 per cent

**Note:** Relative machinabilities can also be calculated on the basis of average removal rates for the standard material and for other workpiece materials.

## 7.3 Machining efficiency

In machining, the greatest efficiency is achieved at the point of lowest cost per cu. cm (volumetric) metal removal. Experimentally, this point is determined by changing one variable (speed or feed), while holding the other constant.

The first step is to select a near-optimum feed; then speed is increased in three stages, and it is determined as to which speed is the most economical. Selection of the near-optimum feed is based on the engineer's knowledge, gained through extensive previous testing and experience of the capabilities of work material and equipment. After this first series of operations — the 'speed search' — speed is held constant and feed is varied in three increments to determine which is the most economical — the 'feed search'.

The number of cu.cm of metal removed before a predetermined wearland developed on the edge of a tool (the basis on which tool life is judged) provides a measure of efficiency.

Normally, the factors included in the determination of machining costs are: tool usage cost, tool change cost and operating cost. Operating cost is based on a standard cost rate per minute for all operations. Tool change cost is obtained by the use of a specific rate of tool changing that had been assigned to each operation. Tool usage cost includes the cost of new tools. The cost of regrinding operation has a specific, assigned rate of tool usage.

## 7.4 Solved examples

***Example 7.3***

In a machining efficiency test on turning, the following data were obtained for *speed search.*

| | | | |
|---|---|---|---|
| Speed,m/min. | 38 | 51 | 63 |
| Speed, rpm | 245 | 327 | 408 |
| Feed, mm/rev. | 0.22 | 0.22 | 0.22 |
| Feed, mm/min. | 53.9 | 71.9 | 89.7 |
| Tool life, $cm^3$ | 590 | 410 | 148 |
| Rate, $cm^3$/min. | 21.96 | 29.34 | 36.5 |

Tool usage cost = Rs. 2.58

Tool change cost = Rs. 1.00

Operating cost = Rs. 1.16 per min.

Find the optimum speed.

***Solution***

**(a) At speed = 38 m/min.**

$$\text{Time to remove one cm}^3 \text{ of metal} = \frac{\text{Tool life (cm}^3)}{\text{Removal rate (cm}^3/\text{min.)}}$$

$= 590/21.96 = 26.87$ min. to remove 590 $cm^3$

or 26.87/590 = 0.05 min. to remove 1 $cm^3$.

**Note:** The above value is also the reciprocal of the removal rate $cm^3$ min., i.e. 1/21.96 = 0.05 min./$cm^3$)

**Cost/$cm^3$**

Operating cost = Rs. 1.16 × 0.05 = 0.06

Tool change cost = Rs. 100/590 = 0.0017

Tool usage cost = Rs. 2.58/590 = 0.0044

Total cost = Rs. 0.066 per $cm^3$.

**(b) At speed 51 m/min.**

Time to remove/cm$^3$ = 1/29.34 = 0.034 min./cm$^3$

**Cost/cm$^3$**

| | | | | |
|---|---|---|---|---|
| Operating cost | = | Rs. 1.16 × 0.034 | = | 0.03944 |
| Tool change cost | = | Rs. 1.00/410 | = | 0.00244 |
| Tool usage cost | = | Rs. 2.58/410 | = | 0.00629 |
| Total cost | = | Rs. 0.048 (per cm$^3$) | | |

**(c) At speed 63 m/min.**

Time to remove/cm$^3$ = 1/36.55 = 0.027 min./cm$^3$

**Cost /cm$^3$**

| | | | | |
|---|---|---|---|---|
| Operating cost | = | Rs. 1.16 × 0.027 | = | 0.03132 |
| Tool change cost | = | Rs. 1.00/148 | = | 0.00676 |
| Tool usage cost | = | Rs. 2.58/148 | = | 0.01743 |
| Total cost | = | Rs. 0.056 per/cm$^3$ | | |

The total cost is minimum at speed 51 m/min.

Optimum speed = 51 m/min., and

Total cost = Rs. 0.048/cm$^3$.

### *Example 7.4*

In a face milling test, the following data were obtained for a feed search.

| Feed, mm/rev. | 0.26 | 0.33 | 0.41 |
|---|---|---|---|
| Feed, mm/min. | 11.18 | 14.19 | 17.63 |
| Speed m/min. | 12.60 | 12.60 | 12.60 |
| Tool life, cm$^3$ | 200.00 | 213.00 | 120.00 |
| Rate cm$^3$/min. | 2.92 | 3.75 | 4.57 |

Tool usage cost = Rs. 21.50

Tool change cost = Rs. 2.00

Operating cost = Rs. 1.16 per min.

Find the optimum feed.

***Solution***

**(a) At feed = 0.26 mm/rev.**

Time to remove/$cm^3$ = 1/2.92 = 0.3425 min./$cm^3$

Cost/$cm^3$

| | | | | |
|---|---|---|---|---|
| Operating cost | = | Rs. 1.16 × 0.3425 | = | 0.3973 |
| Tool change cost | = | Rs. 2.00/200 | = | 0.01 |
| Tool usage cost | = | Rs. 21.50/200 = 0.1075 | | |
| Total cost | = | Rs. 0.515/$cm^3$ | | |

**(b) At feed = 0.33 mm/rev.**

Time to remove /$cm^3$ = 1/3.75 = 0.27 min./$cm^3$

Cost/$cm^3$

| | | | | |
|---|---|---|---|---|
| Operating cost | = | Rs. 1.16 × 0.27 | = | 0.3132 |
| Tool change cost | = | Rs. 2.00/213 | = | 0.00939 |
| Tool, usage cost | = | Rs. 21.50/213 | = | 0.10094 |
| Total cost | = | Rs. 0.424/$cm^3$ | | |

**(c) At feed = 0.41 mm/rev.**

Time to remove/$cm^3$ = 1/4.57 = 0.219 min./$cm^3$

Cost/$cm^3$

| | | | | |
|---|---|---|---|---|
| Operating cost | = | Rs. 1.16 × 0.219 | = | 0.25404 |
| Tool change cost | = | Rs. 2.00/120 | = | 0.01667 |

Tool usage cost = Rs. 21.50/120 = 0.17917

Total cost = Rs. 0.445/cm$^3$

The tool cost is minimum at feed = 0.33 mm/rev.

Optimum feed = 0.33 mm/rev.

Minimum cost = Rs. 0.424/cm$^3$

## 7.5 Machining economics

In factory situations, one frequently encounters the problem of selection of cutting conditions, tool and workpiece materials, etc. The machining parameters will definitely affect the production rate as well as the total cost involved in producing a part. Initially proposed by Gilbert (1950), machining economics analysis largely concerns itself with selection of machining parameters for an optimum production cost or production rate.

Again tool life becomes significant in this context since the cost of the tools influences the machining cost considerably, i.e.

$$vt^n = C \tag{i}$$

where

$v$ = cutting speed

$t$ = tool life

$n$ and $C$ = constants.

At high cutting speeds, machine and labour costs will be low, but with high tool costs. Conversely, for low cutting speeds, tool cost will be low with high machine and labour costs. The problem concerns with finding the optimum cutting speed. Consider turning operation.

Let

$t_c$ = machining time per part

Also

$$t_c = (\pi DL)/v.f \tag{ii}$$

where

$D$ = dia. of workpiece,

$L$ = axial length of work to be cut

$v$ = cutting speed

$f$ = feed

If $t$ = tool life for the cutting conditions, the costs involved are:

| | | |
|---|---|---|
| Direct labour and machine cost | = | $X_1 t_c$ |
| Tool changing cost per part | = | $X_1 t_d t_c / t$ |
| Tool cost per part | = | $X_2 t_c / t$ |

Total cost per part,

$$TC = X_1 t_c + X_1 t_d \left(\frac{t_c}{t}\right) + X_2 \left(\frac{t_c}{t}\right)$$

where

$X_1$ = machine and operator costs with overhead(Rs/min.)

$t_d$ = 'down time' in minutes to change a tool or the tool changing time.

$X_2$ = mean cost of the cutting edge or the tool cost

**For minimum cost**

Substituting for $t_c$ and $t$ from equations (i) and (ii), and making $d(TC)/dv$ = 0, the tool life for minimum cost is found as

$$t_0 = \left[\frac{1}{n} - 1\right] \left[\frac{X_1 t_d + X_2}{X_1}\right]$$

The corresponding cutting speed,

$$v_0 = \frac{C}{(t_0)^n}$$

or

$$v_0 = C\left[\frac{1}{\frac{1}{n}-1}\right]^n \left[\frac{X_1}{X_1 t_d + X_2}\right]^n$$

**For maximum production rate**

The total machining time is

$$T = t_c + t_d(t_c/t) + t_w$$

where

$t_c$ = machining time

$t_d$ = tool changing time

$t$ = tool life, min.

$t_w$ = work changing time

Again substitute for $t_c$ and $t$ from equations (i) and (ii) and make $dT/dv$ = 0. For maximum production rate, optimum tool life is given by

$$t_0' = t_d\left[\frac{1}{n}-1\right]$$

The corresponding cutting speed is,

$$v_0' = \frac{C}{(t_0')^n}$$

or,

$$v_0' = \frac{C}{[(1/n-1)t_d]^n}$$

Thus,

$$\frac{t_0'}{t_0} = \frac{t_d}{[t_d + X_2/X_1]}$$

Hence the optimum tool life for the production rate will be lower than that for minimum cost per part, and the converse holds true for optimum cutting velocities (refer Fig.7.1).

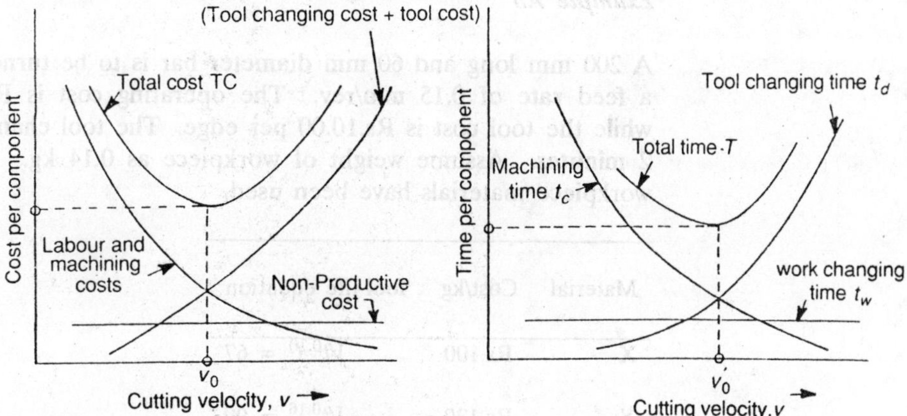


(a) Optimum cutting velocity for minimum cost.

(b) Optimum cutting velocity for maximum cutting rate.

Note: Generally $v_0' > v_0$

**Fig.7.1 Optimum cutting velocities**

## Machinability index based on cost

The most commonly used machinability index, as discussed earlier, is with reference to a 60 minute tool life, i.e.

$$M_{60} = (v_{60})_1/(v_{60})_2$$

Shaw suggests that the machinability index based on cost is a better index, as

$$M_0 = (TC_2)_0/(TC_1)_0$$

where $(TC_1)_0$ is the minimum cost per part for a given tool, work material or cutting fluid, and $(TC_2)_0$ is the corresponding minimum cost per part for the second tool, work material or cutting fluid.

The above equation may also be written as

$$M_0 = \frac{[X_1 t_{co}/(1-n)]_2}{[X_1 t_{co}/(1-n)]_1} \quad \text{or} \quad M_0 = \frac{C_1(t_0)_2^{n_2}(1-n_1)}{C_2(t_0)_1^{n_1}(1-n_2)}$$

Similarly, the machinability index based on a given tool life $M_T$ is given by

$$M_T = (v_t)_1/(v_t)_2 = (C_1/C_2)t^{(n_2-n_1)}$$

$M_0$ and $M_T$ do not differ very much for $n_1$ and $n_2$ are appropriately the same. If $n_1$ and $n_2$ differ widely, the two machinability criteria are not equivalent.

## 7.6 Solved examples

*Example 7.5*

A 200 mm long and 60 mm diameter bar is to be turned on a lathe with a feed rate of 0.15 mm/rev. The operating cost is Rs.0.50 per minute while the tool cost is Rs.10.00 per edge. The tool changing time is about 2 minutes. Assume weight of workpiece as 0.14 kg. The following two workpiece materials have been used.

| Material | Cost/kg | Tool-life equation |
|---|---|---|
| X | Rs.100 | $Vt^{0.10} = 67$ |
| Y | Rs.120 | $Vt^{0.16} = 90$ |

(a) Calculate tool-life values and optimum cutting velocities for minimum cost with no consideration for material cost, and maximum production-rate criteria for both workpiece materials. State which material should be chosen for total minimum cost. (b) If maximum production rate is the criterion, what will be the difference in total cost?

*Solution*

$f$ = 0.15 mm/rev. $D$ = 60 mm, $L$ = 200 mm

Operating cost $X_1$ = Rs. 0.50 per min.

Tool cost $X_2$ = Rs. 10.00 per edge

$t_2$ = 2 min.

**(a) Minimum cost criterion**

*Tool-life basis*

For material $X$: $n = 0.10$

$$(t_0)_X = \left(\frac{1}{0.10} - 1\right)\left(\frac{0.5 \times 2 + 10}{0.5}\right) = 198 \text{ min.}$$

For material $Y$: $n = 16$

$$(t_0)_Y = \left(\frac{1}{0.16} - 1\right)\left(\frac{0.5 \times 2 + 10}{0.5}\right) = 115.5 \text{ min.}$$

*Cutting velocity criterion*

For material $X$: $n = 0.10$, $C = 67$

$$(v_0)_X = 67\left[\frac{1}{(1/0.10)-1}\right]^{0.1}\left[\frac{0.5}{0.5\times 2+10}\right]^{0.1} = 39.5 \text{ m/min.}$$

For material $Y$: $n = 0.16$, $C = 90$

$$(v_0)_Y = 90\left[\frac{1}{(1/0.16)-1}\right]^{0.16}\left[\frac{0.5}{0.5\times 2+10}\right]^{0.16} = 42.1 \text{ m/min.}$$

**Maximum production criterion**

*Tool-life values*

For material $X$: $n = 0.10$

$$(t_0')_X = \left(\frac{1}{0.1}-1\right)2 = 18\text{min.}$$

For material $Y$: $n = 0.16$

$$(t_0')_Y = \left(\frac{\cdot 1}{0.16}-1\right)2 = 10.5\text{min.}$$

*Cutting velocity criterion*

For material $X$: $n = 0.10$, $c = 67$

$$(v_0')_X = \frac{67}{[((1/0.1)-1)\,2]^{0.1}} = 50.15 \text{ m/min.}$$

For material $Y$: $n = 0.16$, $c = 90$

$$(v_0')_Y = \frac{90}{[((1/0.16)-1)\,2]^{0.16}} = 61.8 \text{ m/min.}$$

**Total cost**

*(i) without considering material cost*

Minimum cost criterion: $(TC)_0 = t_{co}\left(\dfrac{X_1}{1-n}\right)$

For material $X$: $n = 0.10$, $v_0 = 39.5$ m/min.

$$[t_{co}]X = \frac{\pi DL}{f} \cdot \frac{1}{(v_0)X} = \left(\pi \times \frac{60}{1000} \times \frac{200}{0.15}\right) \frac{1}{39.5} = 6.365 \text{ min.}$$

$$[T_{Co}]X = \frac{X_1}{1-n} \cdot t_{co} = \frac{0.5}{1-0.1} \times 6.365 = \text{Rs } 3.536$$

For material *Y*: $n = 0.16$

$$[t_{co}]_Y = 251.43/42.1 = 5.972 \text{ min.}$$

$$[T_{co}]_Y = \frac{0.5}{(1-0.16)} \times 5.972 = \text{Rs. } 3.555$$

*(ii) Material cost*

Weight of workpiece = 0.14 kg.

Material cost for *X* = 100 × 0.14 = Rs. 14.00

Material cost for *Y* = 120 × 0.14 = Rs. 16.80

(iii) Total cost including material cost

Material *X* = (machining cost) + (material cost) = 3.536 + 14

= Rs. 17.536

Material *Y* = (machining cost) + (material cost) = 3.535 + 16.8

= Rs. 20.355

Hence material *X* is better than material *Y* and must be chosen.

**(b) Cost for maximum production criterion**

Material *X*:

$$(t'_{co})_X = 251.43/50.15 = 5.014 \text{ min.}$$

since

$$\frac{\pi DL}{f} = \pi \times \frac{60}{1000} \times \frac{200}{0.15} = 251.43\text{m}$$

Material *Y*:

$$(t'_{co})_Y = 251.43/61.8 = 4.068 \text{ min.}$$

Total cost $TC'$ is given by

$$TC' = X_1 t'_{co} + X_1 t_d \left(\frac{t'_{co}}{t'_0}\right) + X_2 \left(\frac{t'_{co}}{t_0}\right)$$

$$[TC']_X = 0.5 \times 5.014 + 0.5 \times 2 \times (5.014/18) + 10 \times (5.014/18) = \text{Rs.}\ 5.571$$

Similarly,

$$[TC']_Y = 0.5 \times 4.068 + 0.5 \times 2 \times (4.068/10.5) + 10 \times (4.068/10.5) = \text{Rs.}6.296$$

Additional cost for material $X = [TC']_X - [TC]_X = 5.571 - 3.536 =$ Rs. 2.035

Additional cost for material $Y = [TC']_Y - [TC]_Y = 6.296 - 3.555 =$ Rs. 2.741

## 7.7 Exercise problems

7.1 In assessing a suitable grade of carbide tool the following data were obtained in turning 8640 steel 190 BHN:

| Carbide grade | Tool life min. | Cutting speed m/min. |
|---|---|---|
| M | 43 | 120 |
| | 18 | 180 |
| P | 17 | 150 |
| | 43 | 90 |

Determine which carbide grade is better taking $v_{40}$ as the criterion.

7.2 In a machining efficiency test on turning, the following data were obtained for a feed search:

| | | | |
|---|---|---|---|
| Feed,mm/rev. | 0.20 | 0.22 | 0.24 |
| Feed,mm/min. | 65.4 | 71.9 | 78.5 |
| Speed m/min. | 51 | 51 | 51 |
| Tool life cu.cm | 360 | 410 | 82 |
| Rate,cm$^3$/min. | 27.20 | 29.34 | 31.63 |

Tool usage cost = Rs. 2.58
Tool charge cost = Rs. 1.00
Operating cost = Rs. 1.16 per min.

Find the optimum feed.

7.3 In a face milling test, the following data were obtained for 'speed search':

| | | | |
|---|---|---|---|
| Speed m/min. | 10.65 | 12.6 | 15.3 |
| Speed, rpm | 36 | 43 | 52 |
| Feed, mm/rev | 0.33 | 0.33 | 0.33 |
| Feed, mm/min. | 11.88 | 14.19 | 17.16 |
| Tool life, $cm^3$ | 200 | 213 | 107 |
| Rate, $cm^3$/min. | 2.92 | 3.75 | 4.57 |

Tool usage cost = Rs. 21.50
Tool change cost = Rs. 2.00
Operating cost = Rs. 1.16 per min.

Calculate the optimum speed.

7.4 A 100 mm long 35 mm dia. bar is to be turned at a feed rate of 0.26 mm/rev. The operating cost is Rs.10.00 per min. and the tool cost is Rs.75.00 per edge. The tool changing time is 4 minutes. A carbide tool is used with two cutting fluids for which the values of $n$ estimates in tool-life equation are:

Cutting fluid I: $n = 0.22$ and $C = 67$

Cutting fluid II: $n = 0.32$ and $C = 67$

Find which cutting fluid is better based on relative cost.

7.5 If in the previous problem, the criterion had been maximum production rate, which one would have been the better cutting fluid.

7.6 A 250 mm long, 40 mm dia., alloy workpiece is to be turned at a feed rate of 0.1 mm/rev. Two tool materials are to be analysed: namely HSS and Carbide tools. The data for the two tool materials are as follows:

| | Tool life min. | Cutting speed m/min. |
|---|---|---|
| HSS | 15 | 40 |
| | 35 | 30 |
| Carbide | 15 | 140 |
| | 45 | 90 |

The HSS costs an average of Rs.25.00 per edge while carbide costs Rs.60.00 per edge. The tool changing time is 3 minutes. Take the better operating cost as Rs.5.00 per minute. Find the better tool material based on minimum cost for machining.

# 8 Cutting fluids

## 8.1 Introduction

Cutting fluids are applied to the tool–workpiece–chip zone in several metal cutting operations to improve the machining performance. These improvements are dependent upon several variables, such as tool and work materials, the type of cutting fluid and to a large extent on cutting conditions.

### *Functions of a cutting fluid*

Basically, the functions which a cutting fluid is expected to fulfil are the following:

(a) to cool the workpiece and tool;

(b) to reduce friction;

(c) to protect the workpiece against rusting;

(d) to provide anti-weld properties;

(e) to wash away the chips.

The relative significance of these functions depends on the workpiece material, cutting rate, type of cutting tool material and the part finish required.

### *Action of the cutting fluid*

The primary function of a cutting fluid is to control the heat in the metal cutting process. This is achieved in two ways:

(a) by the straight cooling action, i.e. carrying away heat generated in cutting, and

(b) by the lubricating action, i.e. reducing the heat generated by reducing the amount of friction.

There are three significant heat generation sources in a metal cutting operation (Fig.8.1), as discussed in Chapter 5.

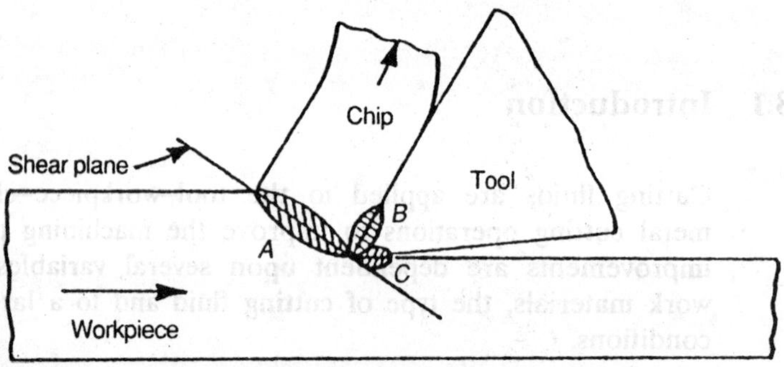


*A* – Shear zone (60% of heat)
*B* – Chip - tool zone (30% of heat)
*C* – Tool-work zone (10% of heat)

**Fig.8.1** Sources of heat in metal cutting

**(a) Shear zone**
As the chips are formed by plastic deformation during the shearing process, the metal portion immediately ahead of the cutting edge of the tool is severely compressed, resulting in high temperatures enabling plastic flow. This process requires tremendous power, and approximately 97 per cent of the useful work done during metal cutting is released as heat.

As the atoms in the metal ahead of the tool are disturbed, the friction involved in the shear zone is estimated to account for 60 per cent or more of the total heat generated.

**(b) Tool–chip interface**

As the tool continues to push through the workpiece, a chip eventually slides up the rake face of the tool. This sliding creates 'external friction', releasing heat which is estimated to be about 30 per cent of the total heat generated in metal cutting.

**(c) Tool–workpiece interface**

As the flank of the tool slides over the cut surface, it too produces friction and releases heat — the remaining 10 per cent or so. As the tool wears, the percentages of heat liberated in the various zones are likely to vary considerably.

There is also the problem of built-up edge formation, which is a transient wedge-shaped mass of metal that is much harder than the workpiece. If the built-up edge is large and flat along the tool face, it decreases the effective rake angle of the cutting tool, demanding more power to cut the metal. This also results in excessive flank wear and cratering of the rake face and also contributes to high surface roughness. However, if the built-up edge is small and sharp, the effective rake angle is increased, thus requiring lower cutting force and also the cutting edge is protected. One of the objectives of the cutting fluid is to control the amount of built-up edge.

To perform the first function of the cutting fluid, which is cooling, the liquid has to be most effective in dissipating heat or in other words it must have a high specific heat, a high heat of vapourization and high thermal conductivity. Oil is a poor liquid in these respects. Water is the best cooler, but it promotes or contributes to rust and has zero lubricity. Due to these factors chemical coolants and water-based emulsions are widely used practically.

The second function, that of lubricating, is not well understood. However, the concept of shear angle and coefficient of friction between chip and tool explain the phenomenon fairly well as briefly described below.

During machining, for a given work material, cutting tool and metal removal rate, the amount of heat produced in the shear zone largely depends on the size of the shear angle (Fig.8.2). If this shear angle is small, then the shear plane runs out a considerable distance ahead of the tool, so that the metal removed is deformed into a short, thick chip. This severe cutting action generates considerable heat. But if the shear angle is large, the shear path is short, thus resulting in a longer, thinner chip and hence considerably less heat.

It should also be noted that the size of the shear angle is controlled directly by the coefficient of friction between the sliding chip and the rake face of the tool. The lower the friction, the larger the shear angle. This is where the action of cutting fluid is significant.

If the friction between the chip and rake face is reduced by the application of a lubricating type cutting fluid, then the heat due to friction in this zone is also reduced. In addition, this reduction in friction causes the shear angle to become larger and hence the heat of plastic deformation, the major source of heat, is also reduced.

The cutting fluid also controls the built-up edge on the tool by reducing the friction between the chip and the tool, thus minimising the chip-to-tool welding responsible for the built-up edge.

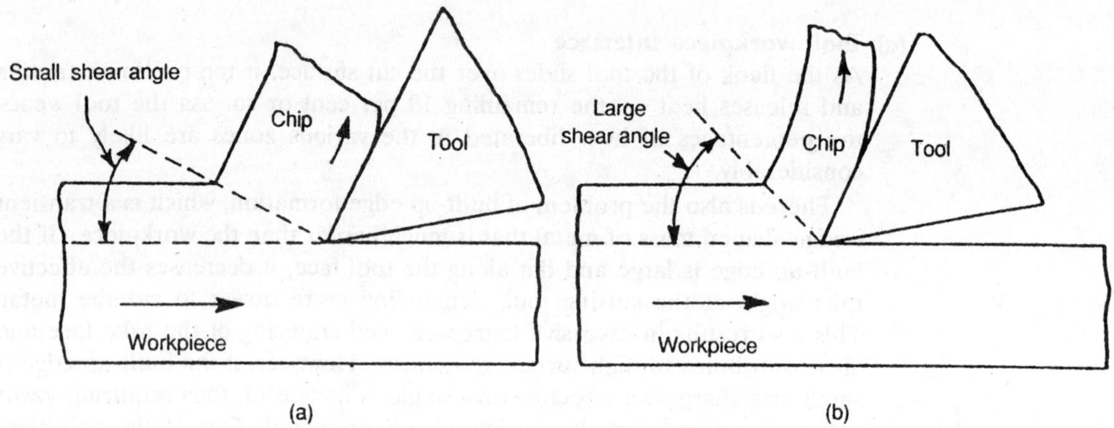


Fig.8.2 Effect of shear angle on heat generation

### *Mechanism of lubricating action*

In most metal cutting operations, the fluid film lubrication is ineffective due to high pressures in the cutting zone. Under such a condition, metal-to-metal contact can be prevented by using lubricants containing additives that result in the formation of an absorbed film. Such lubricants are called extreme-pressure lubricants. This absorbed film, composed of lubricant molecules which have chemically combined with the metal's surface atomic structure, is tough and resists removal even at high pressures and high sliding velocity. This type of lubrication is called boundary lubrication, since the lubrication is provided at the boundary or interface of the two surfaces in contact. Such films are often only three or four molecules in effect, a few millionths of a mm.

Figure 8.3 illustrates the two paths for the cutting fluid to the cutting edge, i.e., through the interspaces between the chip and the rake face, or between the workpiece and the tool flank. The quantity of cutting fluid which gets into the cutting zone is limited due to (a) the chip and workpiece moving in directions opposite to the fluid flow, and (b) the extreme thinness of the labyrinth formed by the surface irregularities, discouraging copious fluid flow.

Capillary action probably plays an important role in getting the cutting fluid to penetrate part of the way (or all the way) to the cutting edge. The liquid vaporizes and reaches the cutting edge as a gas because of high temperatures at the chip-tool interface. This gas provides a pressure separation between the chip and the rake face and also carries the additives that form the absorbed film to the edge.

Proper selection of additives will promote formation of absorbed films on the freshly cut metal. These films are more easily sheared than the parent metal, thereby protecting the rake face from pressure-welding. The commonly used additives are sulphur and chlorine.

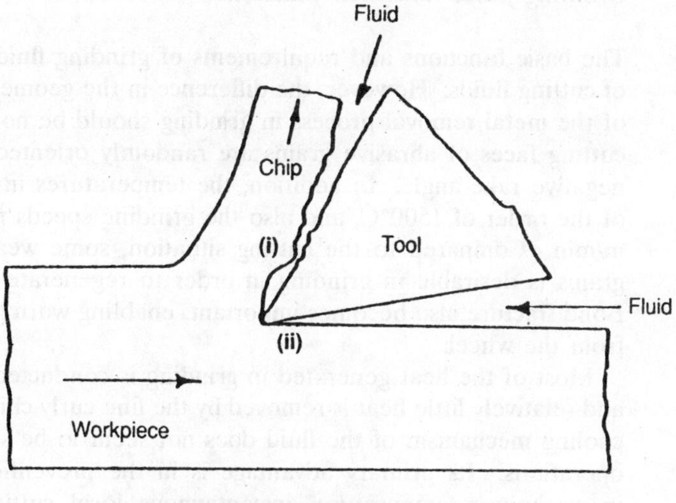


Fig.8.3 Paths for the cutting fluid to the cutting edge

*Cutting process conditions*

Proper application of cutting fluid in the cutting zone can greatly improve the machining performance. Investigations and reports indicate that when turning with high-speed steel tools, tool life can be doubled by applying cutting fluids at the tool flank rather than by conventional flooding. Carbide tool life could be increased by flooding at the chip interface as well as from the bottom up along the tool flank.

The optimum quantity and type of additive is also important. A lubricating film may not form if the reaction is too weak, and on the other hand if its is too strong a reaction, it may chemically attack both the tool and the workpiece.

Though the functions of a cutting fluid include both cooling and lubricating actions, the relative significance of each is also affected by the machining process itself. At low cutting speeds, chemical action can be very predominant. However, as the cutting speed increases, there is less time for the fluid to get to the cutting edge and less time for chemical action and hence friction-reducing capability decrease with increasing speed.

Thus, at high speeds, good cooling capability is of prime importance, while at low speeds good lubricating capability is the prime requisite. An optimum cutting fluid combines both these properties to the highest degree possible.

*Grinding fluids and their functions*

The basic functions and requirements of grinding fluids are similar to that of cutting fluids. However, the difference in the geometry and the dynamics of the metal removal process in grinding should be noted. In grinding, the cutting faces of abrasive grains are randomly oriented and usually have a negative rake angle. In addition, the temperatures in grinding are higher, of the order of 1500°C, and also the grinding speeds may range upto 5000 m/min. Compared to the cutting situation, some wear by fracture of the grains is desirable in grinding in order to regenerate sharp cutting edges. Bond fracture also becomes important, enabling worn grains to get expelled from the wheel.

Most of the heat generated in grinding is conducted into the workpiece, and relatively little heat is removed by the fine curly chips or the wheel. The cooling mechanism of the fluid does not seem to be significant in grinding operations. Its primary advantage is in the prevention of a gradual rise in workpiece temperature; instantaneous local cutting temperatures are probably not significantly reduced by wet grinding. However, chemically active fluids containing sulphur or chlorine additives are effective in reducing cutting forces, improving surface finish and increasing grinding-wheel life. Hence the primary function of grinding fluids is lubrication rather than cooling, though there exist the possibility of enhanced grain fracture due to reaction with the fluid additives.

## 8.2 Types of cutting and grinding fluids

There are four basic types of cutting and grinding fluids that are widely used:

(a) cutting oils,

(b) emulsifiable oils,

(c) chemical fluids,

(d) gaseous products.

**(a) Cutting oils**

Cutting oils are made from mineral oil and may be used either as straight (uncompounded), or as compounded, with polar additives like lard oil, and/or as chemically active additives like sulphur and/or chlorine.

The application of straight mineral oils is restricted to very light-duty operations on high machinability metals.

Among the compounded cutting oils, napthenic-based oils are a good example. They are used because of their greater compatibility with additives. The polar additives enhance the cutting fluids load-carrying capacity or cutting capabilities. Lard oil, castor oil and sperm oil are some of the common polar additives. However, polar additives have the disadvantages of formation of disagreeable odours and a tendency to gum.

Commonly used chemical additives or extreme-pressure lubricants(EP additives) contain sulphur and/or chlorine. These provide a tougher and stable film of lubrication at the chip–tool interface.

The compounded cutting oils usually contain a combination of both types of additives to cater to the wide ranging needs of industry. Examples include: (1) fatty-mineral-oil blend, (2) sulphurised fatty mineral oil, (3) chlorinated fatty or non-fatty mineral oil, (4) sulphurised mineral oil, (5) sulpho-chlorinated fatty-oil blend, (6) any combination of the above oils, sometimes with other metal salts or solid lubricants.

The compounded oils are applied to low-speed, low-feed on difficult-to-machine metals or in form-grinding from the solid.

**(b) Emulsifiable oils**

Also called soluble oils, water-miscible fluids or emulsifiable cutting fluids, these oils are in fact oil droplets suspended in water, blending the oil with emulsifying agents and other materials. Addition of polar additives and/or EP additives enhances the lubricating capability of the emulsions.

In appearances, these range from milky to clear. Normally these fluids are applied at high-cutting speeds with low pressures, providing both cooling and lubrication.

The merits of emulsifiable oils over straight cutting oils are:

(1) higher reduction of heat thus allowing higher cutting speeds;

(2) cleaner working conditions;

(3) greater economy — being largely water-based;

(4) better operator preference — cooler and cleaner parts;

(5) health and safety benefits — no fire hazard, and reduction of oil misting, etc.

(6) sufficient in-process rust control and rancidity control.

The applications include practically all light, moderate and heavy-duty cutting operations except in the case of extremely difficult-to-machine metals, and also for all grinding operations, excluding form grinding.

(c) Chemical fluids

These fluids are blends of a number of chemical agents in water. These agents include:

(1) amines and nitrites for rust prevention,

(2) nitrates for nitrite stabilization

(3) phosphates and borates, for water softening

(4) soaps and wetting agents, for lubrication and reduction of surface tension,

(5) phosphorous, chlorine, and sulphur compounds for chemical lubrication,

(6) glycols, and

(7) germicides to control growth of bacteria.

The chemical fluids contain no mineral oil and they form either true solutions in water or extremely fine colloidal solutions.

Also called synthetic fluids, they consist of two general groups: those with and without wetting agents.

Synthetic fluids with wetting agents have the properties of lubricity, low surface tension, good rust inhibition, and leave a liquid residue. These fluids allow machine tool parts, like machine slides, turrets and other moving parts, to function smoothly.

Synthetic fluids without wetting agents provide excellent rust control, but little or no lubricity. These are applied in rough-grinding operations.

Semi-synthetic fluids contain a small amount of mineral oil plus additives to improve lubricating properties, incorporating the qualities of both synthetic fluid and emulsifiable oils.

Sometimes 2 to 10 per cent concentration of chlorine, sulphur or other additives are added to both synthetic and semi-synthetic fluids to impart extreme-pressure or boundary-lubrication effects. Hence these fluids are used in more difficult and tough machining and grinding applications.

The merits of synthetic and semi-synthetic fluids are:

(1) rapid heat dissipation,

(2) good size control,

(3) good detergent properties,

(4) high workpiece visibility,

(5) easily removable, light, residual films,

(6) easy mixing with little agitation,

(7) good resistance to rancidity leading to enhanced machine life,

(8) easy control of concentration.

However, some of the demerits are:

(1) lack of lubricity (synthetic fluids),

(2) high detergency, irritating sensitive hands, and

(3) tendency to foam in high-agitation operations.

**(d) Gaseous fluids**

Air is the most commonly used gaseous cutting fluid as applied in dry cutting, where the cooling, and lubricating action of air is taken for granted.

Air can also be used as a compressed gas to provide better cooling. The stream of compressed air directed at the cutting edge removes more heat by forced convection and, in addition, blows the chips away.

Other gases used are argon, helium and nitrogen. Their chief action is one of preventing oxidation of workpiece and chip. However, these gases are used only in very special applications because of their high cost.

Other examples include gases with boiling points below room temperature, such as Freon or carbon dioxide, which are compressed and sprayed at the cutting zone, imparting evaporative cooling to very low temperatures ($< 0°$ F).

**Other fluids**

These include limited application of chlorinated solvents such as carbon tetrachloride and trichloro ethane. These highly volatile products wet well, dissipate heat rapidly and produce the low-shear-strength film needed on difficult metals. However, being highly toxic, they require to be used on premises with excellent ventilation.

## 8.3 Selection of the cutting fluid

Proper selection of cutting fluid depends on the workpiece material and its machinability rating, as well as the type of metal-cutting operation selected for increased effectiveness.

A typical cutting fluid recommendations chart is given in Table 8.1 for the well-known machining operations:

**Table 8.1** Cutting fluid recommendations

| Severity | Operation | Machinability ratings | | | | | |
|---|---|---|---|---|---|---|---|
| | | Class 1 | Class 2 | Class 3 | Class 4 | Class 5 | Class 6 |
| 1 | Broaching | A | A | A,J | A,K | D | C |
| 2 | Tapping | A,B | A,B | A,B | A,B | H,K | H,K |
| 3 | Threading | B,C | B,C | B,C | B,C | D,G | D,H |
| 4 | Reaming | D | C | B | A | F | G |
| 5 | Milling | E,C,D | E,C,D | E,C,D | C,B | E,H to K | E,H to K |
| 6 | Drilling | E,D | E,C | E,B | E,A | E,D | E,D |
| 7 | Pláning, shoping, turning, surface grinding, sawing | E | E | E | E | E | E |
| 8 | Thread grinding | A,B | A,B | A,B | A,B | | E |

**Note:** A - High sulphur mineral fatty oil, B - Medium sulphur, medium chlorine mineral fatty oil, C - Low sulphur, medium chlorine mineral fatty oil, D- Chlorinated mineral oil, E - Water miscible fluids (light to heavy duty as needed) F,G,H,J K - Mineral fatty oils (F has highest fatty oil content, K the lowest).

The machinability rating used to classify the workpiece materials are based on AISI 1112* steel (BHN 180 approx.) as 100 per cent machinable.

**Ferrous metals**

Class 1 — 70 per cent or higher

Class 2 — 50 per cent to 70 per cent

Class 3 — 40 per cent to 50 per cent

Class 4 — 40 per cent or lower

**Non-ferrous metals**

Class 5 — 100 per cent or higher

Class 6 — below 100 per cent

Also note water-based fluids are not to be used on magnesium.

**Cutting fluids for heat-resisting alloys**

Exotic alloys are tougher metals with higher resistance to high temperatures. These are composed of Ni, Cr, Mo Co, W, Ti, Fe and other elements.

---

AISI 1112: American Iron and Steel Institute classification system

They include precipitation-hardening stainless steels, iron-nickel-chromium-molybdenum alloys (e.g. Discaloy), nickel-based alloys (e.g. Inconel, Hastalloy), cobalt-based alloys (e.g. S-816 and HS 25) and titanium alloys. These superalloys, used in the aerospace industry, require the superior heavy-duty cutting fluids listed below:

| Cutting conditions | Objectives | Cutting fluid |
|---|---|---|
| Lighter, more moderate speeds | Cooling | EP emulsifiable oil with rich concentration. |
| Extra severe,low speed operation built-up edge | Lubricaticn prevention | Heavy duty cutting oils (Sulphchloronated oil blends) |
| Ni content | To prevent intergranular corrosion | Mineral oils with a content of Nickel. |

**Cutting fluids for non metallics**

Popular under this group are thermoplastic and thermosetting plastics. The chief objective in this context is cooling with some lubrication.

| Type of plastic | objective | Cutting fluid |
|---|---|---|
| Thermoplastic | Cooling to prevent softening/melting | Aqueous emulsion or solution, air blast |
| Thermosetting | Coolant to avoid charring | Aqueous cutting fluids |
| Threading | – | Light viscosity, fatty oil blend, and soft soap in a heavy solution |

# 9 Advances in cutting tool materials

## 9.1 Introduction

A significant feature of the modern manufacturing industry is the development of improved, machines cutting tools, and production processes. The cutting tool plays a pivotal role in any metal-cutting operations. Over the years, considerable research has lead to the evolution of new varieties of tool materials in the race for higher productivity. Progress from carbon tool steels, high-speed steels, cast alloys to carbides and ceramics has made possible the use of higher cutting speeds at each stage of development, because of improvements achieved in the tool material and machine tools.

A summary of the milestones in the evolution of cutting tool materials, along with the increase in cutting speeds achieved in use, is shown in Fig.9.1.

Till 1900, carbon tool steel, in a hardened state, was largely used in machining. At the turn of the century, high-speed steel was introduced, and today, it is available in several types. The cast cobalt-base tools introduced around 1915, are employed for machining operations at much higher cutting speeds.

Sintered carbides were introduced in and around 1930, which today are extremely popular in most of the machining operations. Being modified by further innovation, 'coated carbides' are being introduced in many factories.

Shortage of tungsten has led to the development of 'cermets', that are solid TiC and TiN.

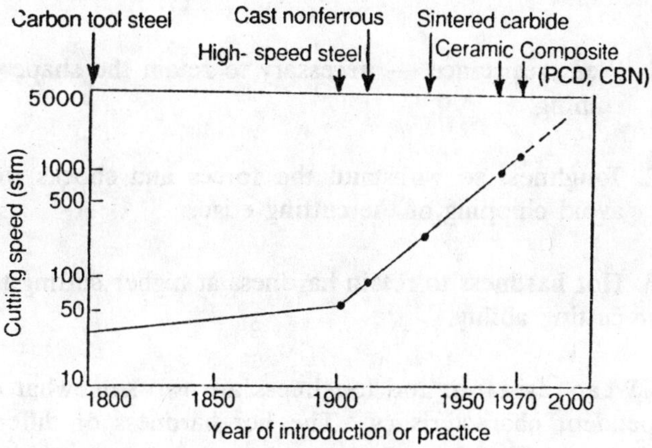


**Fig.9.1 Evolution of tool materials**

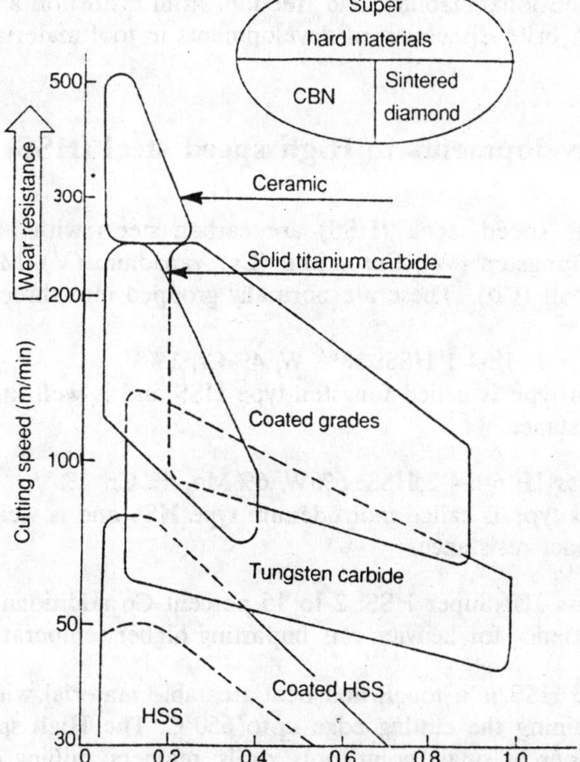


**Fig.9.2 Comparison with reference to hot hardness or wear resistance and toughness**

**Properties of cutting tool materials**

The search for new cutting tool materials has been guided by three significant factors:

1. Wear resistance — necessary to retain the shape and efficiency in machining.
2. Toughness to withstand the forces and shocks in interrupted cuts, to avoid chipping of the cutting edge.
3. Hot hardness to retain hardness at higher cutting temperatures and thus cutting ability.

Wear resistance and toughness are two somewhat contradictory interdependent characteristics. The hot hardness of different tool materials is shown in Fig.9.2.

In addition, the other properties of importance are coefficient of thermal expansion, thermal conductivity, grindability, weldability, hardenability, dimensional stability, and freedom from distortion after heat treatment.

A brief discussion of developments in tool materials is given below.

## 9.2 Developments in High speed steel (HSS) tools

High speed steels (HSS) are carbon steels with alloying elements such as Tungsten (W), Chromium (Cr) Vanadium (V), Molybdenum (Mo) and Cobalt (Co). These are normally grouped into three classes:

**Class I:** 18-4-1 HSS: 18% W, 4%Cr, 1%V

This type is called tungsten-type HSS and is well known for air and heat resistance.

**Class II:** 6-6-4-2 HSS: 6%W, 6%Mo, 4%Cr, 2%V

This type is called molybdenum type HSS and is well known for wear and impact resistance.

**Class III:** Super HSS: 2 to 15 percent Co additionally to increase cutting efficiency for heavier cuts imparting higher temperatures.

The HSS is a tough and heat treatable material with high 'red hardness' retaining the cutting edge upto 650°C. The High speed steels find applications as single point tools, drills, reamers, milling cutters. These can be sharpened by grinding with Aluminium Oxide wheels, economical compared to carbide tools and perform fairly well. The hardness is about 65 to 67 $R_c$. These are used at 20 to 30 surface m/min for most steels.

The notable recent developments are briefly discussed below:

**(a) Sintered HSS**

High speed steels are used extensively for cutting and forming tools. However, the cast HSS can limit toughness, present heat treating problems and decrease grindability.

The alternate sintered HSS, though expensive has superior strength and toughness. The powder metallurgy process produces a finer grain structure and avoids the carbide clusters that limit the strength in cast HSS. There is less chance of distortion or cracking during heat treatment, thus allowing a higher hardness. The improved grindabililty, in spite of high alloy and carbide contents, makes tool-making and resharpening easy, with less possibility of damage due to burning, for example, in tools which need accurate finishing because of their intricate geometry.

Due to homogeneity and uniform hardness, sintered HSS gives more consistent wear-life over the entire edge of a given tool. The finer grains result in tougher tools, having greater resistance to chipping, a major cause of cutting-edge breakdown. Tool life is longer and productivity is increased because higher speeds and/or feeds are possible.

The PM steels are especially useful when the tool-shape is complex, e.g. hobs, form tools, milling cutters, end mills, etc.

**(b) Ion-plated HSS with $Al_2O_3$**

In this innovation, $Al_2O_3$ coating is deposited on the HSS by pulsed ion plating techniques — an extension of vacuum-coating technology.

Claimed to be an economical process, the tools can be produced for a little additional cost. The tools have the surface characteristics of a refractory oxide, with the flexibility and price of HSS. There is a remarkable increase in tool life of the ion-plated tools, compared to ordinary tools in turning, milling, threading die or tap applications over a wide range of workpiece materials.

**(c) TiN coated HSS**

TiN coatings are being introduced for HSS twist drills and taps. The tools are coated by using the physical vapour deposition (PVD) process.

The beneficial effects include longer life, higher productivity and reduced power consumption, and these accrue from the characteristics of the coatings as given below:

(i) The coating is approximately three times harder than the base tool steel.

(ii) The coating adds a measure of lubricity, which improves chip flow, resulting in less heat generation.

(iii) The coating acts as a barrier between the drill and the chip, inhibiting microwelding of the chip to the base tool.

The best applications are those with higher cutting speeds with a slight increase in chip load per revolution, resulting in increase in tool life and productivity.

## 9.3 Developments in carbide inserts

**Manufacturing carbide inserts**

The manufacturing process starts with mining and milling tungsten to produce a tungsten concentrate, which is usually chemically processed to form ammonium paratungstate. Hydrogen is used to reduce the substance to form metallic tungsten powder. Approximately 6 per cent carbon(by weight) is added, the mixture is blended, and then heated in a furnace to form tungstem carbide(WC) powder.

After screening, blending and sampling, cobalt is added, together with any other additives, and the ingredients are ball-milled together for 1 to 5 days, generally with a volatile solvent. After ball-milling, the mixture is dried, and paraffin is added to hold the material together for compacting.

The process used for such smaller products as inserts consists of palletizing and granulating the powder to make it flow readily into moulds in automatic pill presses for compacting. Then it is dewaxed to remove the paraffin and presintered. Presintering does not cause shrinkage, but does provide sufficient green strength. A few products undergo a shaping operation after presintering. It is then sintered by the liquid-phase process at 1300–1600°C, depending on the grade of carbide in hydrogen or vacuum.

**Effect of alloying elements**

The term 'cemented carbide' refers to the fact that a metallic carbide is actually bonded or cemented together with a matrix of a lower-melting-point metallic element. Cemented carbide consists of tungsten carbide mixed with cobalt in powder form so that the mixture can subsequently be pressed and sintered.

Titanium carbide (TiC) is used as an additive to WC-based material for improved crater-resistance in steel machining. Tantalum carbide (TaC) is used as an ingredient to inihibit grain growth and it also has the effect of increasing high-temperature resistance to plastic deformation and of decreasing coefficient of friction at high temperatures. The TaC addition forms a solid solution with some of the tungsten carbide.

It may also be noted that the hardness of cemented tungsten carbide decreases with a higher cobalt content, but a finer grain structure produces a harder cemented carbide with the same cobalt content. Higher hardness ensures greater abrasion resistance, but the variation is not directly proportional to cobalt content. Abrasion resistance is at its optimum when the cobalt content is about 45 per cent, below which abrasion-resistance decreases, because individual WC grains are not held together tightly enough. Generally the cobalt content is increased for increased strength and toughness, and this poses the important question of trade-off between strength and abrasion-resistance. Also, it is to be mentioned that fine-grained materials generally have a higher traverse rupture strength compared to coarse-grained materials.

In the ISO system of classification of cemented carbides, *P* designates a broad category of ferrous metals producing long chips; *K* is for ferrous metals yielding short chips, non-ferrous metals and non metallics, and *M* is an intermediate class for ferrous metals with long or short chips and non-ferrous metals. Higher numerals in this system indicate increasing toughness or increasing feeds, and decreasing hardness and wear resistance or decreasing machining speeds.

### 9.3.1 *Improved tungsten carbide*

Edge preparation seems to be a significant factor, which is as important as correct grade selection in achieving optimum cutting-tool performance. Typically, the life of a tungsten carbide edge can be increased by as much as 200 per cent by simply honing the cutting edge to remove notches — the minute surface imperfections that serve as starting places for cracks, edge chipping or breaks. While the degree of honing largely depends upon the various conditions of use, the key factor is hone uniformity.

It is also possible to achieve significant performance improvement, mainly through even more stringent quality control and improvements in the manufacturing processes, in other words, through process innovation. Essential measures include reduction in grain size variation by the prevention of discontinuous grain growth and the refinement and even distribution of the mixed carbide phase. At the same time the solubility of the carbides in the cementing metal phase is improved, so that the strength increases.

By employing rod milling instead of ball milling, one can achieve more precise control of grain size. Here, with improved uniformity, the alloyed powder resists grain growth in sintering, which in turn leads to better strength and edge wear, and improved thermal characteristics in the final product.

Unique cutting tool geometries can also contribute to the demand for higher speeds and feeds. One can introduce a positive/negative insert in a form that gives a negative cutting tool a positive cutting action. A double positive configuration, enables the insert to take deeper cuts at higher feeds with no increase in horse power. Critical to the performance of this tool is a conical contour that curls chips both lengthwise and across the width. This results in a relatively freer chip flow, reduced heat, and extended insert life.

### 9.3.2 *Coated carbides*

While applying the cemented carbide grades, a balance was sought between wear resistance and toughness. In other words, increased wear resistance was achieved at a reduced level of toughness and vice versa.

This objective resulted in the development of coated carbides for improving wear resistance, while retaining adequate toughness. In these coated carbides, a microscopic layer of wear resistant, i.e. titanium carbide/ titanium nitride, is chemically coated over the tough carbide substrate to attain a single grade of carbide providing the property of both high wear resistance and toughness.

**(a) Titanium carbide coating**
A thin layer of titanium carbide of 4 to 8$\mu$m thickness and of 0.2$\mu$m grain size is coated over a tungsten carbide substrate by the vaporization technique, with no cobalt binder. The layer is metallurgically bonded to the substrate. It has a microhardness of up to 3000 kg/mm, 50 per cent harder than the base carbides.

The cutting forces are reduced due to very low friction. It becomes cost effective by using increasing feed rates and hence metal removal.

**Applications**
(1) TiC coatings are good for light and semi-finished cuts on materials that tend to alloy or weld to the binder in carbides.

(2) They have limited applications in interrupted cutting because of the sensitivity of the coating to cracking.

(3) They are not recommended for high alloy and super alloys and for light alloys of aluminium and magnesium.

**(b) Titanium nitride coating**
A layer of about 7 to 8 $\mu$m pure TiN of very fine grain size, without a binder, is chemically bonded to a tough carbide base, providing a gold colour. It has a higher resistance to crater wear than TiC coating, and a much higher tool-life, because of its lower coefficient of friction.

This TiN coating finds application in general metal removal applications and in finish-machining of steels.

**(c) Double coatings, TiC and TiN**
The drawback with TiN coating, though less brittle than TiC coating, is that it does not have much adhesive strength and does not bind strongly to the substrate. This is overcome by double-coating or multi-coating. In this type of coating, there is a layer of TiC with strong adhesion to the substrate, next to the carbide layer. This layer is followed by an interpenetrating carbo nitride layer and then finally by a TiN coating.

The resultant coating is strong, less brittle and stable. It combines the good flank-wear resistance property of TiC with the crater resistance of TiN. This results in an increased cutting performance of 25 to 50 per cent compared to ordinary TiN coated bits.

**(d) Aluminium oxide coating**

A controlled thickness of 7 to 8 $\mu$m aluminium oxide is deposited as vapor on the carbide substrate of the steel machining grade to obtain an $Al_2O_3$ coating. It can be effectively used in areas where ceramic tools fail because of lower strength and also in the higher speed range where TiC and TiN coated tools fail due to their oxidation. Wear resistance of this material is high because of good heat dissipation.

An $Al_2O_3$ coated tool operates at about twice the speed used for the TiC or TiN-coated carbides. This material has found use in machining cast iron and other ferrous substances, an area traditionally dominated by ceramics.

**(e) Double coatings, TiC–$Al_2O_3$**

The dual coating, generally, consists of depositing on top of TiC of thickness 4–5 $\mu$m, with an $Al_2O_3$ of thickness 1 - 2$\mu$m.

It combines wear resistance with toughness. These inserts are suitable for use at intermediate speeds between that of TiC-coated and of ceramic inserts. TiC–$Al_2O_3$ coating can perform well at higher speed ranges where TiC and TiN are ineffective due to the tendency to oxidize. Aluminium has high thermal stability and an extremely high rate of heat dissipation.

However, the coating tends to fracture when subjected to high impact loading. Also, the coating is largely ineffective in the lower speed range, 3 m/sec being the approximate dividing line, and also for small feeds. In addition, careful edge honing is needed.

**(f) Cubic boron nitride (CBN) coating**

CBN coatings use amorphous boron nitride which contains microcrystals of CBN. Just a 1$\mu$m coating of the material makes hard cutting tool materials harder still. In terms of Knoop (25 g) hardness, for example, the coating increases the hardness of TiN coated carbide from 1300–1650 to 2200–3100, $Al_2O_3$ coated carbide from 1200–1600 to 1600–2200, and sialon ceramic from 1400–1700 to 2100–2800.

Innovative CBN coated inserts are likely to find popular application.

## 9.4 Cermet cutting tools

Recently, TiC cermet tools and TiC–TiN cermet tools have become increasingly significant in machining because of their high wear resistance at elevated temperatures and applicability in high-speed machining. Also, these tools have fewer problems with regard to availability of TiC and TiN compared to tungsten carbide tools.

TiC cermet is a cutting tool material consisting of TiC, WC, Ni and Mo.

TiC–TiN cermet is another cutting tool material consisting of TiC, TiN, TaN, Ni and Mo.

**Characteristics of TiC–TiN cermets**

(a) The bonding materials used are nickel and molybdenum. TiC and TiN have greater solubility in Ni and Mo than WC in cobalt, thus resulting in high strength of the material, with good resistance to crater wear and reduced friction between chip and tool.

(b) Due to high thermal conductivity, cutting temperatures are lower.

(c) Due to low density, about one-third to half, when compared to WC alloys, it has low heat absorption, thus extending tool-life.

(d) These tools exhibit higher hot hardness.

(e) They do not form built-up edge on their rake faces, contributing to good surface finish.

(f) They have high resistance to flank wear.

(g) They can be used at higher cutting speeds where a longer tool-life, is required, e.g., 450 m/min. along light to moderate feeds and cutting depths.

**Applications**

(1) On annealed carbon and low alloy steels,

(2) on hard alloy steels, and

(3) on high temperature alloys with a poor machinability index.

## 9.5 Ceramics (cemented oxides)

**Manufacturing aspects**

Ceramics are produced by processing bauxite into a dense crystalline form known as alpha alumina. The tools are produced either by cold pressing in steel and carbide dies, where the finely divided powders are compressed into the required form and then sintered, or by the hot pressing method where forming and sintering (to a temperature just below the fusion point) are combined by applying pressure and heat simultaneously. Up to 10 additives like oxides of magnesium and chromium, may be added to obtain superior quality tools. The blanks are then finish ground with diamond impregnated wheels. To get strong, hard and highly wear resistant tools, it is necessary to control the grain size, density and percentage of impurities.

**Properties**

(a) Ceramics are hard with a high degree of compressive strength even at elevated temperatures.

(b) They have good abrasion resistance, resistance to cratering, low friction coefficient, and are not sensitive to the higher range of temperatures encountered in machining.

(c) They can retain cutting edge hardness up to about 1400°C and exhibit uniform strength up to 1200°C. Hence ceramics are used at higher cutting speeds and at higher temperatures compared to other tool materials.

(d) Because of poor wettability, they are used on high abrasive and reactive materials, at higher cutting speeds without the formation of a built-up edge. However, brazing is difficult on steel shanks, except by using epoxy resins.

(e) They are acid resistant, non-magnetic, non-conducting and non-corrosive. Resistance to reactivity with workpiece material is high, thus minimizing built-up edge and tool wear.

(f) An improved manufacturing technique has lead to use of ceramics in interrupted cuts, though it has a low transverse rupture strength, about one-half to one-third of that of carbides.

**Machine tool requirements**

A machine tool of high rigidity is necessary because of the brittleness of ceramics. Vibration and chatter should be eliminated wherever possible. The tool-holders should be rigid.

Exploitation of potentialities of ceramic tools demand high-speed machining. A thorough change in the design of machine tools and their elements is necessary, providing high-speed ranges and horsepower, with rigidity and accurate balancing of machine tool parts and work-holding devices.

**Applications**

(1) Ceramics are employed for increasing productivity and lowering the costs, because of their higher hot hardness and greater resistance to wear.

(2) Ceramics eliminate finishing operations like grinding, since they provide good surface finish and quality.

**Examples**

**(1) Cast iron, noted for its abrasive characteristics, can be machined to a smooth bright finish.**

**(2) Heat treated steel as hard as 65 Rc can be finished up to 0.5$\mu$m surface finish.**

**(3) High temperature alloys such as hastalloy, stellite and monel can be machined.**

**(4) Also used for roll turning, long tube boring, cylinder liner boring, etc.**

## 9.6 Diamond

Diamond, because of its high modulus of elasticity, chemical inertness and exceptionally high hardness, is ideal for obtaining fine surface finish and accuracy. Though the initial cost of diamond is high when compared to HSS or carbides, the cost per piece machined with diamond is invariably much lower. Under proper conditions, diamond can machine 10,000–50,000 pieces, or sometimes even 100,000 pieces in set-ups where carbides can machine only 300–400 pieces before it needs resharpening.

Diamond as a cutting tool material is useful in two forms — as a single crystal diamond tool as well as a polycrystalline diamond tool.

### 9.6.1 *Single crystal diamond*

Today high precision is demanded in the finishing process of precise parts of a magnetic memory device, laser equipment, electrostatic copier, printing machine, etc. Non-ferrous materials, such as aluminium, copper and resin, are used for such parts. The single crystal diamond tool has low affinity to these materials and a very sharp cutting edge, and is therefore suitable for such precision machining.

However, high precision machine tools should be developed to eliminate factors attributable to the wear caused by the machine tools such as vibration.

Some of the relevant properties of the single crystal diamond are given below:

**(i) High thermal conductivity, resulting in low temperatures**

**(ii) Chemically inert and takes high polish. Hence chips do not adhere to its surface when machining non-ferrous and non-metallic surfaces.**

(iii) High hot hardness, but excessive heat causes diamond to crack and oxidation of diamond starts at around 800°C . Hence abundant, uninterrupted supply of cutting fluid is necessary with light feeds.

(iv) Cutting edge is extremely smooth and accurate, hence it is used for precision applications.

(v) Extremely brittle, and hence it chips or fractures, if it is not handled properly. It should be well protected from shock-loading and used on machines with minimum vibration or chatter.

### *9.6.2 Polycrystalline diamond (PCD)*

Polycrystalline diamond has been widely accepted in areas where tungsten carbide was used earlier.

The polycrystalline diamond is a synthesized integral mass of randomly oriented diamond particles in a metal matrix, having a very hard isotropic structure. Being composed of millions of tiny, randomly oriented diamond crystals fused together, it has wear-resistance due to the hardness of the crystals and also strength and toughness from the random orientation. This enables the structure to withstand the mechanical shock encountered in machining by dissipating the energy uniformly.

The tool blank is made up of a layer of thin polycrystalline diamond bonded to a tungsten carbide substrate by way of an intermediate refractory metallic layer. This layer also absorbs stresses which may result, for instance, from the differing thermal properties of the polycrystalline diamond zone and the carbide substrate.

**Applications**

Compact tools can be used in machining non-ferrous metals and alloys, carbon, ceramics, glass, reinforced plastics, rubbers, plastics and resins, wood and aluminium oxide.

They can be used effectively to machine glass reinforced plastic, with consequent reduction in production time, labour costs and labour involved. The successful applications include those in turning synthetic resin-bonded fabric, glass fibre tubing and optical fibre material. They can also be used for machining moulded phenolic components for the electrical, aircraft and hydraulic industries which use chemical resistant cases and containers. Tool life is reported to have increased by a factor of 120 compared to conventional carbide tooling with improved accuracy.

Copper/mica components which are used in electric motors are suitably machined by the diamond compacts. Tool life is reported to have increased almost five times with consistent surface finish.

Polycrystalline diamond can replace the use of natural diamond very effectively, for dressing of grinding wheels of a wider range of sizes and grades.

It is also used for precious metals like gold, silver and platinum. The applications include machining of alloy pistons containing higher silica content, and sintered bearings.

**Cutting conditions**
The cutting geometry of polycrystalline tools closely follows that of tungsten carbide, the only significant difference being in rake angles, where positive rake angles are normally used. Polycrystalline compacts can normally be used with a zero rake. This is because a sharper edge has a longer life, and the low coefficient of friction at the diamond layer aids chip flow and avoids built-up edges. On certain materials, however, mainly copper and pure aluminium, a positive rake angle is required.

Cutting speeds for diamond should be as high as possible, the speed being limited by the onset of vibrations, and feeds should be low.

**Advantages**
(1) Abrasion resistance of polycrystalline diamond is equal or superior to natural diamond because of its composite structure.

(2) It is not subjected to directional hardness variations and hence its abrasion resistance is high and consistent from piece to piece.

(3) Its homogeneous nature, ensures that the compact wears uniformly at a relatively slow rate.

(4) It can take cuts comparable with the equivalent tungsten carbide tool.

(5) It has a long tool life on difficult-to-machine materials. (With carbides, these materials usually have a high conventional tool consumption, high rejection rate, poor consistency and a great deal of expensive downtime).

(6) The compacts reduce the rejection rate considerably, give consistent results over long periods, improve surface finish and reduce downtime on tool changes. Thus production can be increased, extensive down time reduced and scarce skilled labor better utilized.

(7) The compacts have the ability to combine roughing and finishing operations.

**Disadvantages**
Polycrystalline diamond costs about fifty times more than carbide. But there are few applications where it will achieve fifty times the work. Further, polycrystalline diamond is viable in those applications where other factors such as shock resistance and consistency make its use economical.

## 9.7 Cubic boron nitride (CBN)

CBN was originally developed as an alternative to synthetic and natural diamond, especially in grinding ferrous materials, since diamond, being a form of carbon, is not that thermally very stable, and at high temperatures readily reacts with iron. It was used initially in the tool and cutter grinding of high speed steels, where there were problems with conventional abrasive tools.

CBN consists of atoms of nitrogen and boron, with a special structural configuration similar to diamond.

**Properties**
CBN is ideally suited for use as a cutting tool material for machining exceptionally hard steels in view of the following considerations :

(a) It has a knoop hardness of about 4,800 kg/mm and is second in hardness next only to diamond.

(b) It retains its hardness at temperatures above 1,000°C.

(c) It does not readily oxidize.

(d) It is chemically inert to carbon containing materials.

**Applications**
Made in the form of indexable inserts and blanks of standard shape and size, they are capable of machining hardened tool steels, chilled cast iron, high-strength alloys, and heat-resistant alloys. The indexable inserts can be used on standard tool-holders. The blanks can be brazed onto steel shanks, form ground and then used.

On ferrous materials, the compacts perform better when the hardness is greater than 45 Rc. They perform well on chilled cast iron and steel rolls of hardness greater than 67 Rc. With light cuts the surface finish obtained is often as smooth as the ground surface, eliminating in some cases the subsequent grinding operations.

CBN can also be used for machining non-ferrous metals like brass and duralumin at cutting velocities of 250–400 m/min.

## 9.8 Sialon

Sialon is the family name for a range of new ceramic alloys. The name is derived from the material's principal constituents — silicon, aluminium, oxygen and nitrogen. Its remarkable resistance to high temperatures, and its tolerance of thermal and mechanical shocks makes it a very attractive tooling material, though yet to find popular applications.

Sialon cutting tools are made using a process similar to the one used for the production of cemented carbides and alumina tool tips. Already prepared, very fine, high purity, Sialon powder is mixed with additives and binders. It is then pressed into either pellets or slabs and sintered. It can also be hot pressed. Since the properties obtained are similar in both the cases, cold pressing is preferred because it is more economical.

Sialon tool is strong enough to withstand the stresses developed during the process of machining. The hot hardness is 960 vickers at 950°C, compared to the average hardness of 1,650 vickers at room temperature.

It is used as a cutting tool for a range of ferrous metals and super alloys such as medium carbon steel, cast iron and Ni-based super alloys.

The most remarkable feature of Sialon is its ability to cope with high feed rates, where it out-performs hot pressed ceramics significantly. This merit is combined with its tolerance of high cutting speed. These factors offer considerable potential for increased productivity.

A chip-breaker plate under the tip clamp is recommended for distributing locking forces over a larger area and improving clamping. It is necessary to use the strongest possible tip geometry, longest practical tip radius and a positive lead angle.

Sialon has shown greatly enhanced metal removal capabilities and reduced throughput times on some of the longer components made from difficult materials used in the aero engineering industry.

Though it is slightly costlier than traditional ceramic tools and considerably more expensive than conventional carbides, the extra cost can be recovered by the enhanced metal removal rates and tool-life.

# 10 Chatter and its significance

## 10.1 Types of chatter

Chatter or vibration in a turning operation will lower the surface finish, generate excessive noise and lead to premature tool failure through edge chipping. There are two basic types of chatter — forced vibration and self-excited vibration.

### (a) Forced vibration

Generally, forced vibration results from the continuing application of an external periodic force. Sources of forced vibration in a turning operation include spindle imbalance, gear drive irregularities, operating machine tools in the surrounding area, electric motors, oil pumps, and insert entry impacts in interrupted cutting.

This type of chatter is external to the metal removal operation and the entire machine tool, primarily, should be carefully analyzed. A change in any of the operating conditions may not have significance for this type of chatter. Increase in feed may have a favourable effect, since this will increase preload on machine members and thus tend to dampen forced vibration. Such vibration can sometimes be reduced by increasing cutting forces in the direction in which the deflection is occurring. This tends to load-up the system components, and thus has a damping effect. Normally, radial forces should be increased since a tubular or rod-like part is more likely to deflect in the bending direction, than along its axis. Also boring bars are normally positioned with their axes parallel to that of the part, and these are much more likely to deflect in the radial direction. The remedial measures to increase radial force include: (i) increasing load angle, (ii) changing from positive to negative rake geometry, (iii) using an insert with a large nose radius, and (iv) using an insert with a hone or T-land.

**(b) Self-excited vibration**

Self-excited vibration results from the instability that is inherent in any machining operation. This instability is caused by the interaction of the structural dynamics of the machine tool and the forces generated in the chip removal process. In any process where substantial energy is transmitted and mechanical damping is low, even a very small amount of energy is sufficient to produce large amplitude vibrations. Initially, the instability would have had no forces associated with it, but such forces build up over a period of time.

For example, self-excited chatter could be initiated if some small disturbance,such as a sand inclusion or hard spot, cause the tool or insert to jump slightly, leaving a small impression on the workpiece surface. In the next revolution, the insert is forced to take a slightly deeper cut, that will cause it to jump again, leaving yet another impression. Depending on the stability of the system, these impressions will either gradually die out, or will be specified till a serious chatter problem manifests.

Occasionally, self-excited vibration could be reduced by adjusting cutting speed. Any machine tool has greater stiffness at certain frequencies. By experimenting with changes in cutting speed, the corresponding frequency attributing to greater stiffness of the machine tool can be determined.

Sometimes, an increase in feed rate can help in controlling chatter if 0° lead angle tooling is employed since it increases preload on machine members. However, for a tooling with a substantial lead angle, reducing feed rate may be beneficial, though productivity will be reduced, since a reduction in feed rate will lower radial force.

Also, self-excited vibration will occur only if depth of cut exceeds certain threshold value. In other words, the vibration amplitude will be of the order of say 0.25 to 0.4 mm above the threshold value, and of about 0.1 mm or less, for the depth of cut below the threshold value. Hence if depth of cut is maintained above the threshold value, changes in it will have little effect on the magnitude of chatter. Depth of cut should be reduced only as a last measure, since it reduces productivity.

Since self-excited vibration in its simplest sense is amplified tool or workpiece deflection, it can often be controlled by reducing the forces that cause the tool or workpiece to deflect. Any deflection in turning/boring operations is mostly caused by radial forces. These forces can be reduced by measures such as (a) reducing lead angle, (b) changing from negative to positive rake, (c) reducing the nose radius, or (d) using an insert with an unhoned edge.

## 10.2 Machine tool fixture and workpiece stiffness

Lack of stiffness in the machine tool fixture and workpiece may not actually cause chatter, but can be a significant contributing factor to both types of chatter. Play in the spindle bearings, slides, feed drives, fixture, etc. should be reduced to the minimum. The workpiece, due to its own inherent instability, may vibrate and cause chatter. It may be possible to dampen these vibrations by wrapping a member belt or hose around it. Plaster of paris or any other suitable substance may be used as a filler to provide stability, and this may be particularly appropriate for machining parts with vanes or propellers.

## 10.3 Determination of the type of chatter

The type of chatter can be determined by measuring the wavelength of the chatter marks on the workpiece surface. The wavelength is equal to the disturbance between corresponding points on chatter marks as in Fig.10.1.

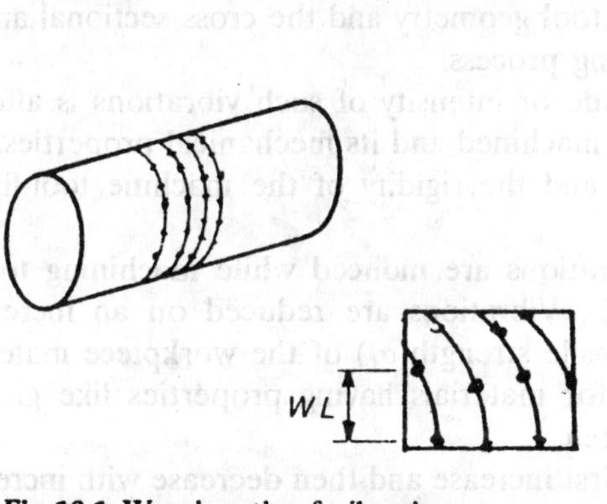


**Fig.10.1 Wavelength of vibration**

The frequency of vibration can be calculated by the expression

$$f = v/(WL)$$

where, $f$ = vibration frequency(cycles per second), $v$ = cutting speed (mm/sec), $WL$ = wavelength of vibration (mm).

If the marks are caused by forced vibrations, the frequency of vibration will correspond to the frequency of the source of the vibrations, or occasionally to a simple multiple of the frequency of the forcing agent or source. The frequency of vibration is compared to the running speed of all rotating parts on the machine tool and other machining parts in the surroundings. If the frequency of vibration is neither equal to, nor a simple multiple of the rotating speed of some unit that is part of the machine tool, then the case is one of self-excited vibration.

**Forced vibrations**

Forced vibrations originate due to a periodic excitation of forces which may be: (a) variable forces acting on the system as a result of intermittent or interrupted machining, for example, in turning a shaft having a longitudinal slot, (b) centrifugal forces of inertia of unbalanced rotating masses, the blanks, chuck, pulleys, electric motor rotors,etc., and (c) impact forces caused by faults or manufacturing errors on the work surfaces of components of the mechanism for transmitting motion, for example, wear of the parts in the mechanism, manufacturing errors of toothed gearing, sudden engagements or switching over, etc.

**Self-excited vibrations**

Self-excited vibrations are more complex and occur more frequently in metal cutting.

Some of the causes of self-excited vibrations are: (a) variability of frictional forces between the chip and tool and between the tool and workpiece, (b) non-uniform work-hardening of the layer being machined across its thickness, and (c) instability of the built-up edge that leads to changes in the tool geometry and the cross-sectional area of the uncut chip in the machining process.

The amplitude or intensity of such vibrations is affected by the type of material being machined and its mechanical properties, cutting parameters, tool geometry and the rigidity of the machine tool-fixture-tool-workpiece complex.

Heavier vibrations are induced while machining tough grades of steel, than cast iron. Vibrations are reduced on an increase in the hardness (BHN) and tensile strength($\sigma_t$) of the workpiece material. Also vibrations are increased for materials having properties like greater elongation and reduction in area.

Vibrations first increase and then decrease with increase in cutting speed. The effect of the rate of feed on vibrations is less than that of the cutting speed or depth of cut. With an increase in feed (uncut chip thickness), vibrations are reduced — if feed is less than the depth of cut. Vibrations are increased with an increase in the rate of feed — if feed is larger than depth of cut. Also, for a single unit increase in depth of cut, i.e., the uncut chip width, vibrations increase in longitudinal turning.

## 10.4 Geometry

Vibrations can be heavier if the principal cutting edge angle, $k_r$, also called the plan approach angle, is small, because of the decrease in thickness and increase in width of uncut chip and the increase of the radial force for a smaller $k_r$. For increased radial forces, the force causing deflection between the work and the carriage unit of a lathe is also higher. Therefore, for turning long thin shafts, i.e. shafts with low rigidity, it is appropriate to use single-point tools with a large principal cutting edge angle. In addition to increasing the $k_r$ to 90°, rests are used in practice to reduce the force of deflection and vibration. These special devices are called vibration dampers. The end-cutting edge angle affects vibration in a similar way, but to a lesser degree, and the vibrations are more intense for smaller angles.

Also, as the nose radius is increased, there is increased vibration, due to increase in the width of the uncut chip. As a result its average thickness reduces and radial force increases.

The vibrations are found to be less for grooved tools, while flank wear leads to a heavier vibration.

## 10.5 Rigidity

Vibration is less for a machine tool-fixture-tool-workpiece complex of higher rigidity. For example, in longitudinal turning, heaviest vibrations occur when the tool is in the middle of the workpiece, since the work deflection by the forces acting on it will be greatest due to its minimum rigidity. When the workpiece is turned near the tail or tool of the lathe, vibrations are lower, and they are further reduced when turning is done near the headstock.

Vibrations are heavier when the tailstock overhang is more, since the rigidity then is comparatively low.

Similarly, vibrations are less for greater rigidity of the tailstock centre. Results are good for an ordinary dead centre. However, for higher speeds, live centres are used that often reduce the rigidity by 70 to 75 per cent.

Larger the overhang of the tool from the tool-holder and smaller the cross-sectional dimensions of the tool shank, lower will be the rigidity of the system, inducing greater vibrations. Vibrations are highly influenced by the tool overhang for increased cutting speeds.

In view of the side effects , great care should be taken to tackle vibrations, while identifying the causes as discussed. For example, if $k_r$ is increased, it reduces vibrations, but it also accelerates tool wear. Similarly, it is not advisable to use a large rake angle, or a large end-cutting edge angle, or a small nose radius, since the output will be lowered.

Suitable measures to tackle vibration include: (a) insertion of elastic pads, make of materials like rubber, between the driving stud and the lathe dog while turning between centres, or under jaws of the chuck while turning in a chuck, and (b) the use of special devices called vibration dampers, that retard the development of vibrations by increasing the forces of resistance in the machine tool-fixture-tool-workpiece complex.

# 11 Surface roughness

## 11.1 Introduction

**In any machining operation, surface integrity is one of the important outputs. Generally, surface integrity involves several variables, such as surface finish, freedom from cracks, chemical change, thermal damage, including burn, transformation and over tempering, and adverse or tensile residual stress. However, surface finish is the most important variable especially in finishing operations.**

**Generally surface roughness is expressed by the characteristic maximum peak-to-valley roughness ($R_{max}$ or $R_t$) or by the arithmetic average or centre line average ($R_a$) values. The values of $R_t$ and $R_a$ for different machining operations are given in Table 11.1.**

**Refer Table 11.1.**

**Table 11.1 $R_t$ and $R_a$ obtained for different machining operations**

| Finishing operation | $R_{max}$ or $R_t \mu m$ | $R_a$ $\mu m$ |
|---|---|---|
| Very rough surfaces (castings etc.) | $\approx 10^3$ | 12500 |
| Rough machining | 250 to 2500 | $\approx 25$ |
| Medium machining (e.g. rough grind) | 50 to 250 | $\approx 10$ |
| Fine machining (e.g fine grind) | 5 to 10 | 0.80 to 2.5 |
| Very fine grind (turned) | 0.5 to 5.0 | 0.13 to 0.8 |
| Honed | 1 to 2 | 0.05 to 0.3 |
| Lapped, polished | 0.05 to 1 | $\approx 0.1$ |
| Fine metallographic polish | $\approx 0.3$ | 0.03 |

In any machining operation, the final surface roughness is the result of two factors:

**(a) Ideal surface roughness**
This is a result of the geometry of the tool and the feed. However, it is achieved only when built-up edge, chatter, inaccuracies in spindles and slides, etc. are eliminated. As summarised later, the roughness values can often be calculated or estimated.

**(b) Natural surface roughness**
This is a result of the irregularities in the cutting operation and often forms a large proportion of the actual roughness. The factors that commonly contribute to natural surface roughness in practice are:

(1) the occurrence of a built-up edge;

(2) the occurrence of chatter or vibrations of the machine tool;

(3) inaccuracies in machine tool movements, such as the movement of the machine-tool saddle;

(4) irregularities in the feed mechanism;

(5) defects in the structure of the work materials;

(6) discontinuous chip formation when machining brittle materials;

(7) tearing of the work material when ductile metals are cut at low cutting speeds;

(8) surface damage caused by chip flow etc;

(9) inaccuracies in the manufacture of cutting tools such as of a cutter, and

(10) material flow at the surface.

## 11.2 Theoretical surface roughness

Let

$f$ = feed, mm/rev.

$r$ = nose radius, mm

$k_r$ = principal cutting edge angle

$k_r' =$ end cutting edge angle

$R_{max} =$ theoretical maximum height of roughness

$R_a =$ theoretical arithmetical mean value of roughness.

**(a) Single-point radiused turning tool (refer Fig.11.1)**

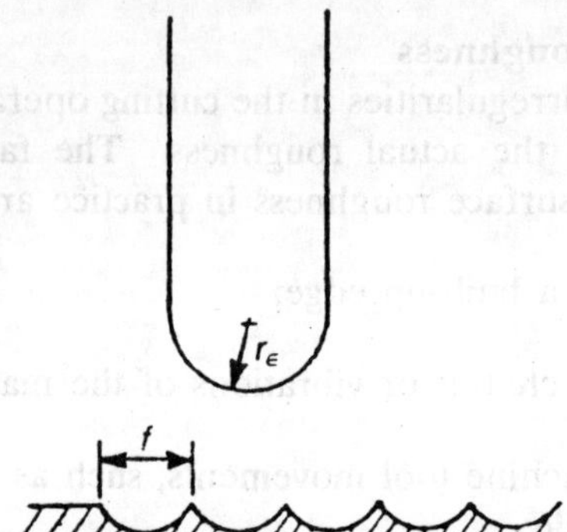


Fig.11.1 Surface roughness with a non-radiused tool

$$R_{max} = f^2/(8r)$$

$$R_a = (0.0321 f^2)/r$$

**(b) Single-point turning tool (refer Fig.11.2)**

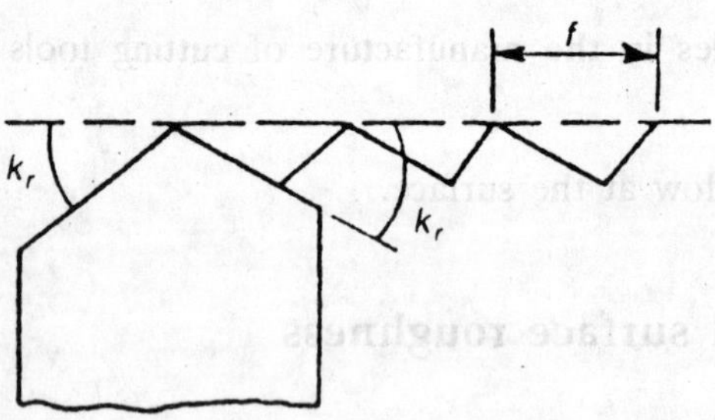


Fig.11.2 Surface roughness with a non-radiused tool

$$R_{max} = \frac{f}{\cot k_r + \cot k_r'}$$

$$R_a = \frac{f}{4(\cot k_r + \cot k_r')}$$

The above equations hold good only when

$$(f/r) \gg 1$$

**(c) Cylindrical or slab milling**

Let

$d_t$ = dia. of cutter, mm

$v_f$ = feed speed, mm /tooth

$n_f$ = rotational frequency of cutters/sec/tooth

$f_1$ = feed, mm /rev. = $v_f/n_t$

$z$ = number of teeth in a cutter

$$R_{max} = \frac{f_1^2}{(4D)}$$

$$R_a = \frac{0.0642}{d_t}\left(\frac{v_f}{n_t}\right)^2$$

Another general equation commonly used is,

$$R_{max} = \frac{f_t^2}{[(d_t/2) \pm (f_t z)/\pi]}$$

where the plus sign is for up-milling and the negative sign is for down-milling and $f_t$ = feed/tooth. Note that cutting efficiency '$C$' is expressed as the ratio of measured roughness to theoretical roughness, i.e.

$$C = \frac{R_{max}(\text{measured})}{R_{max}(\text{theoretical})}$$

However the above are only simplified estimates, since these ignore the natural surface roughness factors that defy quantification, when considered, but otherwise irrelevant in practical applications.

## 11.3 Effect of tool geometry and cutting parameters on surface roughness

**(a) Effect of nose radius and feed rate**

Nose radius and feed rate are the operating parameters that have the greatest significance on average roughness height typically in turning or boring operations. These two govern the minimum theoretical roughness, the one that would be achieved if the impression formed on the workpiece by the tool had been an exact mirror image of the contour of the tool with no deflection of either the workpiece or the tool. Generally, increasing nose radius improves surface finish, just as reducing feed rate also improves surface finish.

However, because of the significant effect that feed rate has on overall efficiency of the operation, it is selected based not on surface finish, but rather because of its effect on tool life as discussed in Chapter 6. The nose radius, on the other hand, is selected to achieve specific surface finish requirements.

**(b) Effect of cutting speed**

Most machined surfaces have a higher average roughness than the theoretical one, especially in operations where work material adheres to the cutting edges. The built-up edge material tears and galls the workpiece, and eventually collapses, possibly to be deposited on the finished surface. This feature is especially common in the case of soft, gummy workpiece materials.

Increasing the cutting speed can reduce actual roughness. At low cutting speeds, shear angle is low and hence cutting forces are high. Additionally, a specific section of the workpiece is in contact with the cutting tool for a relatively long period of time. Both these conditions contribute to built-up edge, and that leads to tearing and galling.

**(c) Effect of rake angle**

When a higher rake angle, either more positive or less negative, is used, shear angle is increased, and hence cutting force is reduced. There is less tendency for workpiece material to adhere to the tool and therefore surface finish usually improves. Such an effect is most notable in ductile materials.

**(d) Effect of tool changing**

A dull tool has a large contact area, since the entire flank wearland of the tool or insert is in contact with the workpiece. Cutting forces and heat generated are high, and the large wearland tends to rip out workpiece fragments. Dull tools can be easily identified when roughness readings are irregular from part to part. It is practical to change the tool or index the insert before the recommended maximum flank wear is reached.

**(e) Effect of coolant**

Coolant reduces the temperature at the tool–chip interface and hence reduces the tendency of workpiece material to adhere to the tool. However, coolant residue contaminates the contact surface between the tool and workpiece, and interferes with metallurgical reactions that may cause the tool to perform erratically. Hence the most appropriate coolant should be selected and effectively applied.

## 11.4 Solved examples

*Example 11.1*

What corner radius should be ground on a tool with a rounded corner to givé an arithmetical mean surface roughness of 10 $\mu$m, when turning under ideal conditions with a feed of 0.25 mm /rev.? What will be the expected maximum height of roughness ?

***Solution***

$$R_a = 10\mu m = 10 \times 10^{-3} \text{ mm}$$

$$f = 0.25\text{mm /rev.}$$

$$R_a = 0.0321 f^2/r_\epsilon$$

$$\text{or,} \quad 10 \times 10^{-3} = \frac{0.0321 \times 0.25^2}{r_\epsilon}$$

$$\therefore \quad r_\epsilon = 0.0321 \times 0.0625 \times 10^2$$

$$= 0.2\text{mm}$$

$$R_{max} = f^2/(8r_\epsilon) = 0.25^2/(8 \times 0.2)$$

$$= 0.039 \text{ mm} \quad \text{or } 39\mu m$$

*Example 11.2*

When turning a cylindrical workpiece, two different tools are used. In one tool, no nose radius is provided, the side cutting and edge cutting angles being 30° and 7° respectively. In the other tool, a nose radius of 0.7 mm is provided. The feed used in both cases is 0.125 mm /rev. Find out the theoretical maximum height of unevenness in the generated surfaces. Find also the theoretical arithmetical mean value of roughness.

***Solution***

***Tool 1***

$f = 0.125$ mm./rev.

Side cutting edge angle $\psi = 30°$.

$k_r = 90 - 30 = 60°$ and $k_r' = 7°$.

$$R_{max} = f(\cot k_r + \cot k_r')$$

$$= 0.125/\ (\cot 60° + \cot 7°)$$

$$= 0.014 \text{ mm} \quad \text{or } 14\mu\text{m}.$$

$$R_a = R_{max}/4$$

$$= 0.014/4$$

$$= 0.0035 \text{ or } 3.5\mu\text{m}.$$

*Tool 2*

$$f = 0.125 \text{ mm /rev.}$$

$$r_\epsilon = 0.7 \text{ mm}$$

$$R_{max} = f^2/(8r_\epsilon)$$

$$= 0.125^2/(8 \times 0.7)$$

$$= 0.0028 \text{ mm. or } 2.8\mu\text{m}.$$

$$R_a = (0.0321 f^2)/r_\epsilon$$

$$= (0.0321 \times 0.125^2)/0.7$$

$$= 0.0007 \text{ mm. or } 0.7\mu\text{m}.$$

Therefore the second tool is better, since its $R_{max}$ and $R_a$ values are smaller than that for the first tool.

## 11.5 Exercise problems

11.1 A turning tool with a sharp corner and a principal cutting edge angle of 60° is to be used at a feed of 0.05 mm./rev. What side cutting edge angle should be provided to obtain an arithmetical mean surface roughness under ideal conditions of 3$\mu$m? Also calculate the theoretical maximum height of unevenness.

11.2 A 150 mm dia. slab-milling cutter has 10 teeth and is used at a feed of 1.5 mm/sec. Estimate the 'ideal' arithmetical mean surface roughness when rotational frequency of the cutter is 3 sec/tooth. Estimate also the theoretical maximum height of roughness.

# 12 Chip breakers

## 12.1 Introduction

The controlling and breaking of chips is essential in any machining operation due to its significance with reference to personal safety, possible damage to equipment and product, handling and disposal of swarf after machining, cutting forces, temperature and tool life.

Chip breaker refer to a modification of the tool face to control or break the chip, consisting of either an integral groove or an integral or attached obstruction. Chip curvature is an important factor in this context and the chip curl may be increased by use of the chip breaker.

However, it should be noted that in addition to the design of a good chip breaker, it is necessary to have a correct tool geometry enabling the chip to follow the proper path across the tool face.

## 12.2 Types of chip breakers

**(1) Integral obstruction type chip breaker (Fig 12.1)**

Let,

$l_n$ = chip-breaker distance

$h$ = chip-breaker height

$a_o$ = chip thickness

$r_{\text{chip}}$ = radius of chip curvature

$l_f$ = contact length between chip and tool

Then,

$$r_{\text{chip}} = \frac{(l_n - a_o)^2}{2h} + \frac{h}{2}$$

when

$$l_f \approx a_o.$$

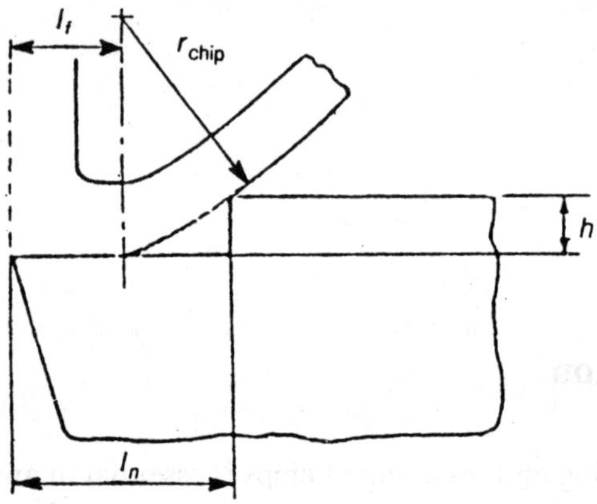


Fig.12.1 Integral obstruction type

**(2) Attached obstruction-type chip breaker (Fig.12.2)**

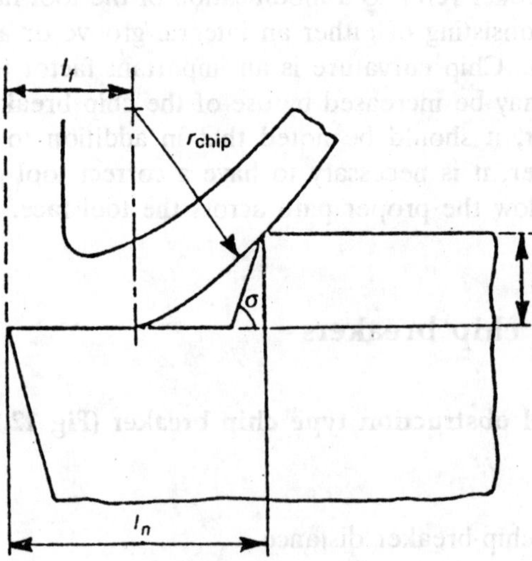


Fig.12.2 Attached obstruction type

The radius of chip curvature is given by

$$r_{\text{chip}} = [(l_n - a_o) - h \cot \sigma)] \cot \frac{\sigma}{2}$$

where

$\sigma$ = chip-breaker wedge angle

A modified method suggested by Nakayama and M C Shaw (refer Fig.12.3).

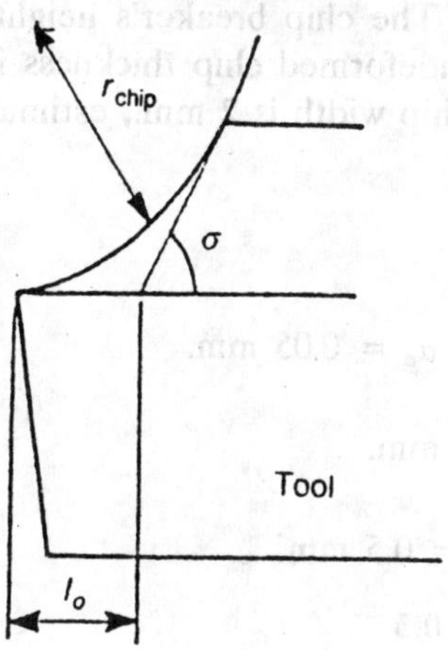


Fig.12.3 Type with no contact length

$$l_o = \text{offset distance} = \frac{r_{\text{chip}}}{\cot(\sigma/2)}$$

**Note:** In case(2), the effect of $l_f$ is neglected.

**(3) Groove-type chip breaker (refer Fig.12.4)**

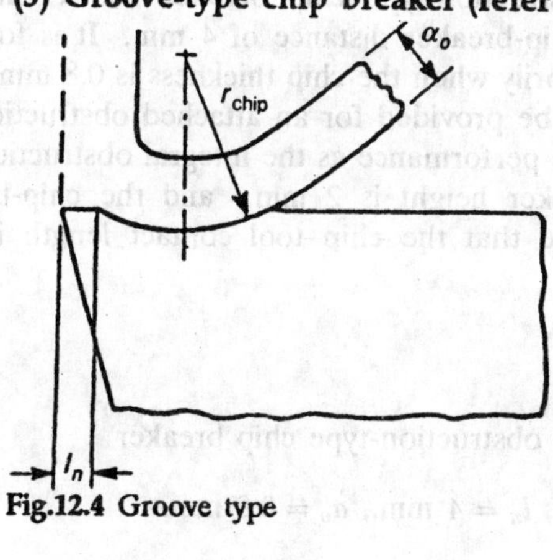


Fig.12.4 Groove type

Let $l_n$ = chip-breaker land width, $q_n$ = chip-breaker groove radius, then $r_{chip} = q_n$, if $l_n < a_o$.

## 12.3 Solved examples

### *Example 12.1*

A single-point cutting tool is fitted with an integral obstruction-type chip breaker and is provided with a positive, principal cutting edge angle so that a helical chip is produced. The chip breaker's height is 0.5 mm. and its distance is 1.5 mm. The undeformed chip thickness is 0.05 mm. and the cutting ratio is 0.2. If the chip width is 2 mm., estimate the radius of chip curvature.

*Solution*

Undeformed chip thickness $a_c$ = 0.05 mm.

$$a_o = \frac{a_c}{r_c} = \frac{0.05}{0.2} = 0.25 \text{ mm.}$$

$l_n$ = 1.5 mm. and $h$ = 0.5 mm.

$$r_{chip} = \frac{(1.5 - 0.25)^2}{2 \times 0.5} + \frac{0.5}{2}$$

$$= (1.25)^2 + 0.25 = 1.5625 + 0.25 = 1.8125 \text{ mm.}$$

Therefore chip curvature radius = 1.8125 mm.

### *Example 12.2*

An integral obstruction-type chip breaker has a chip-breaker height of 1 mm. and a chip-breaker distance of 4 mm. It is found that the chip is broken satisfactorily when the chip thickness is 0.8 mm. What chip-breaker distance should be provided for an attached obstruction-type chip breaker to give the same performance as the integral obstruction-type chip breaker, if the chip-breaker height is 2 mm. and the chip-breaker wedge angle is 45°? Assume that the chip–tool contact length is equal to the chip thickness.

*Solution*

For the integral obstruction-type chip breaker

$$h = 1 \text{ mm.},\ l_n = 4 \text{ mm.},\ a_o = 0.8 \text{ mm.}$$

$$r_{\text{chip}} = \frac{(4-0.8)^2}{2 \times 1} + \frac{1}{2} = 5.12 + 0.5 = 5.62 \text{ mm.}$$

For an attached obstruction-type chip breaker

$$h = 2 \text{ mm.}, \ \sigma = 45°, \ l_n = ?$$

For a performance similar to that of the integral type, take $r_{\text{chip}} = 5.62$ mm. (as calculated above)

$$r_{\text{chip}} = [(l_n - a_o) - h \cot \sigma] \cot \sigma / 2$$

or

$$\begin{aligned} 5.62 &= [(l_n - 0.8) - 2 \cot 45°] \cot 22.5° \\ &= [l_n - 0.8 - 2 \times 1]2.4142 \\ &= (l_n - 2.8)2.4142 \\ \therefore l_n &= \frac{5.62}{2.4142} + 2.8 = 5.13 \text{ mm.} \end{aligned}$$

## 12.4 Exercise problems

12.1 When machining brass at a cutting speed of 15m/min. at a chip thickness of 1.0 mm., radius of chip curvature was found to be 4.2 mm. Find the height of the integral obstruction-type chip breaker, if the chip breaker distance is 3.43 mm. Also calculate the offset distance of a clamped chip-breaker for equivalent performance, if the wedge angle is 45°.

12.2 During machining of Cr–Mo steel, chip-flow radius was found to be 6.6 mm. at limiting value of chip thickness of 0.5 mm. Calculate the offset distance necessary for a clamped chip breaker with a wedge angle of 45°. What will be the offset distance if the wedge angle is changed to 60° or 30°?.

# 13 Aspects of single-point tool design

## 13.1 Introduction

The design method for lathe tools or single-point tools is briefly outlined in this section to illustrate how metal-cutting theory and other aspects are to be taken into consideration for achieving effectiveness in production. The method is discussed with reference to cemented carbide tools.

The machining or cutting is done by a tip of cemented carbide that is secured in place in the tool shank by brazing directly to the shank or by clamping the inserts mechanically. The other methods include securing by means of cutting forces or by mechanically clamping a blade on which the tip is brazed.

## 13.2 Brazed carbide tool

Three types of cross-sections are used for the tool shank; (1) the rectangular cross-section, which is the most popular, since the reduction in strength of this shank section when a seat is cut for the tip is less than for other cross-sections; (2) the square cross-section which offers better resistance to complicated bending deformation; the applications include boring tools, tools used in automatic turret lathes and in cases where the distance from the centre line of the lathe to the supporting surface of the tool is too small to accommodate a rectangular shank; (3) the round shanks used for boring, threading, relieving and other tools and such shanks have the advantage of being turned easily to impart new geometry by grinding.

The design of the tool shank is dictated by the cutting force, shank material, tool overhang, and other factors. The following formula can be used to determine side $b$ or diameter $d$ of the tool shank:

For square shank, where $h$ = height of the shank and $h = b$

$$b = \left[\frac{6F_z l}{\sigma_{bp}}\right]^{1/3}$$

For rectangular shank, where $h \simeq 1.6b$,

$$b = \left[\frac{6F_z l}{2.56\sigma_{bp}}\right]^{1/3}$$

For round shank,

$$d = \left[\frac{10F_z l}{\sigma_{bp}}\right]^{1/3}$$

where $F_z$ = cutting force, N (kgf), $l$ = tool overhang m(mm), $\sigma_{bp}$ = permissible bending stress of the shank material, MPa (kgf/mm$^2$).

$\sigma_{bp}$ is about 200 to 300 MPa i.e. about 20 to 30 kgf/mm$^2$, for unhardened carbon steel shank and the values are twice as much for hardened carbon steel shanks. Also, half the above values are to be used for high-speed turning and intermittent chip removal.

For cut-off tools, the critical cross-section is neck, the place where the shank body terminates in the tool head, and for a ratio of $(b/h) \simeq 1/6$,

$$b = \left[\frac{F_z l}{6\sigma_{bp}}\right]^{1/3}$$

Now, the maximum load determined by the tool strength for the tool shank is given by $F_{zp}$.

(a) For the rectangular shank,

$$F_{zp} = \frac{bh^2\sigma_{bp}}{6l}$$

(b) For the round shank,

$$F_{zp} = \frac{\pi d^2\sigma_{bp}}{32l} \simeq \frac{d^2\sigma_{bp}}{10l}$$

The maximum load based on tool rigidity considering deflection is given by

$$F_{zp} = \frac{3fEI}{l^3}$$

where

$f$ = permissible deflection of the tool, mm

= $0.1 \times 10^{-3}$ m or 0.1 mm, for rough turning

= $0.05 \times 10^{-3}$ m or 0.05 mm, for finishing

$E$ = Young's modulus of shank material

$I$ = moment of inertia of shank cross-section

= $bh^3/12$, for a rectangular cross-section ($b \times h$)

= $0.05\ d^4$, for a round cross-section

$l$ = distance from the tool nose to the place of critical cross-section (overhang).

The actual force $F_z$ should be less than or equal to $F_{zp}$ or $F_{zr}$.

The tool geometry is determined from reference works on machinability data or by experimental work based on metal-cutting theories.

## 13.3 Mechanically clamped inserts

Today polyhedral *throw-away* inserts are available in triangular, square, pentagonal and hexagonal forms for carbides, ceramics, etc. These inserts are used in special tool holders having appropriate recess/pocket, where the insert is placed and mechanically clamped. These inserts are not resharpened. With the dulling of one cutting edge, the insert is indexed for the next cutting edge in operation. Once all the cutting edges are used, the insert is replaced by a new one.

The special tool holders with the pockets and clamping means determine the cutting edge angles, rake angles and relief angles by themselves, for a particular form of the insert.

The forces $F_{zp}$ and $F_{zr}$ can be estimated as above and these should be more than or equal to the actual force $F_z$ that should be computed otherwise for a specific operation.

In practice, the tool shanks are readily or commercially available in standard sizes: for example, 25mm × 25mm or 10mm × 10mm In such cases, it is advisable to estimate the maximum permissible load due to machining and accordingly select the cutting conditions for a given type of insert. Similar analysis holds good for brazed tool holder.

Conversely, for a given set of required or chosen cutting conditions, the problem will be one of ensuring a particular tool holder as technically sufficient with reference to strength of the shank as well as rigidity of the shank criteria.

The above features are illustrated in the following example.

*Example*

Estimate the maximum permissible load for a carbon steel square shank of 25 × 25mm² cross-section. Discuss further regarding selection of cutting conditions, when carbide triangular insert is used in the shank for turning alloy steel workpiece. Assume the following:

Young's modulus of shank material = $2 \times 10^5$ MPa

Limiting bending stress for shank material = 250 MPa

Permissible deflection = 0.8mm

Tool overhang = 10mm

*Solution*

*1. Strength of tool shank as criterion ($F_{zp1}$):*

$$F_{zp1} = \frac{bh^2\sigma_{bp}}{6l}, \text{ (Note: } b=h \text{ for square shank)}$$

$$= \frac{25 \times 25^2 \times 250}{6 \times 10}, \text{ (Note: 1 MPa = } 10^6\text{N/m}^2 \text{ or 1 N/mm}^2)$$

$$= 0.065 \times 10^6\text{N or 0.065 MN.}$$

*2. Shank rigidity as criterion ($F_{zp2}$):*

$$F_{zp2} = \frac{3fEI}{l^3} \text{ (Note: } I = (b^4/12) \text{ for square shank)}$$

$$= \frac{3 \times 0.08 \times 2 \times 10^5}{10^3} \times \frac{25^4}{12}$$

$$= 15.6 \times 10^6\text{N or 15.6 MN.}$$

The selection of cutting conditions should be so done that the cutting force that will be induced during machining should not exceed the above estimated loads. Again the cutting force may be found by dynamometry-based experiments for a given set of parameters, though time-consuming, expensive and laborious. Conversely, the cutting force may be estimated by specific energy considerations in machining, provided appropriate data is available or from records based on past experimental work.

Typical tool-insert and tool-holder manufacturers supply catalogues and manuals. In such occasions, the selection of indexable inserts or tool holders is done by referring to the corresponding 'identification system'.

**Insert identification system**

The International Standards Organisations (ISO) Insert identification system is briefly discussed as follows, though most of the manufacturers have their own system of standards.

*Example:*

| T | N | M | G | – 22 | 04 | 12 | E | –48 |
|---|---|---|---|---|---|---|---|---|
| 1 | 2 | 3 | 4 | 5 | 6 | 7 | 8 | 9 |

The various characters have been briefly outlined as below:
1. Shape, 2. Relief angle, 3. Tolerance, 4. Type of insert, 5. Cutting edge length, 6. Thickness, 7. Radius, 8. Cutting edge, 9. Chip groove geometry.

The first letter refers to the shape of the insert. In the example, T indicates a triangular insert. Other symbols include S for square, C for Rhombic 80°, D for Rhombic 55°, K for Rhomboidal 55°, and R for Round.

The second letter refers to the relief angle. N refers to 0°. The other codes are C for 7°, T for 10°, and P for 11°.

The third letter refers to tolerances, and these may vary with insert size.

The fourth one indicates the type of insert. In the example, G refers to an insert with cylindrical hole, with chip-breakers on two sides. The other codes are:

N = Without hole and chip-breakers.

F = Without hole and with chip-breaker on two sides.

R = Without hole, chip-breaker on one side.

A = With cylindrical hole, without chip-breaker.

M = With cylindrical hole, with chip-breaker on one side.

X = Special design.

The fifth one indicates the cutting edge length. In the example, being discussed, the cutting edge length is 22mm. Other kinds are 9.52mm. indicated by 09 and 12.7mm. by 12. For round inserts, diameters are indicated preceded by a 0.

The sixth letter refers to thickness of the insert. For example, 4.76mm. indicated by 04.

The seventh character refers to radius, in 1/10mm. In the example 12 indicates a radius of 1.2mm.

The eighth feature refers to the type of the cutting edge finish. E refers to edge rounded. The other codes are:

F = Sharp.

H = Indicates nominal hone in tolerance mode, when used with numeral.

J = Polished cutting surface only.

S = Primary land chamfered and edge rounded.

T = Primary land chamfered.

Finally, the ninth character refers to the chip groove geometry, the first digit to the relative feed range and the second digit to the relative force range. The number range for each is 1 to 9, 1 indicating 'very low' and 9 indicating 'very high'. For example, in 48, 4 indicates 'medium' feed and 8 indicates 'high' force.

**Tool holder identification system**

The selection of tool holder largely depends on the manual or catalogue of the manufacturer and unfortunately there is no standardized system commonly followed. However, the typical features involved are discussed below, by referring to a particular manufacturer.

*Example:*

| M | T | F | N | R | S | −16 | −4 | D |
|---|---|---|---|---|---|---|---|---|
| 1 | 2 | 3 | 4 | 5 | 6 | 7 | 8 | 9 |

The first character refers to method of holding. In the example, M indicates multiple lock assembly (pin and clamp lock). Other codes include C for clamp-lock assembly, P for pin-lock assembly, S for screw lock, and T for Tee-lock tool holders.

The second one refers to insert shape. In the example, T represents triangle. The other codes are C for 80° Diamond, D for 55° Diamond, L for rectangle, R for Round, S for Square and V for 35° Diamond.

The third letter is regarding the toolholder style. In the example, F refers to offset shank with 0° end cutting edge angle. The symbols range from A to Z and imply type of shank and end or side cutting edge angle.

The fourth character represents rake attitude, N for negative, O for neutral and P for positive rakes.

The fifth character is with reference to 'hand of tool', L for left, N for neutral and R for right.

The sixth one is with reference to pocket style, S representing single-wall pocket construction, and vacant letter position representing full-pocket construction.

The seventh one refers to tool holder shank size. For square shanks, the number represents the number which is sixteenths of width and height. For rectangular shanks, the first digit represents the number that is one-eighths of width, and the second digit represents the number which is one-fourth of height. These refer to inch unit.

The eighth one represents insert size. Rectangle and parallelogram inserts require two digits, the first digit for number of one-eighths in width and the second digit for number of quarters in length.

The ninth one is with reference to the qualified surface and length. In the example, D represents qualified back and end, 6 inches long.

## 13.4 Tool-in-use angles

The tool geometry discussed in Chapter 2 is basically what is called tool-in-hand angles. However, the recent ISO Draft gives more importance to defining the geometry of cutting tools in terms of their effective geometry, i.e. the geometry that exists when the tool is actually performing the cutting operation, and the angles are defined with reference to the tool-in-use system. It should be noted that ISO also recognizes the tool-in-hand system of angles for their practical implications for tool generation so that the manufacture and inspection of tools become easy.

The chapter also considers the single-point cutting tool for turning operations. There are two different factors that affect the effective geometry of the single-point cutting tool.

### (a) Cutting speed angle, $\eta$

The tool-in-use system of planes is located relative to the machine reference system set of axes, since for a turning operation, the direction of primary motion and the direction of feed motion coincide with the axes of the machine reference system (Fig.13.1). The cutting speed angle '$\eta$' is given as, $\tan\eta = (v_f/v_c) = (f/\pi d)$, where, $v_f$ = feed velocity, $v_c$ = cutting velocity,

$d$ = diameter of the part. However, $\eta$ will change the effective or working angles, which are different from the original tool-in-hand angles, particularly if the feed is high. Figure 13.2 illustrates the effective geometry for a single-point turning tool.

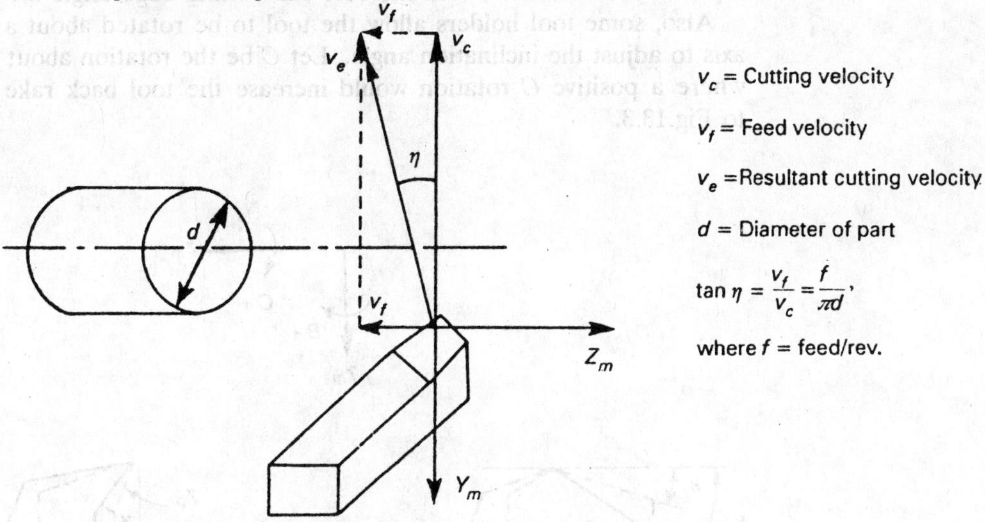


**Fig.13.1** Cutting speed angle

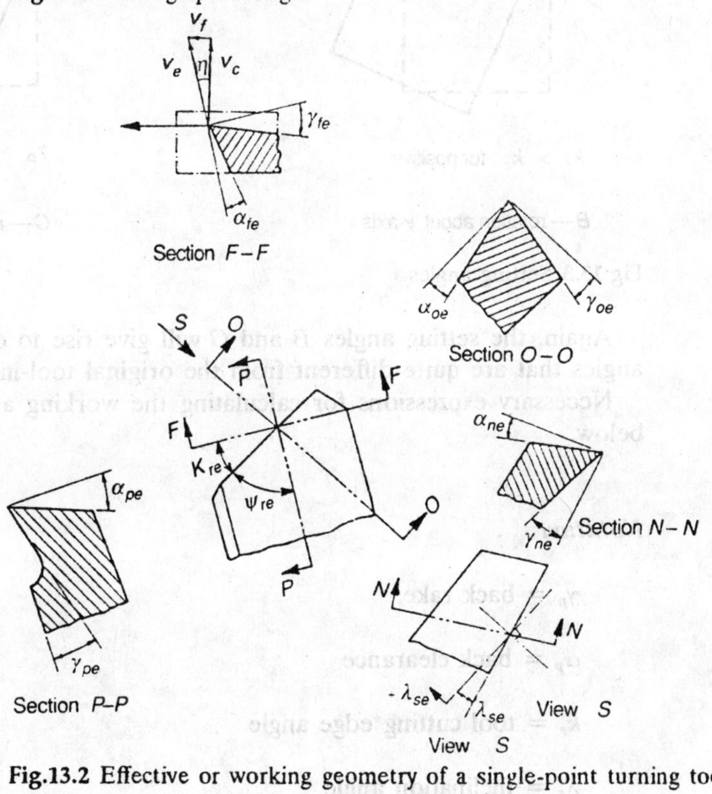


**Fig.13.2** Effective or working geometry of a single-point turning tool

**(b) Setting angles**

The tool can generally be rotated about the tool post, i.e., the $Y$-axis of the machine reference system. Let $B$ be the rotation, about the $Y$-axis, when a positive $B$ rotation would increase the cutting edge angle $k_r$.

Also, some tool holders allow the tool to be rotated about a horizontal axis to adjust the inclination angle. Let $C$ be the rotation about the $Z$-axis, where a positive $C$ rotation would increase the tool back rake $\gamma_p$. Refer to Fig.13.3.

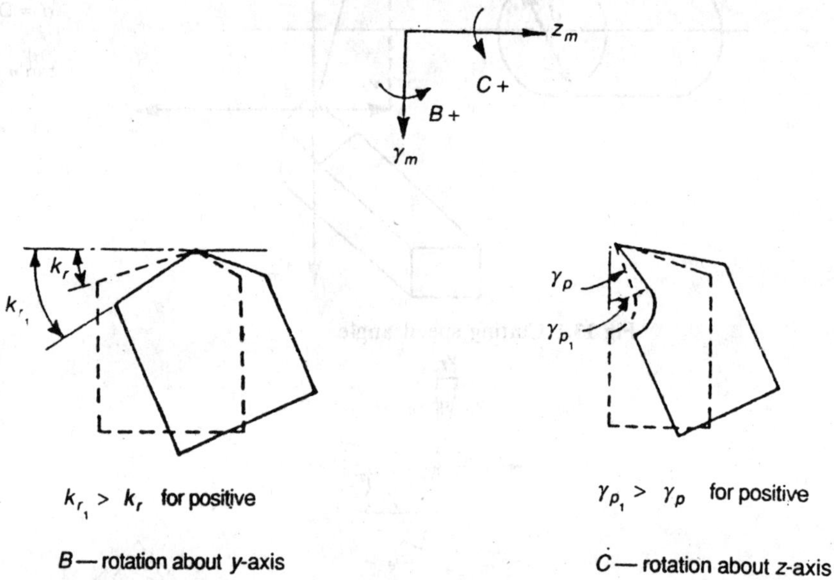


Fig.13.3 Setting angles

Again, the setting angles $B$ and $C$ will give rise to effective or working angles that are quite different from the original tool-in-hand angles.

Necessary expressions for calculating the working angles are described below.

***Notation***

$\gamma_p$ = back rake,

$\alpha_p$ = back clearance

$k_r$ = tool cutting edge angle

$\lambda_s$ = inclination angle

$\gamma_o$ = orthogonal rake

$\gamma_n$ = normal rake

$\alpha_o$ = orthogonal clearance

$\alpha_n$ = normal clearance

$\gamma_f$ = side rake

$\alpha_f$ = side clearance

The following equations can be used when $\gamma_p$, $\gamma_f$, $\alpha_p$, $\alpha_f$ and $k_r$ are known.

**(a) Effect of setting angles, *B* and *C***

Let $\gamma_{pm}$, $\gamma_{fm}$, $\alpha_{pm}$, $\alpha_{fm}$, $k_{rm}$ and $\lambda_{sm}$ be the changed corresponding angles with the introduction of setting angles *B* and *C*.

$$\tan\gamma_{fm} = [\tan\lambda_{sm}\sin(\theta+B)]/\sin(W-\theta)$$

$$\cot\alpha_{fm} = [\tan\lambda_{sm}\sin(\theta_1+B)]/\sin(W-\theta_1)$$

$$k_{rm} = -(W+B)$$

$$\tan\gamma_{pm} = [\tan\lambda_{sm}\cos(\theta+B)]/\sin(W-\theta)$$

$$\cot\alpha_{pm} = [\tan\lambda_{sm}\cos(\theta_1+B)]/\sin(W-\theta_1)$$

where,

$$\tan\lambda_{sm} = \frac{[\sin k_r\tan C+\tan\lambda_s]\sin W}{[\sin k_r-\tan\lambda_s\tan C]}$$

$$\tan W = \cos C\tan k_r - \frac{\cos C\tan k_r}{\cos k_r}$$

$$\tan\theta = \frac{\sin k_r\tan\gamma_f}{\cos C[\tan\lambda_s+\sin k_r\tan C+\cos k_r\tan\gamma_f]}$$

$$\tan\theta_1 = \frac{\sin k_r\cot\alpha_f}{\cos C[\tan\lambda_s+\sin k_r\tan C+\cos k_r\cot\alpha_f]}$$

**Note:** $\gamma_{pm}$, $\gamma_{fm}$, $\alpha_{pm}$, $\alpha_{fm}$, $k_{rm}$ and $\lambda_{sm}$ will be same as the corresponding $\gamma_p$, $\gamma_f$, $\alpha_p$, $\alpha_f$, $k_r$ and $\lambda_s$ when *B* and *C* are both equal to zero.

**(b) Effect of resultant cutting speed angle, $\eta$**

Let $\gamma_{pe}$, $\gamma_{fe}$, $\alpha_{pe}$, $\alpha_{fe}$, and $k_{re}$ be the corresponding angles while considering effect of feed introducing the resultant cutting speed angle $\eta$.

$$\gamma_{fe} = \gamma_{fm} + \eta$$

$$\alpha_{fe} = \alpha_{fm} - \eta$$

$$\tan k_{re} = \frac{\tan k_{rm}}{\cos\eta - \sin\eta[\tan k_{rm}\tan\gamma_{pm} - \tan\gamma_{fm}]}$$

$$\tan\gamma_{pe} = \frac{\tan\gamma_{pm}}{\cos\eta - \tan\gamma_{fm}\sin\eta}$$

$$\cot\alpha_{pe} = \frac{\cot\alpha_{pm}}{\cos\eta - \cot\alpha_{fm}\sin\eta}$$

**Note:** $\gamma_{pe}$, $\gamma_{fe}$, $\alpha_{pe}$, $\alpha_{fe}$ and $k_{re}$ will be same as the corresponding $\gamma_{pm}$, $\gamma_{fm}$, $\alpha_{pm}$, $\alpha_{fm}$, and $k_{rm}$, if $\eta$ is assumed to be zero, i.e. when feed is very low.

**(c) Working angles or effective angles**

Let $\lambda_{se}$, $\gamma_{ne}$, $\gamma_{oe}$, $\alpha_{ne}$, $\alpha_{oe}$ be the resulting corresponding working or effective angles on introduction of setting angles $B$ and $C$ and the resultant cutting speed angle $\eta$.

$$\tan\lambda_{se} = \sin k_{re}\tan\gamma_{pe} - \cos k_{re}\tan\gamma_{fe}$$

$$\tan\gamma_{ne} = \frac{\cos\lambda_{se}\tan\gamma_{fe}}{\sin k_{re}} + \frac{\sin\lambda_{se}}{\tan k_{re}}$$

$$\text{or, } \tan\gamma_{ne} = \cos\lambda_{se}\tan\gamma_{oe}$$

$$\tan\gamma_{oe} = \cos k_{re}\tan\gamma_{pe} + \sin k_{re}\tan\gamma_{fe}$$

$$\cot\alpha_{ne} = \cos\lambda_{se}\cot\alpha_{oe}$$

$$\tan\alpha_{oe} = \frac{1}{[\cos k_{re}\cos\alpha_{pe} + \sin k_{re}\cot\alpha_{fe}]}$$

**(d) Tool-in-hand angles**

The inter-relations among tool-in-hand angles as discussed in Chapter 2 are given below for ready reference.

$$\tan\lambda_s = \sin k_r\tan\gamma_p - \cos k_r\tan\gamma_f$$

$$\tan\gamma_n = \frac{\cos\lambda_s\tan\gamma_f}{\sin k_r} + \frac{\sin\lambda_s}{\tan k_r}$$

$$\text{or, } \tan\gamma_n = \cos\lambda_s \tan\gamma_o$$

$$\tan\gamma_o = \cos k_r \tan\gamma_p + \sin k_r \tan\gamma_f$$

$$\tan\alpha_n = \frac{\sin k_r}{\cos\lambda_s \cot\alpha_f + \cos k_r \sin\lambda_s}$$

$$\text{or, } \cot\alpha_n = \cos\lambda_s \cot\alpha_o$$

$$\tan\alpha_o = \frac{1}{\cos k_r \cot\alpha_p + \sin k_r \cot\alpha_f}$$

## 13.5 Solved examples

*Example 13.1*

In a turning operation of chilled cast iron with coated carbide of 50 mm dia. at 2 mm depth of cut, the following data is applicable.

Feed = 2 mm/rev; Back rake = –6°

Side rake = –8°; Side cutting edge angle = 15°

Calculate the working normal rake and working inclination angle of the tool-in-use system and compare it with corresponding tool-in-hand angles.

***Solution***

Given:

$$\gamma_{fm} = -8^\circ, \gamma_{pm} = -6^\circ, \psi = 15^\circ$$

Dia. $d$ = 50 mm, $f$ = 2 mm/rev.

$$k_{rm} = 90^\circ - 15^\circ = 75^\circ.$$

Let $\eta$ = the resultant cutting speed angle. Then,

$$\tan\eta = f/(\pi d)$$

$$= 2/(\pi \times 50) = 0.0127$$

$$\text{or, } \eta = 0.73^\circ \text{ or } 44'.$$

$$\tan k_{re} = \frac{\tan k_{rm}}{\cos\eta - \sin\eta(\tan k_{rm}\tan\gamma_{pm} - \tan\gamma_{fm})}$$

$$= \frac{\tan 75^\circ}{\cos 44' - \sin 44'[\tan 75^\circ \tan(-6^\circ) - \tan(-8^\circ)]}$$

$$= 3.7205 \quad \text{or} \quad k_{re} = 74^\circ 57'$$

$$\tan\gamma_{pe} = \frac{\tan\gamma_{pm}}{\cos\eta - \tan\gamma_{fm}\sin\eta}$$

$$= \frac{\tan(-6^\circ)}{\cos 44' - \tan(-8^\circ)\sin 44'}$$

$$= -0.1049$$

$$\text{or, } \gamma_{pe} = -5^\circ 59'.$$

Therefore,

$$\gamma_{fe} = \gamma_{fm} + \eta = -8^\circ + 44' = -7^\circ 16'$$

**Tool-in-use angles**

$$\tan\lambda_{se} = \sin k_{re}\tan\gamma_{pe} - \cos k_{re}\tan\gamma_{fe}$$

$$= \sin(74^\circ 59')\tan(-5^\circ 59')\tan(-7^\circ 16')$$

$$= (0.9657)(-0.1049) - (0.2613)(-0.1275)$$

$$= -0.1013 + 0.0333 = -0.0680$$

$$\text{or, } \lambda_{se} = -3^\circ 54'.$$

$$\tan\gamma_{oe} = \cos k_{re}\tan\gamma_{pe} + \sin k_{re}\tan\gamma_{fe}$$

$$= \cos(-3^\circ 54')\tan(-8^\circ 33') + \sin(-3^\circ 54')\tan(-7^\circ 16')$$

$$= (0.9977)(-0.1505) = -0.1505$$

$$\text{or, } \gamma_{oe} = -8^\circ 32'.$$

$$\tan\gamma_{ne} = \cos\lambda_{se}\tan\gamma_{oe}$$

$$= -0.1501.$$

$$\text{or, } \gamma_{ne} = -8^\circ 32'.$$

**Tool-in-hand angles**

$$\begin{aligned}
\tan \lambda_s &= \sin k_r \tan \gamma_{pm} - \cos k_r \tan \gamma_f \\
&= \sin 75^\circ \tan(-6^\circ) - \cos 75^\circ \tan(-8^\circ) \\
&= (0.9659)(-0.1051) - (0.2588)(-0.1405) \\
&= -0.1015 + 0.0364 = -0.0651 \\
\text{or, } \lambda_s &= -3^\circ 43'. \\
\tan \gamma_o &= \cos k_r \tan \gamma_p + \sin k_r \tan \gamma_f \\
&= \cos 75^\circ \tan(-6^\circ) + \sin 75^\circ \tan(-8^\circ) \\
&= (0.2588)(-0.1051) + (0.9659)(-0.1405) \\
&= -0.0272 - 0.1357 = -0.1629 \\
\text{or, } \gamma_o &= -9^\circ 15' \\
\tan \gamma_n &= \cos \lambda_s \tan \gamma_o \\
&= \cos(-3^\circ 43') \tan(-9^\circ 15') \\
&= (0.9979)(-1.1629) = -0.1625 \\
\text{or, } \gamma_n &= -9^\circ 14'.
\end{aligned}$$

**To sum up**

| Tool-in-use angles | Tool-in-hand angles |
|---|---|
| $\gamma_{ne} = -8^\circ 32'$ | $\gamma_n = -9^\circ 14'$ |
| $\gamma_{oe} = -8^\circ 33'$ | $\gamma_o = -9^\circ 15'$ |
| $\lambda_{se} = -3^\circ 54'$ | $\lambda_s = -3^\circ 43'$ |

*Example 13.2*

A carbide tool has the following geometry:

| | |
|---|---|
| Back rake | $= -7^\circ$ |
| Side rake | $= -5^\circ$ |
| Side cutting edge angle | $= 15^\circ$ |

Calculate the working angles if the setting angles are,

$B = +3°$, $C = -2°$

What will be the working angles, if a resultant cutting speed angle of 1° is also considered?

***Solution***

Given: $\gamma_p = -7°$, $\gamma_f = -5°$, $\psi = 15°$ or $k_r = 90° - 15° = 75°$

To find $\lambda_s$, $\gamma_o$ and $\gamma_n$, we have

$$\tan \lambda_s = \sin k_r \tan \gamma_p - \cos k_r \tan \gamma_f$$

$$= \sin 75° \tan(-7°) - \cos 75° \tan(-5°)$$

$$= -0.1186 + 0.0226 = 0.0960$$

$$\text{or, } \lambda_s = -5°30'.$$

$$\tan \gamma_o = \cos k_r \tan \gamma_p + \sin k_r \tan \gamma_f$$

$$= \cos 75° \tan(-7°) + \sin 75° \tan(-5°)$$

$$= (0.2588)(-0.1228) + (0.9659)(-0.0875)$$

$$= -0.0318 - 0.0845$$

$$= -0.1163$$

$$\text{or, } \gamma_o = -6°38'.$$

$$\tan \gamma_n = \cos \lambda_s \tan \gamma_o$$

$$= \cos(-5°30') \tan(-6°38')$$

$$= (0.9954)(-0.1163)$$

$$= -0.1157$$

$$\text{or, } \gamma_n = -6°36'.$$

Now,

$B = +3°$, $C = -2°$, $k_r = 75°$, $\gamma_p = -7°$, $\gamma_f = -5°$, $\lambda_s = -5°30'$

To find $W$ and $\theta$, we have

$$\tan W = \cos C \tan k_r - \frac{\cos C \tan k_r}{\cos k_r}$$

$$= \cos(-2°) \tan 75° - \frac{\cos(-2°) \tan 75°}{\cos 75°}$$

$$= (0.9994)(3.7321) - \frac{(0.9994)(3.7321)}{0.2588}$$

$$= 3.7298 - 14.4119 = -10.6821$$

$$W = -84°40'$$

$$\tan \theta = \frac{\sin k_r \tan \gamma_f}{\cos C(\tan \lambda_s + \sin k_r \tan C + \cos k_r \tan \gamma_f)}$$

$$= \frac{\sin 75° \tan(-5°)}{\cos(-2°)[\tan(-5°30') + \sin 75° \tan(-2°) + \cos 75° \tan(-5°)]}$$

$$= \frac{(-0.0845)}{(0.9994)(-0.0960 - 0.0337 - 0.0226)}.$$

On simplification, we get $\theta = 29°2'$.

To find $\lambda_{sm}$, we have

$$\tan \lambda_{sm} = \frac{[\sin k_r \tan C + \tan \lambda_s] \sin W}{\sin k_r - \tan \lambda_s \tan C}$$

$$= \frac{[\sin 75° \tan(-2°) + \tan(-5°30')] \sin(-84°40')}{\sin 75° - \tan(-5°30') \tan(-2°)}$$

$$= \frac{(-0.0337 - 0.0960)(-0.9957)}{(0.9659 + 0.0033)} = 0.1332.$$

$$\text{or, } \lambda_{sm} = 7°36'.$$

Now, to find $\gamma_{fm}$, $\gamma_{pm}$ and $k_{rm}$, we have

$$\tan \gamma_{fm} = \frac{\tan \lambda_{sm} \sin(\theta + B)}{\sin(W - \theta)}$$

$$= \frac{\tan 7°36' \sin(29°2' + 3°)}{\sin(-84°40' - 29°2')}$$

$$= \frac{(0.1332)(0.5304)}{-0.9157} = -0.0771$$

or, $\gamma_{fm} = -4°25'$.

Similarly,

$$\gamma_{pm} = -7°2'$$

$$k_{rm} = -(W + B) = -(-84°40' + 3°) = 81°40'.$$

**Case 1**

$$\eta = 0°; \quad \gamma_{fe} = \gamma_{fm} = -4°25'$$

$$\gamma_{pe} = \gamma_{pm} = -7°2'; \quad k_{re} = k_{rm} = 81°40'$$

**Working angles**

$$\begin{aligned}
\tan \lambda_{se} &= \sin k_{re} \tan \gamma_{pe} - \cos k_{re} \tan \gamma_{fe} \\
&= \sin 81°40' \tan(-7°2') - \cos 81°40' \tan(-4°25') \\
&= (0.9895)(-0.1234) - (0.1473)(-0.0771) \\
&= -0.1221 - 0.0114 = -0.1335
\end{aligned}$$

$$\text{or, } \lambda_{se} = -7°36'$$

$$\begin{aligned}
\tan \gamma_{oe} &= \cos k_{re} \tan \gamma_{pe} + \sin k_{re} \tan \gamma_{fe} \\
&= \cos 81°40' \tan(-7°2') + \sin 81°40' \tan(-4°25') \\
&= (0.1473)(-0.1234) + (0.9895)(-0.0771) \\
&= -0.0182 - 0.0763 \\
&= -0.0945
\end{aligned}$$

$$\text{or, } \gamma_{oe} = -5°24'$$

$$\begin{aligned}
\tan \gamma_{ne} &= \cos \lambda_{se} \tan \gamma_{oe} \\
&= \cos(-7°36') \tan(-5°24') \\
&= (0.9912)(-0.0945) = -0.0937
\end{aligned}$$

$$\text{or, } \gamma_{ne} = -5°21'$$

**Case 2**

$\eta = 1°$; $\gamma_{fm} = -4°25'$; $\gamma_{pm} = -7°2'$; and $k_{rm} = 81°40'$.

To find $k_{re}, \gamma_{pe}$ and $\gamma_{fe}$,

$$\tan k_{re} = \frac{\tan k_{rm}}{\cos\eta - \sin\eta[\tan k_{rm}\tan\gamma_{pm} - \tan\gamma_{fm}]}$$

$$= \frac{\tan 81°40'}{\cos 1° - \sin 1°[\tan 81°40' \tan(-7°2') - \tan(-4°25')]}$$

$$= \frac{6.7720}{0.9998 - 0.0175(-0.8357 + 0.0771)} = 6.6851$$

$$\text{or, } k_{re} = 81°30'$$

$$\tan\gamma_{pe} = \frac{\tan\gamma_{pm}}{\cos\eta - \tan\gamma_{fm}\sin\eta}$$

$$= \frac{\tan(-7°2')}{\cos 1° - \tan(-4°25')\sin 1°}$$

$$= \frac{-0.1234}{0.9998 + 0.0013} = -0.1233.$$

$$\text{or, } \gamma_{pe} = -7°2'$$

$$\gamma_{fe} = \gamma_{fm} + \eta$$

$$= -4°25' + 1° = -3°25'.$$

**Working angles**

Now

$\gamma_{pe} = -7°2'$; $\gamma_{fe} = -3°25'$ and $k_{re} = 81°30'$.

$$\tan\lambda_{se} = \sin k_{re}\tan\gamma_{pe} - \cos k_{re}\tan\gamma_{fe}$$

$$= \sin 81°30' \tan(-7°) - \cos 81°30' \tan(-3°25')$$

$$= (0.9890)(-0.1233) - (0.1478)(-0.0422)$$

$$= -0.1219 + 0.0062 = -0.1157$$

$$\text{or, } \lambda_{se} = -6°36\,.$$

$$\begin{aligned}
\tan\gamma_{oe} &= \cos k_{re}\tan\gamma_{pe} - \sin k_{re}\tan\gamma_{fe} \\
&= \cos 81°31'\tan(-7°2') + \sin 81°30'\tan(-3°25') \\
&= (0.1478)(-0.1233) + (0.9890)(-0.0422) \\
&= -0.0599. \\
\text{or, } \gamma_{oe} &= -3°26'. \\
\tan\gamma_{ne} &= \cos\lambda_{se}\tan\gamma_{oe} \\
&= \cos(-6°36')\tan(-3°26') \\
&= (0.9934)(-0.0599) = -0.0595 \\
\text{or, } \gamma_{ne} &= -3°24'.
\end{aligned}$$

**To sum up**

| Tool-in-hand angles | Tool-in-use angles | |
|---|---|---|
| | $\eta = 0°$ | $\eta = 1°$ |
| $\gamma_n = -6°36'$ | $\gamma_{ne} = -5°21'$ | $\gamma_{ne} = -3°24'$ |
| $\gamma_o = -6°38'$ | $\gamma_{oe} = -5°24'$ | $\gamma_{oe} = -3°26'$ |
| $\lambda_s = -5°30'$ | $\lambda_{se} = -7°36'$ | $\lambda_{se} = -6°36'$ |

## 13.6 Exercise problems

13.1 A single point turning tool has a back rake of 5°, a side rake of 13° and a side cutting edge angle of 15°. Calculate the inclination angle, orthogonal rake and normal rake in tool-in-hand system.

If the above tool is rotated about the tool post by 5° which tends to increase the side cutting edge angle, and also rotated about the spindle axis by 7° which tends to increase the tool back rake, calculate the tool-in-use system of working angles, i.e. the working inclination angle, working orthogonal rake and working normal rake.

13.2 A double carbide tool has the following geometry:

Inclination angle = −5°
Orthogonal rake = 10°
Cutting edge angle = 75°

Calculate the corresponding working angles, if the setting angles are $B = +7°$, $C = +4°$; what will be the working angles, if a resultant cutting speed angle of 0.90° is also considered?

# 14 Machining non-metals and hard materials

## 14.1 Polymer-based products

In recent years, polymer based products are becoming, a new class of commonly used engineering material. These non-metallic products will find more applications in future, especially in the engineering industries.

Polymers are long-chain molecules composed of many organic atoms. There are two main groups of materials which are relevant to our study: (1) plastics, though plastics may be a mixture of polymers with additives and/or fillers, (2) elastomers.

Plastics are synthetic materials made from chemical raw materials called manomers. For example, polyethylene is made from the manomer (one chemical unit), ethylene, reacting with other manomer molecules to form long chains of repeated ethylene units.

**(a) Thermoplastic composites**
These are thermoplastics reinforced with high-strength, high-modulus fibres to increase strength and stiffness, toughness, and dimensional stability. Glass fibres, carbon fibres and aramid fibres are common examples.

**(b) Thermoset composites**
Glass fibre is the most widely used reinforcement. Other notable reinforcements include carbon, graphite, boron and aramid (Kevlar). These composites are finding greater application in new areas such as automobile body panels, seats and panels, printed-circuit boards, gears, aircraft

components, demanding light weight, high strength and excellent fatigue performance.

**(c) Elastomers and rubbers**

Elastomers include natural rubber and synthetic materials such as neoprene, nitride, styrene butadiene and lutadiene rubber. Elastomers are used in engineering applications dealing with shock absorption, noise and vibration control, sealing, corrosion protection, abrasion and friction reduction, electrical and thermal insulation, and load bearing.

## 14.2 Other hard materials

**(a) Ceramics**

Ceramics are basically inorganic, non-metallic materials processed or consolidated at high temperatures. They consist of metallic and non-metallic materials that are compounds of oxides, fluorides, carbides, nitrides, and borides. These find application in erosion-resistant centrifugal pumps, heat exchangers, mechanical seals, cutting tools, nozzles, heat shields for spacecrafts and other allied areas. Some examples of engineering ceramics are alumina, silicon carbide, silicon nitride, tungsten carbide, etc.

**(b) Nickel-based super alloys**

These superalloys are often specified for high-strength applications at high temperatures up to 2000° F. Inconel, Monel, Hastalloy, Waspaloy are important Nickel-based super alloys.

**(c) Refractory metals**

Refractory metals are characterized by extremely high melting points that range well above those of iron, cobalt and nickel, and are used in applications requiring high-temperature strength and corrosion resistance. Widely used refractory metals include tungsten, tantalum, molybdenum and columbium (niobium).

**(d) High-strength, low-alloy steel**

High-strength, low-alloy (HSLA) steels are being increasingly used in the automotive industry to reduce the weight of the parts. The high strength is due to ultrafine grain sizes and precipitation mechanisms with low alloy contents. The alloying elements are columbium (0.02 per cent), vanadium (0.05 per cent), aluminium (0.02 per cent) and Titanium (0.05 per cent).

## 14.3 Machining thermoplastics

Machining of thermoplastics is common when the tolerances required cannot be met economically by moulding or where low production runs do not justify the mould-cost. Machining is good because, in addition to producing flat surfaces, it can produce very small parts, thin sections, shapes difficult to mould, and parts that could go through several design changes.

While machining thermoplastics, the following are the principal differences to be considered with reference to metals:

**(a) Lower modulus of elasticity**

Thermoplastics are relatively resilient; so the forces involved in holding and cutting must be adjusted accordingly, and the material must be supported to avoid distortion.

**(b) Plastic memory**

Elastic recovery occurs in plastic materials both during and after machining, and the cutting tool must be provided with enough clearance to compensate for this. Otherwise, the expansion of the compressed plastic as it recovers, will increase the friction between the recovered cut surface and the relief surface of the cutting tool. In addition to generating heat, this rubbing causes tool wear.

Unless necessary precautions are taken, elastic recovery, after machining, can result in drilled or tapered holes that are smaller than the diameter of the drill or in turned diameters that become larger than they were during machining.

**(c)Low thermal conductivity**

Almost all the heat generated by the machining friction between the plastic and the tool will be absorbed by the latter. Even the little heat conducted to plastic raises the temperature of the surface layer significantly, and this heat must be minimized or removed by the coolant.

**(d) Thermal expansion**

The coefficient of thermal expansion of plastics are greater, by a factor of about ten, than those of metals. The expansion of the plastic as a result of the heat generated, generates further heat due to increased friction. Sufficient clearance angles are necessary to minimize melting.

**(e) Softening point**

Since the softening, deformation and degradation temperatures are relatively low for plastics, gumming, dislocation, poor tolerance control, and poor finish are common if the frictional heat is allowed to build-up during generation. The heat build-up becomes critical with plastics which have lower melting points.

Appropriate tool geometry and optimum speeds and feeds can, to a large extent, reduce the heat build-up. Additionally, it is recommended that a suitable coolant be used, especially for high speed or automatic machining operations. Water soluble oils (with a 1:10 or 1:20 oil-to-water ratio), light-machine oils, or a jet of compressed air can be used as coolants. Care is to be taken in selection to avoid chemical reaction of the coolant with the work. For example, any coolant can be used with TFE-fluroplastic due to its resistance to all chemicals. But polystyrene and polycarbonate can be attacked by fluids containing chlorinated or aromatic hydrocarbons and may stress-crack after prolonged exposure.

The cutting tools for thermoplastics must have sharp, carefully honed cutting edges (of 10 $\mu$ surface finish or even better) and a greater clearance than normally used for machining metals. Though HSS tools work well, carbides are suitable for long production runs. However, the carbide tools must be used on filled plastics such as molybdenum disulfide-filled nylons, glass-reinforced nylons and TFE-fluroplastics with or without ceramic fillers. Carbide tools should be honed on 400 to 600-grit size diamond wheels for maximum smoothness after grinding.

Most of the thermoplastics machine well with a 0° top rake angle, but variation in tooling and physical characteristics of specific works may warrant modifications.

Additionally, clamping and holding pressures must be held to the required minimum, because the thermoplastics deform more easily than metals. If too much pressure is applied, however carefully the piece is machined, it will expand in the area of compression once the clamping pressure is removed, for example with TFE that deforms easily. This is not a crucial factor when it comes to harder thermoplastics.

Though plastics can be machined faster than free-machining brass, tool forces are quite low, and so considerably less collet pressure is needed. For example, in automatic screw machine work, high speeds are involved and the collet pressure just necessary to avoid the work from slipping is enough.

## 14.4 Composites

A composite is a complex material in which two or more distinct, structurally complementary substances, especially metals, ceramics, glass and polymers, combine to produce some structural or functional properties not present in the individual components. The composite materials, the fibre-reinforced metals and plastics, provide impressive strength-to-weight and stiffness-to-weight advantages. These materials find increasing application in aerospace manufacturing, especially in the manufacture of airframes and aircraft engine components, replacing Al, steel and titanium. They consist mostly of graphite or boron filaments in a resin or metal matrix. Table 14.1 gives the comparison of strength limits for different matrix/reinforcing materials.

For example in a boron-filament/epoxy-matrix composite, the filaments improve the matrix's tear resistance, while the flexibility of the matrix offsets the inherent brittleness of the filaments.

**Table 14.1** Comparison of strength limits

| Material | Ultimate strength kg/cm$^2$ | Den-sity gm/cm$^3$ | Specific strength (UTS/density) cm | Elastic modulus $E$ kg/cm$^2$ | Specific modulus ($E$/density) cm |
|---|---|---|---|---|---|
| Mg | 3600 | 1.77 | 2034 | 433,000 | 244,600 |
| Al | 6700 | 2.69 | 2490 | 670,000 | 249,000 |
| Ti | 12000 | 4.44 | 2860 | 1133,000 | 255,180 |
| Fe | 20000 | 7.8 | 2564 | 1977,700 | 253,400 |
| **New fibres and wires** | | | | | |
| Stainless steel | 36000 | 7.8 | 4615 | 1977,700 | 253,551 |
| Be | 11300 | 1.8 | 6278 | 2733,000 | 1518,333 |
| B | 26700 | 2.3 | 11600 | 3677,000 | 1594,347 |
| SiC | 23300 | 3.4 | 6850 | 4333,000 | 1274,411 |
| E-glass | 23300 | 2.5 | 9320 | 700,000 | 280,000 |
| C | 13300 | 1.6 | 8313 | 2667,000 | 1667,000 |

**Examples: Typical:** Boron/epoxy, Boron/Aluminium, Boron/Aluminium-titanium, Graphite/epoxy.

The reinforcing materials are normally in the form of small diameter wires or of still smaller single crystal whiskers. For the comparison of different reinforcing materials, refer to Fig.14.1. The fibres or wires range in diameter from a few microns to 0.25 cm.

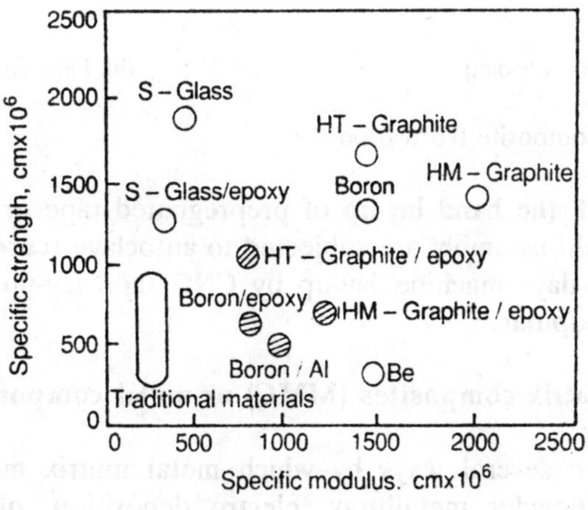


**Fig.14.1** Comparison of materials

The two main categories of composites are resin matrix composites (RMC) and metal matrix composites (MMC).

### Resin matrix composites (RMC) or plastic composites

The usual matrix material is epoxy resin. The reinforcing materials are fibres of graphite or boron. Being combined in a polymer-resin matrix, these fibres or filaments offer scope to reduce weight, minimize machining, increase performance and reduce costs. Weight saving of 20 to 30 per cent or even up to 50 per cent is possible.

First, prior to actual part fabrication, the fibres and resin are combined into a preimpregnated system. Prepregnated fibres or very narrow (3 to 6 mm) prepared tapes are used in filament winding. The fibres are processed through a resin bath, cured for a specific time at a specific temperature to drive off the processing solvents and to cure the resin to appropriate condition and then wound onto a storage reel. For example, certain aircraft components are fabricated from 7 cm wide continuous tape, which is made by winding resin coated fibres onto a mandrel till a complete, unidirectional tape is produced. For broader items, wider mandrels are used, enabling sheets being cut. Preforms for specific shapes can also be used (Fig.14.2).

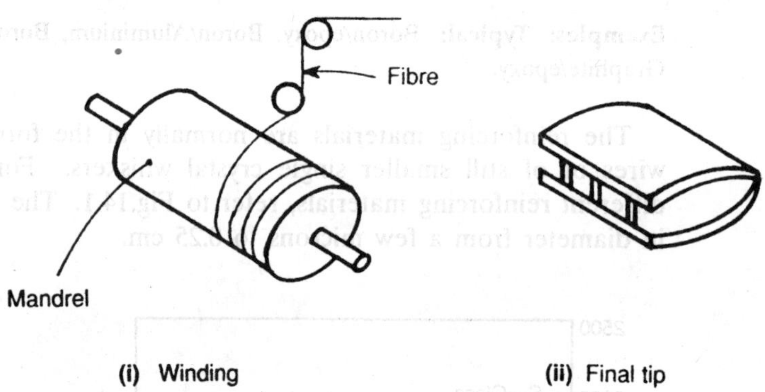


**Fig.14.2** Composite fabrication

Second, the hand lay-up of prepregnated tape or broader items or the final mould assembly are subjected to autoclave (cure) or press lamination.

Now-a-days machine lay-up by CNC tape lay-up machines is also becoming popular.

### Metal matrix composites (MMC) or metal composites

There are several ways by which metal matrix materials are produced namely, powder metallurgy, electro deposition, plasma flame spraying, explosive consolidation, molten-metal impregnation, diffusion bonding, electroforming and rolling. Among them, presently, diffusion bonding is the most important method.

In diffusion bonding, alternative layers of matrix foil and oriented fibres are placed one on top of the other till the required amount of material for the final thickness is assembled. Further, by a combination of heat, pressure and time in a vacuum (typical measures are 400–500°C for one hour at 140 to 600 kg/cm$^2$ in a vacuum of $10^{-3}$ to $10^{-4}$ torr), the matrix is caused to flow around the fibres so that it binds to the next layer of matrix and at the same time, grips the reinforcing fibres very tightly.

Typical among metal matrix composites are the aluminium alloy matrix materials. Titanium matrices enable higher temperature applications. Reinforcing materials include boron, borsic (silicon carbide-coated boron) and silicon carbide in diameters from 0.075 to 0.125 mm as well as beryllium and steel wires in diameters from 0.05 to 0.25 mm. A widely used composite consists of 40 per cent to 50 per cent (by volume) of boron filament in an aluminium alloy matrix.

Generally, these matrices can be bent, joined and otherwise formed to a variety of shapes. However, forming operations requiring an appreciable stretch of the filaments are not possible with boron of low permissible elongation. Hot bending of cross-ply material is easier than bending of unidirectional material, provided the direction of the filaments is at an angle to the bend axis.

Joining of matrices is no problem. Adhesive bonding, mechanical fasteners, brazing and resistance welding are easy.

## 14.5 Machining composites and other hard materials

Though a composite design generally eliminates most of the machining, a little machining like edge routing, drilling of attaching holes, grinding of mating surfaces, etc. is involved. At this stage, however, these materials are extremely difficult to machine.

### (a) Machining boron/epoxy

The main problems in machining boron/epoxy composites arise due to the extreme hardness of boron filaments and the lack of support by the epoxy-resin matrix for these filaments. These factors contribute to very high tool wear and break out of the reinforcing fibres.

Diamond core drills, reamers and blades or tools are one solution. The appropriate non-conventional cutting methods are gas-assisted laser cutting, electrochemical grinding, and ultrasonic cutting techniques with a rotary diamond tool.

### (b) Machining graphite/epoxy composites

Here the problems faced are brittleness of graphite fibres, abrasion of

**the thermosetting epoxy-resin matrix, and surface contamination by cutting fluids.**

**Using carbide tools or diamond tips is one solution. Ultrasonic, abrasive jet and laser machining are other methods. The latest addition is water jet cutting.**

**(c) Machining boron/aluminium composites**

**Carbides and diamond tools are commonly used when machining such composites. Special machining methods such as electro-discharge machining(EDM), wire EDM, electrochemical grinding, ultrasonic machining are other alternatives (see Figs.14.3, 14.4 and 14.5). Chemical milling and electrochemical machining are new additions.**

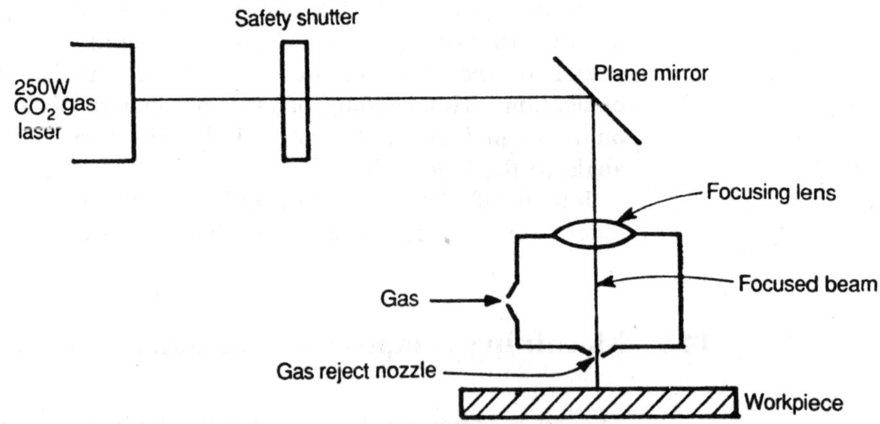


**Fig.14.3 Laser machining**

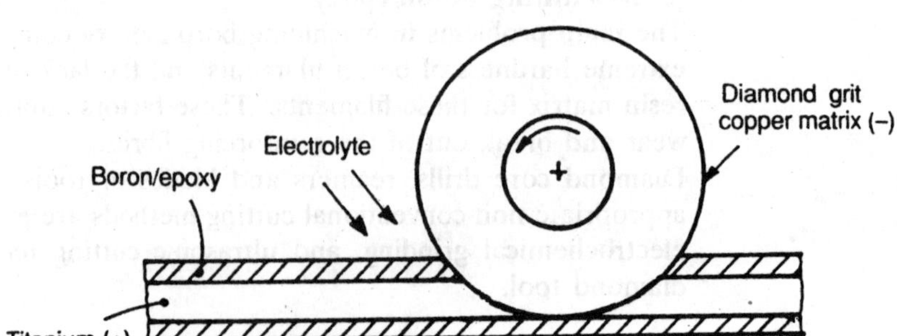


**Fig.14.4 Electrochemical grinding**

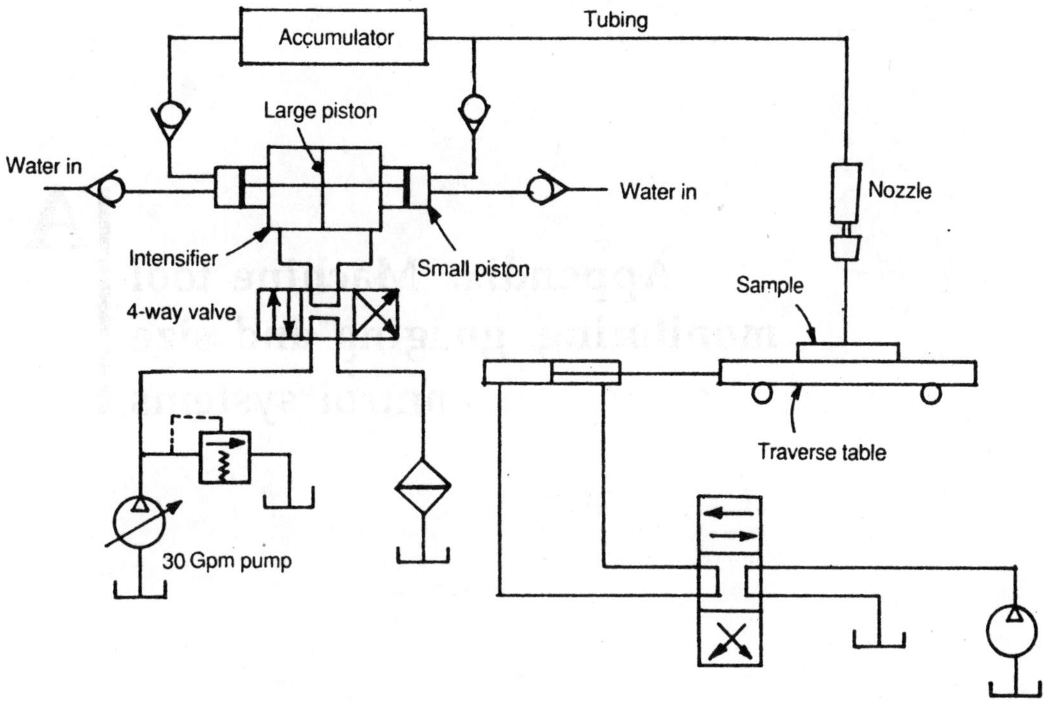


Fig.14.5 Water jet cutting

**(d) Machining other hard materials**

**Appropriately selected tool materials like PCD, CBN, coated carbides, etc. is one method. The other is by special machining methods depending on specific requirements. For more details, refer to concerned chapters (Chapters 9 and Appendix-B).**

A

# Appendix: Machine tool monitoring, guaging and size control systems

## A.1 Machine tool monitoring systems

The machine tool monitoring systems provide a highly efficient means for constant electronic surveillance of machine operations to help protect costly machines, tools and parts against damage. A family of transducers, specially designed for economic monitoring, are added to the machine. Thus practical adaptive control and other cost-saving features can be incorporated into the machining operations.

### *Power monitor*

A power monitor helps to prevent machine and machine tool damage in borings, drilling, milling, turning, grinding, shaping and hobbing operations. By monitoring a.c. or d.c. motor power consumption, the power monitor alerts the operator through audio or visual signals when power limits are exceeded, and shuts down the machine altogether when potential damage is imminent. The desired power limit is set by thumb wheel switches on a typical power monitor. The power reading for automated systems is readily available as an output in analog and digital forms suitable for interfacing with recorder, printer or data acquisition systems.

## *Tool sense machine-tool monitor*

This unit is a unique programmable system that accurately monitors power in machining processes for up to, say, 99 different tools or tool operations with a single control unit. The unit is designed specifically for NC, DNC and CNC machining centres.

In addition to basic monitoring of horse power, the unit is normally provided with optional adaptive control features. This option enables a machine tool to maintain a constant horse power throughout a cut, even through interrupts, tapers, etc. There is also an additional feature to aid in setting up, a 'self-teach' mode that automatically programs the power limits.

The tool sense adaptive control (Fig.A.1) is designed to maintain constant horse power through control of the feed rate over wide input. For example, the adaptive power is, say, programmed to maintain 10 horse power — the maximum needed for the deepest cut. The cut is a ramp, requiring the least power at entry and progressively more power as the cut deepens. Normally without adaptive control, feed rate would be constant, dictated by the maximum depth of cut even though a faster rate is possible at entry. The adaptive control automatically adjusts to these differing conditions, adjusting feed rate as needed with a fixed programmed horse power, thus maximizing productivity.

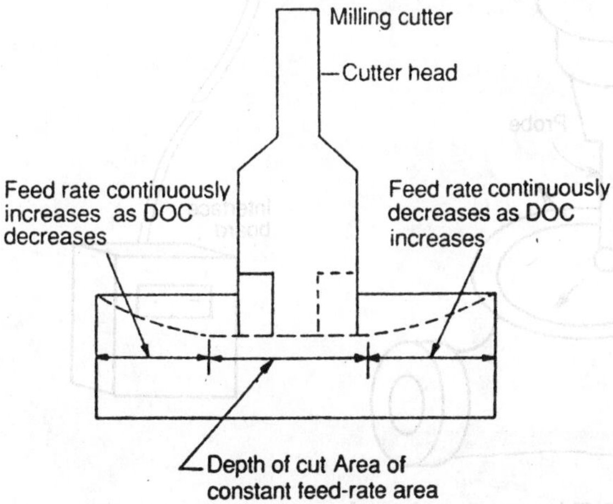


**Fig.A.1 A typical tool sense adaptive control**

## *Statistical tool control (STC) gauge amplifier*

This unit typically determines when to compensate a tool, based on an ongoing average or on the mean of gauge readings for a predetermined group size which ranges from, say, 2 to 10. The unit provides a digital display of the current part being gauged and upon, demand, the statistical average ($x$) or the range ($R$) of the selected group size. Control limits of both $x$ and $R$ can be entered into the STC gauge amplifier. LED's as well as 110 V a.c. outputs are provided to indicate when these limits are exceeded. In addition, the STC gauge module provides a serial interface port and analog output signal to transmit actual gauge readings to other analysis-equipment. This gauge can also store up to 500 readings and transmit them on request.

### *Telemetry touch probes*

Through the use of infrared signal transmission, the touch probes permit fast checking of part parameters on CNC machines. Based on infrared signal transmission, these probes are easily and quickly installed on the CNC without any costly machine modification or space consuming problems.

The system has three components (Refer Fig.A.2):

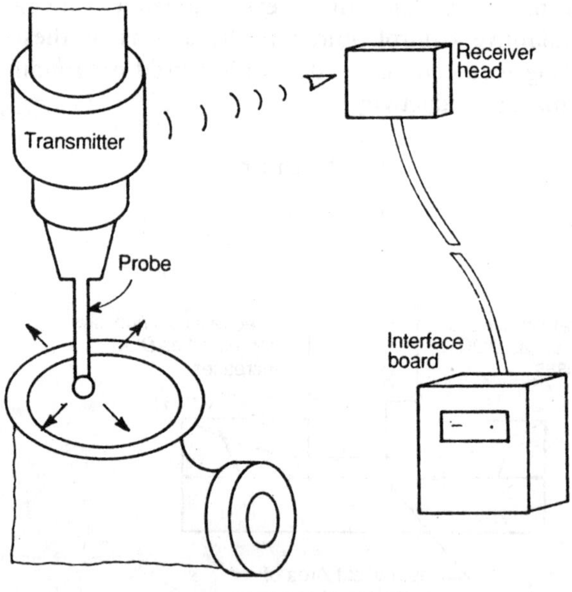


**Fig.A.2** Telemetry touch probe system

(a) a probe with its battery-powered infrared transmitter,

(b) an interface board that is mounted in the CNC control panel connecting the probe system to the CNC.

(c) a receiver head which picks up the infrared signal produced by the probe and transmits it to the interface board.

The machining centre probes are stored in the tool magazine just like any other tool and are loaded with the help of the automatic changer when needed. The turning tool probe and boring bar probe are simply placed in lathe turret pocket like cutting tools. The probes signal the CNC when the stylus is deflected. With the appropriate software, the CNC uses the signal to:

(i) locate and determine part orientation;

(ii) sense surface location;

(iii) establish hole centres as well as diameters;

(iv) regrind the machine ($x$, $y$, $z$ coordinates);

(v) gauge or measure parts for length, depth and diameter;

(vi) probe for and determine broken drills;

(vii) assist the tool-setting and verification.

The probe, in its simplest form, is an extremely accurate electronic switch that is operated by a lithium battery pack for transmission of the probe signal. The probe replaces the mechanical indicator gauge by utilizing the machine control to determine when the workpiece has been contacted. By comparing the actual location which has been touched, to the programmed location of the part program, the CNC can determine the error, if any, in position, size, skew, etc.

When the probe is activated, it begins transmitting a carrier signal to the receiver head via infrared light. When the stylus is deflected, this signal is modulated.

The control interface converts this signal from the receiver head to relay contact that is used to interface to the machine control. In seconds, the probe touches, transmits, and the CNC control translates to assure an uninterrupted, precision machining.

Also, unlike the other surface sensing probes that require a fixed receiver mounted on the machine control and a critical alignment procedure of the probe with the receiver, the telemetry touch probe eliminates the need for spindle orientation because of infrared light transmission. The receiver head may be mounted anywhere.

### *Applications*

(a) In-process inspection.

(b) Automatic regrind or zeroing of the machine, i.e., the probe can assist the machine to correct errors due to thermal drift of the machine part or fixture.

(c) Support the unmanned machining concept: The probe can allow the machine to automatically determine whether the part is present and it is properly oriented; if not, it can correct the part for offsets, thus minimizing the need for extremely accurate fixturing and avoiding costly accidents. The probe can also be used for part identification.

## A.2 Machine control and gauging systems

### *Introduction*

The microprocessor, a digital logic device, is a complex electronic circuit consisting of thousands of microscopic transistors fused onto a tiny silicon chip, often no larger than 3/4 $cm^2$. Presently, the application of microprocessors to electronic gauging has helped to accelerate the transition of part size measurement from inspection room to the manufacturing floor.

The electronic column gauge can, typically, be adapted to the microprocessor to form systems that greatly enhance the measuring and decision-making capability required in many production-proven applications to integrate gauging and inspection with the manufacturing process, and to improve production control and reduce costs.

### *Microprocessor and its significance*

Microprocessor is a product of the present-day silicon chip technology based on the advances in integrated circuit electronics/computer science, that incorporates a very large number of basic digital logic elements on a small area of single wafer of silicon. In contrast, it may be noted that early computers were built of complex circuits using a large number of transistors and valves. The highly reliable and also very economical LSI (Large Scale Integration) chip is the heart of microprocessor system.

Compared to computers with conventional hard wired logical circuites, the microprocessors provide high flexibility and are easily reprogrammable. The microprocessor chip is like Central Processing Unit (CPU) of the 'computer'.

The physical components used to form the microprocessor/computer system are collectively called 'hardware', which include microprocessor or CPU, memory and input/output peripherals. 'Software' comprises program instructions to specify the tasks to be performed by the computer system, both for directing the system operation and for performing particular application tasks.

Digital logic forms the basis of operation of microprocessors using transistor switches in ON (1) or OFF (0) states. Such basic elements of digital logic are referred to as binary digits or bits. In the microprocessor system, a number of bits are combined together to form words. The most common collection consists of 8 bits and is called a *Byte*. The microprocessor system recognizes and decodes different combinations of bits, and depending on the value of these bits, it performs the appropriate action. For example, data value specifying manipulation, and also the instructions to transmit data to a peripheral or compare two data values — all are represented by distinct collections of bits. The system designer/programmer specifies the above necessary instructions. It may be interesting to note that 8 bits (1 byte) will have $2^8$ or 256 combinations and 16 bits will have $2^{16}$ or 65536 different combinations. Examples of 8 bit microprocessors are Intel 8080, Motorola M6800, etc. and of 16 bit microprocessors are Intel 8086, Motorola 68000, Zilog Z-8000 systems. 32 bit microprocessors are also commercially available.

Microprocessor accepts data only in discrete digital form as bits or collection of bits and the real-world devices are not likely to be in this format. Similarly, the data output from microprocessor is also in the digital format, i.e., as a collection of bits, and the devices to which the data are to be output are not always able to accept the digital data.

For example, in a process/machine control system, the input devices would be sensors or transducers, where the physical parameters are converted into an appropriate electrical signal in the form of current or voltage, mostly in a continuous fashion within a specified range, such as between 0 to 10 V. Similarly, most of available actuators can only operate on continuous analog output data, and the output of the microprocessor in digital format must be converted to analog format. In such applications, Analog to Digital (A/D) converters and Digital to Analog (D/A) converters are used as standard units.

Also output signals from many of available transducers are of very low value and cannot be directly input to the microprocesor system. Hence, amplifiers are necessary for amplification of the transducer signal to a level of upto 10 V, before the data are converted and processed in the microprocessor. Similarly, amplifiers are often required for converting the computer signals to the levels required by the actuators.

Data output by the transducers are often contaminated by noise, that is eliminated or reduced by using suitable filters. Also linearizing circuits are used to linearize the transducer data.

Sometimes the system will consist of a large number of transducers or output data to a number of actuators or output devices. One alternative is to use an appropriate number of A/D and D/A converters and connect them to microprocessor chip. However, using a number of converters is expensive and the microprocessor chip has only a limited number of pins to which input/output devices can be connected. This difficulty is overcome by using standard circuits known as Multiplexers and Demultiplexers.

A number of sensors are converted to a multiplexer system which is also linked to a Sample and Hold (S/H) device and an A/D converter circuit. The multiplexers transfer data from a number of lines into a single line so that the data from different transducers can be scanned without increasing heavy system overloads. Thus, in order to pass a signal from a given sensor, the signal value from that particular transducer is input to a S/H circuit which accurately samples that value and keeps it fixed until the value has been input to the A/D circuit and converted into digital format. If it is necessary to sample a large number of variables simultaneously, individual S/H circuites must be used for each signal. The multiplexer will take one value at a time and input it to the A/D converter.

Similarly on the output side from the computer, a number of digital outputs can be connected into analog format by using a single D/A converter and a demultiplexer. The demultiplexer is used to transfer the data from one line to a number of lines. Figure A.3 illustrates a typical multiple input and multiple output microprocessor system.

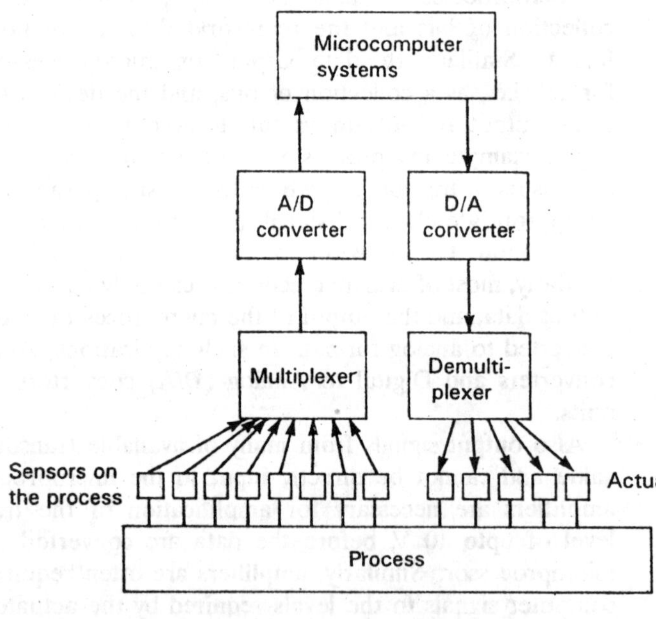


**Fig.A.3 Multiple I/O microprocessor system**

Microprocessor systems find applications in two major groups: (i) information manipulate/retrieval applications such as Computer Aided Design/Production Planning and Control and Routine Data Processing, and (ii) other applications in controlling a process or machine requiring sensors and actuators.

The sensors or transducers are needed to monitor the value of a variable of interest so that the data value can be input to the microprocessor system and an appropriate decision be made. The physical parameters monitored depending on the problem can be such as pressure, temperature, velocity, flow-rate, acceleration, force, displacement, liquid level, strain, mass, frequency of vibration, density, etc.

Also a range of actuators are available for interfacing with the microprocessor system. Examples include solenoids, relays – mechanical or solid state, hydraulic cylinders, pneumatic cylinders, stepping motors, field control d.c. motors, armature control d.c. motors, a.c. motors, and hydraulic motors. Additionally, current to pneumatic (I/P) converters and pneumatic to voltage (P/V) converters are also used for interfacing appropriate actuators.

### *Microprocessor and I/O modules*

A multiplexer module consisting of an eight-bit microprocessor with its control, program and data memory, I/O interface control and bi-directional latches is contained in a unit of the size of a standard column gauge. The single, compact module, for example in a typical system, contains the needed circuitry to acquire and store data from 16 gauge probes.

A bi-directional column gauge bus permits data to be transferred between columns and the microprocessor. After scanning up to 16 probes, the microprocessor can make the necessary measurements, decisions or calculations, etc. The output can be to display or to I/O columns for control purpose.

### *Applications*

**1. Automatic gauging/machine control**

A roller shaft used in a duplicating equipment is given in Fig.A.4. While gauging, the part is rotated through at least one revolution and sorted into 'accept' and 'reject' clauses. Three column gauges are used to measure the diameter at both ends and at a point in the centre of the shaft for Total Indicator Runout (TIR).

The system consists of three column gauges, three I/O columns, and a special function column. Inspection up to about 700 parts/hr is possible for example, indicating the advantages of integrating the machine control and gauge functions in the same system.

**2. Multiplexing probe**

This system referred in Fig.A.5 is designed in the example to measure the diameter and location of two bearing bores relative to a reference hole in tube pump assemblies. Two sets of probes are used in each bore. Each set, consisting of two probes, is used to measure the diameter. Then the same probes are used in a different combination to determine location of the bores.

To determine diameter, measurements from the probes have to be added. To find the location of the bore, measurements from the two gauge probes must be subtracted and then divided by 2. The ability to first add and then subtract measurements is made possible by the microprocessor column. The result is a fixture to provide complete gauging measurements with a minimum number of probes.

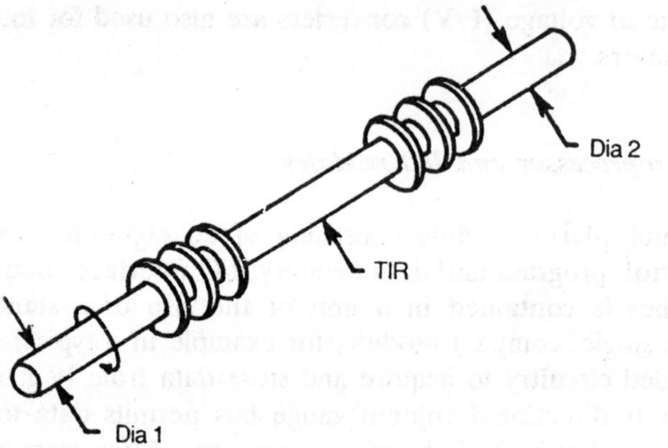


**Fig.A.4** An example for automatic gauging and machine control

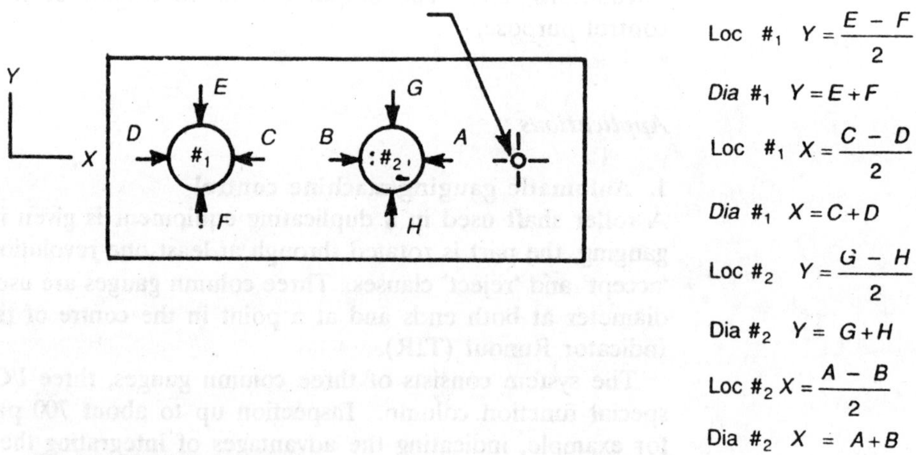


**Fig.A.5** Multiplexing probe

### 3. Part classification

The microprocessor based gauging system given in Fig.A.6, inspects piston parts and, through use of multiplexer control, deflects each part into the correct storage tube according to size. The system provides for a selection of parts classified by size for a subsequent selective assembly operation.

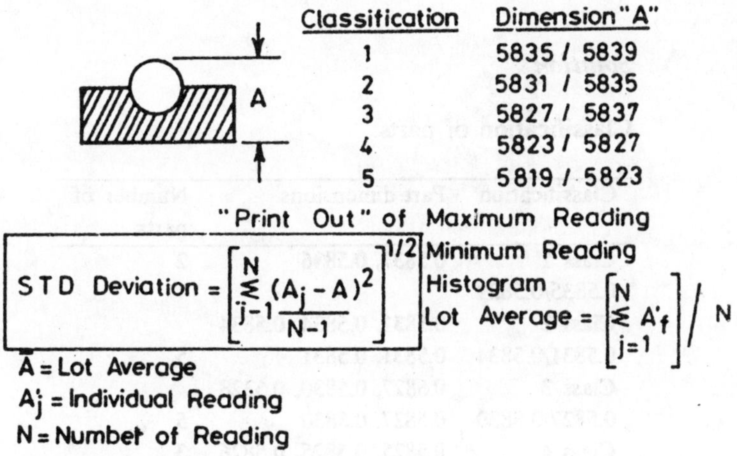


**Fig.A.6** Part classification by size

There is also a microprocessor in the 'printer interface' module in the system which stores the readings from each group of, say, 50 parts and provides in-process statistical analysis of the data and prints the results by means of an alpha-numeric printer. The print-out includes the dimension defining for each of the classifications, a histogram or a plot of the distribution of the parts, the total number of parts in each category, the minimum and maximum readings, average and standard deviation as well as the average plus and minus three times the standard deviation.

Consider the following example.

*Example*

In a gauging system for inspection of piston parts, the following are the data obtained on the critical diameter for 20 parts:

| | | | | |
|---|---|---|---|---|
| 0.5820 | 0.5837 | 0.5827 | 0.5831 | 0.5821 |
| 0.5834 | 0.5825 | 0.5834 | 0.5830 | 0.5821 |
| 0.5831 | 0.5828 | 0.5825 | 0.5820 | 0.5827 |
| 0.5836 | 0.5819 | 0.5830 | 0.5831 | 0.5826 |

Classify and identify number of parts in the following classes:

| Classsification | Dimension range |
|---|---|
| Class 1 | 0.5835/0.5839 |
| 2 | 0.5831/0.5834 |
| 3 | 0.5827/0.5830 |
| 4 | 0.5823/0.5826 |
| 5 | 0.5819/0.5822 |

Find the maximum reading, minimum reading, lot average, standard deviation and the histogram for the data obtained.

***Solution***

Classification of parts:

| Classification | Part dimensions | Number of parts |
|---|---|---|
| Class 1 0.5835/0.5839 | 0.5837, 0.5836 | 2 |
| Class 2 0.5831/0.5834 | 0.5831, 0.5834, 0.5834 0.5831, 0.5831 | 5 |
| Class 3 0.5827/0.5830 | 0.5827, 0.5830, 0.5328 0.5827, 0.5830 | 5 |
| Class 4 0.5823/0.5826 | 0.5825, 0.5825, 0.5826 | 3 |
| Class 5 0.5819/0.5822 | 0.5820, 0.5821, 0.5821 0.5820, 0.5821 | 5 |
| | Total | 20 |

Maximum reading = 0.5837

Minimum reading = 0.5820

$$\text{Lot average} = A = \left[\sum_{j=1}^{N} A_j\right] \Big/ N$$

where

$A_j$ = individual reading

$N$ = Number of readings

$A$ = $[0.5837 + 0.5836 + \ldots + 0.5821]/2$

= 0.5827.

$$\text{Standard deviation, } s = \left[\sum_{j=1}^{N} \frac{(A_j - A)^2}{N-1}\right]^{1/2} = 0.0005.$$

The Histogram for the above example is given in Fig.A.7. Such computations become part of a typical gauging system.

These data provide the operator with a complete analysis of the machine performance as the parts come off the machine. This gauge will continue to process parts until the average, standard deviation or the combination of the two exceeds prescribed limits.

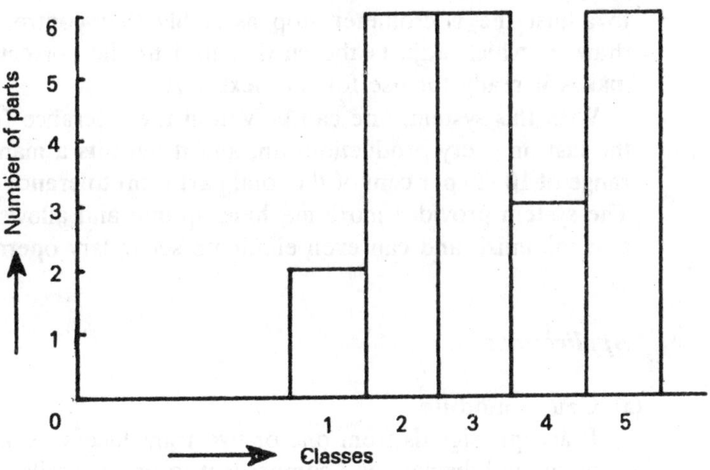


Fig.A.7 Histogram for the sample data

## A.3 Automatic size control system

The automatic size control system aims at avoiding shutdown of the machine for inspection and adjustment of cutting tools, thus eliminating costly downtime and improving the efficiency and quality of the manufacturing operation.

In an automatic size control system, as the workpiece progresses through an automatic machining sequence, or a single-purpose machine, the critical dimensions are measured electronically. Size information, relayed from the measuring probe of an inspection station with a compensator, is then used to make tool adjustments. As dimensions change from part to part, the position of the cutting tool adjusts in response to the control commands to meet tightly defined tolerances within a larger prescribed print tolerance. The system helps in eliminating the problems of confusion, where the operator must monitor multiple operations. Since there is no need to stop the machine between cycles, the cutting tool may be adjusted after machining each part, if necessary. Thus 100 per cent part inspection of initial dimensions are obtained.

A typical system, for example, can maintain an outward or inward adjustment of the cutting edges, ranging from 0.5 microns upto 500 microns. Adjustments can be made with the spindle either rotating or stationary. The cutting edges retract 0.15 cm approximately, after each cut to eliminate drag-out marks.

First, the cutting tool bores the workpiece. The gauge then probes the bore and sends a signal to the gauge amplifier that compares the present size with the required size preset in the control panel. If adjustment is required, a signal is relayed from the compensator panel to a stepper motor to adjust the micrometer stop assembly that controls the motion of the drawbar which adjusts the cutting tool to the corrected setting, and also makes it ready for use for the next part.

With this system, one can be within the tolerance from the first part to the last on every production-run, and it permits a manufacturing tolerance range of 10–20 per cent of the total part print tolerance in most applications. The system provides more machine uptime and allows machining to limits that minimize and can even eliminate secondary operations

### *Applications*

**(a) Gauge module**
It accepts signals from one or two transducers, makes a single measurement, and displays and compares it to preset limits. The data is available in the standard interface to a PC or controller module.

**(b) Compensator module**
It accepts commands from the bus interface to control a mechanical compensation unit and transmits compensation and limit data to either a controller module or a customer's PC. Signals may come from either a controller module or the customer's PC.

**(c) Controller module**
This is used to accomplish special system factors such as calculation of concentricity, runout, and machine control. The unit is customer programmed at the factory for each application and the hardware and software in the PC required to support the gauging/compensation system are minimized.

**(d) I/O module**
It is used to accomplish machine control or interface to a PC or CNC. Other components can include display module.

### *Typical applications*

**(a) Basic auto size system**
In this application, the system is used with a programmable controller, which provides commands for gauging the part, and when and how much the tool is to be compensated (Fig.A.8). Further the gauging and compensation data can be requested to perform other decision-making processes and to operate peripheral devices such as a printer.

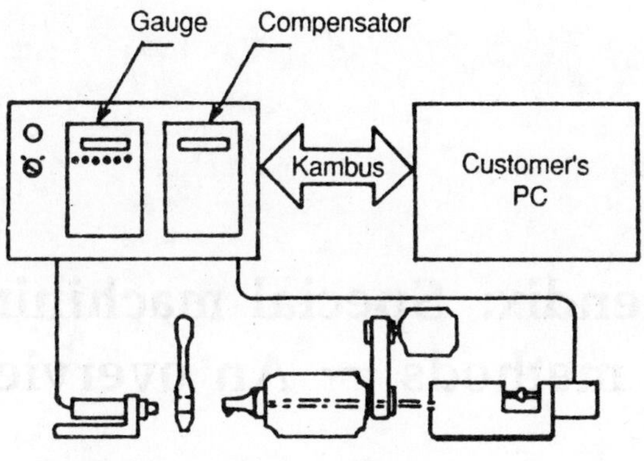


**Fig.A.8** Automatic size gauging system

**(b) CNC interface**

**In this application, as shown in Fig.A.9, the CNC must include parallel interface inputs for axis offset control for use in tool compensation. To compensate for tool wear, the system unit controls gauging of the part and formats data to provide axis offset information to the CNC.**

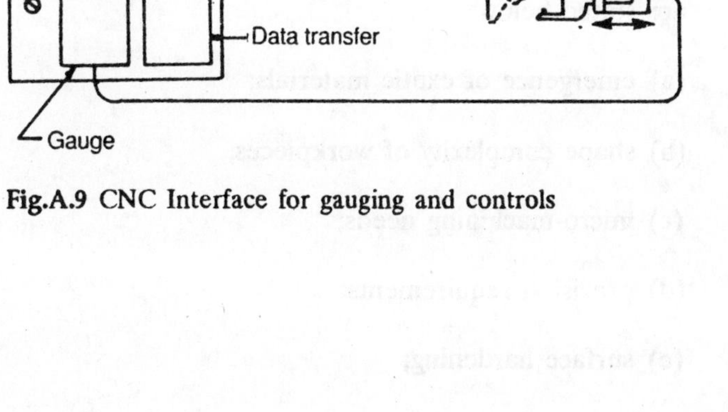


**Fig.A.9** CNC Interface for gauging and controls

# Appendix: Special machining methods — An overview

B

## B.1 Introduction

Special machining processes, also called as non-traditional or chipless processes, refer to a wide range of mechanical, chemical, electrical and thermal material removal processes. These processes were developed after World War II due to changing demands on metal working industry. Some of the major reasons for the development of these alternative machining methods are stated below:

(a) emergence of exotic materials;

(b) shape complexity of workpieces;

(c) micro-machining needs;

(d) precision requirements;

(e) surface hardening;

(f) ease of automation.

**(a) Emergence of exotic materials**
Since the mid-forties, the growth of aircraft, aerospace, nuclear and recently

the semiconductor/computer industries has motivated the development of new types of materials with tough precision requirements.

For example, the space-age alloys, called exotic materials, have high strength-to-weight ratios, with improved corrosion, erosion and temperature resistance. These are also known as high strength temperature resistant (HSTR) materials. Examples of each are given below:

(i) alloy steels;

(ii) stainless steels;

(iii) light-weight metals, e.g., titanium, zirconium and beryllium alloys;

(iv) high temperature alloys, e.g., iron base (Discaloy);

(v) nickel base(Waspaloy), cobalt base (S 816);

(vi) refractory metals, e.g., columbium, molybdenum, tantulum, tungsten;

(vii) metal composites;

(viii) plastic composites.

Though these materials are quite appropriate in the aerospace and allied industries, compared to other materials, they pose problems when it comes to traditional machining. For example, some have low thermal conductivity or low specific heat, contributing to higher cutting temperatures. Some are brittle and tend to strain-harden severely or tend to cause rapid wear of tool materials. A high coefficient of thermal expansion prevents dimensional accuracy. Cutting forces have to be very high or else the productivity is low.

Many of these exotic materials are also difficult to grind because of high wheel wear rate and high residual stresses induced on the work surface.

Traditional machining processes can be used to process these materials, however, at lower speeds and feeds, which results in greatly reduced productivity, thus necessitating the employment of more machines to produce the same number of parts produced when conventional materials are used. There has been some improvement in recent years in the form of new cutting-tool materials like ceramics, polycrystalline or synthetic diamond and CBN (cubic boron nitride) as well as diamond and CBN grinding technology with improved design features of machine tools.

The newer, non-traditional machining methods, to a great extent, provide an alternative, ensuring increased productivity and precision on most occasions. Many of these unconventional machining methods employ material-removal methods that depend more on material properties such as thermal conductivity, melting, temperature, electrical resistivity, atomic valency, etc., rather than on mechanical properties, such as mechanical strength, hardness, toughness, etc., of the workpiece as is the case with traditional machining methods.

In other words, traditional machining technology employs only mechanical energy and non-traditional machining technology employs different types of energy, including chemical, electrical, thermal and mechanical energy. This is one reason for these processes being termed non-traditional or un-conventional. Refer Fig.B.1.

**(b) Shape complexity of workpieces**

Design engineers have been suggesting that parts of complex shapes be stressed close to ultimate material capabilities instead of assembling a large number of parts, to reduce production cost, wherever feasible. The newer machining methods offer a solution in this context by using the 'designing for manufacture' concept.

The favourable factors are geometrical restrictions, simple design requirements, shape complexity and problems related to accessibility in machining. For example, it is easier to drill a circular hole while it is impossible to drill a square hole or a hole of any other shape by traditional drilling. For ECM and EDM, the shape is of no concern.

Similarly, to cut grooves of a depth of a few microns is difficult. But chemical machining can surmount this problem.

CNC facility also largely solves the problem of complexity.

**(c) Micromachining needs**

The trend towards smaller dimensions such as 10–100$\mu$m is a recent one, mainly because of the microelectronic, semiconductor or computer industry. Thus, micromachining is also becoming a new strategic production process. EDM, CHM, EBM are frequently applied for such processes.

**(d) Precision requirements**

There is also a trend towards ultra-precision machining, meaning the achievement of dimensional tolerances in the order of 0.01 $\mu$m and surface roughness of 0.001 $\mu$m (1 nanometre). The dimensions of parts may be as small as 1 $\mu$m. This 'nano-technology' finds application in the semiconductor industry for integrated circuit (IC) elements. The required precision can be obtained by removing atoms or molecules, rather than chips. Ion beam machining is one example. Also, some of the other new processes produce low distortion of surface layer due to mechanical or thermal action.

**(e) Surface hardening**

Some of the new processes like Laser beam method(LBM), electron beam method(EBM), plasma arc method(PAM), etc., are quite effective in controlling the properties of surface layer-by-layer deposition, alloying, ceramic coating, etc. These become a class of new manufacturing processes, though not machining processes.

**(f) Ease of automation**

The introduction of CNC facilities in this era of CAD/CAM and CIM, has the advantages of considerable reduction in production time, decreased production cost, reduced inventory, etc. In addition, NC-controlled laser or electron beam machining, and EDM wire cutting, for example, have enhanced capabilities to cope with a wide range of workpiece shapes with improved precision. These reduce the number of parts being assembled later. For example, a carbide die-plate can be machined by spark erosion on one piece. The traditional method would require the assembly of two or more pieces machined, necessitating a subsequent profile grinding operation.

The new machining methods evolved during the past three or four decades compete with the traditional machining methods in machining the special exotic materials which are used in several industries. A simple classification is by the type of energy involved in the material-removal mechanism as illustrated in Table B.1. The schematic of these machining methods is given in Fig.B.1.

**Table B.1** Classification of non-traditional methods compared with traditional methods

| Non Traditional Methods | | | | Traditional Methods |
|---|---|---|---|---|
| Mech. energy (Erosion) | Chem. energy (Chemical action) | Elec. energy (Electrolytic dissolution) | Thermal energy (Melting and vapourization) | Mech. energy (Shear deformation) |
| Ultrasonic machining (USM) | Chemical machining (CHM) | Electrochemical machining (ECM) | Laser beam machining (LBM) | Turning<br>Drilling |
| Abrasive jet machining (AJM) | | Electro-Chemical grinding (ECG) | Electron beam machining (EBM) | Milling |
| water jet cutting (WJC) | | | Ion beam machining(IBM) | Grinding, etc. |
| Abrasive water jet cutting(AWJC) | | | Plasma arc machining(PAM)<br>Thermal energy method (TEM)<br>electro discharge Machining(EDM) and allied processes. | |

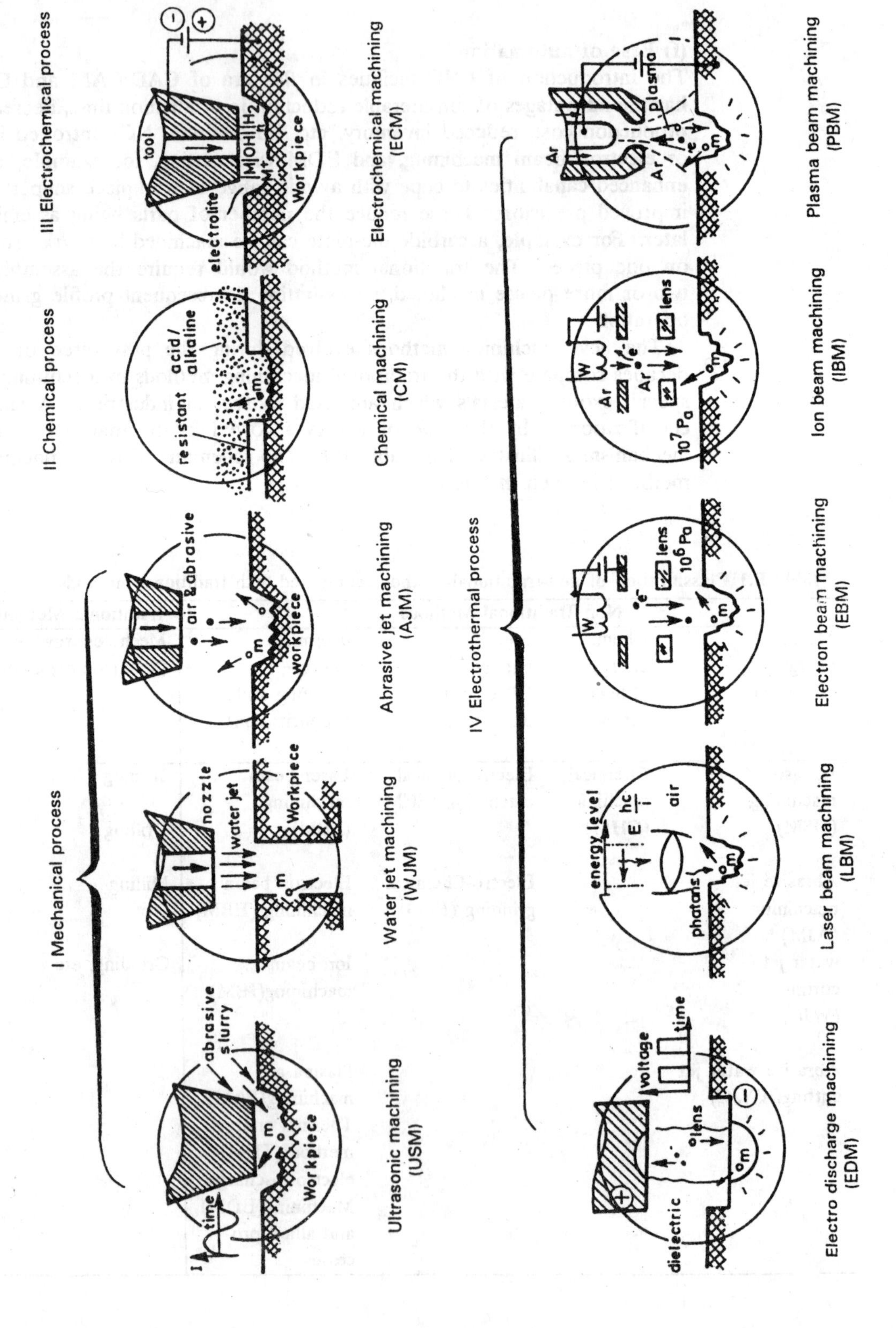


**Fig.B.1** Schematic of special machining methods

The mechanical energy method removes material by 'erosion' in contrast to the traditional metal cutting technique involving 'shear deformation'.

The chemical energy method relies on the metals being vulnerable to attack by some chemicals for erosion.

The electrical energy method makes use of principles of electrolysis or what is called 'anodic dissolution'.

The thermal energy method removes material by melting and vaporization due to thermal changes.

The above methods are called non-traditional methods for the following reasons:

(i) The type of energy and the mechanism involved in these processes are quite different compared to those employed in the traditional machining methods.

(ii) These processes are of recent origin (post-1940) compared to the traditional methods that were in use from the early twentieth century.

(iii) These processes owe their development to the growth of widespread use of space-age/exotic materials.

(iv) These processes also cater to micro-machining requirements, that were almost impossible earlier.

(v) These processes also ensure quite a high degree of accuracy.

The non-traditional machining processes find application when machining all metals and alloys, sometimes even when working with non-metallic materials and composites. The relative non-significance of traditional machining processes can be appreciated because of their lower capability especially when dealing with superalloys and exotic-hard materials.

Table B.2 provides a brief summary of the processes as applicable to certain typical materials. It may be noted that Ultrasonic machining (USM), Abrasive jet machining (AJM), Electron beam method (EBM) and Laser beam method (LBM) find applications on non-metallic materials as well.

**Table B.2** Process applicability to typical materials

| Material | Better Processes |
|---|---|
| Aluminum | CHM, PAM |
| Steel | ECM, CHM, EDM, PAM |
| Superalloys | AJM, ECM, EDM, PAM |
| Refractories | USM, AJM, EDM, EBM |
| Ceramics | USM, AJM, EBM, LBM |
| Plastics | USM, AJM, EBM, LBM |
| Glass | USM, AJM |

## B.2 The special machining processes

Refer to Fig.B.1 for processes 1 to 10 discussed below:

### 1. Ultrasonic machining (USM)

The material removal is by a tool oscillating at ultrasonic frequencies of about 10 to 30 kHz or kc per sec. in an abrasive slurry medium. The material removal is due to impact energy of the abrasives that are driven against the workpiece across the small gap between the tool and part. The ultrasonic vibrations are obtained by a magnetostrictive or piezoelectric transducer, based on changes in length of a material, e.g. a stack of nickel laminations induced by high-frequency alternating current, and hence by applied magnetic field. A properly designed or shaped toolholder or 'horn' serves to amplify the amplitude of output vibrations upto six gains. The connecting body between, transducer and toolholder is made of either titanium or monel, and provides the first mechanical amplification. The final amplitude of vibration is about 0.03 to 0.10 mm. The direction of vibration is along the 'feed'. A feed weight maintains the small gap between the tool and part. The abrasive slurry is introduced and circulated by means of a pump system. The tool, typically of steel, is brazed or soldered to a tool tip that is threaded to the toolholder.

Though $Al_2O_3$ and SiC are also used, Boron carbide, being the hardest of the three, is used as the abrasive, as it is economical. Diamond is the hardest abrasive known, but it is very expensive. Water is the usual abrasive carrier, and the slurry is between 30 and 40% of abrasives by volume in water.

Brittle and hard materials of hardness above 64 Rc, and the ductile ones to some extent, form the materials used. The range of materials include glass, ceramic, germanium, tungsten carbide, tool steel, carbon graphite, ferrite, quartz, boron carbide, mica, plastics and composites.

The typical shapes include drilling of holes of any shape or of a curved axis, or coining operations. The part is moved or rotated to increase the range of shapes, or for threading or trepanning. The size ranges from 0.08 to 110 mm. The depth / diameter ratio is upto 2.5, limited by problems of feeding the slurry and tool wear. The feed rates and removal rates depend on part material, and they are approximately 1.25 $mm^3$/ min. for ceramics and 1.63 $mm^3$/min. for steel. While the process is good for a range of brittle materials, non-metals and non-conductive ones, it has limitations like low removal rates, tool wear and depth of cavity.

### 2. Water jet machining (WJM)

The machining or cutting action in WJM is by a fine, high-pressure, high-velocity stream of water or water-based fluid with additives on the workpiece, removing material and producing a narrow kerf. Also called as Hydrodynamic machining, the system comprises a high-pressure pump, jet cutter system and a filtration unit. The jet nozzle assembly consists of a nozzle holder made of stainless steel and a jewel nozzle made of ruby or sapphire or diamond. The cutter system control includes manual operation, optical tracing systems or CNC. CNC is suitable for continuous, repetitive and precise cutting. The cutting fluid is usually water, but sometimes polymer solution, or water with additives like gylcerine, polyethlene oxide, long chain polymer, is used to produce better jet coherency (when a sharp edge is required).

Water jet machining is largely used to cut non-metallic materials, such as plastic-based composites, e.g., carbon black, kevlor, pc board, etc., fiberglass, plastic materials like acrylic, polyester, polyethelene, polycarbonate, thermoplastics, etc., green or fired alumina ceramic tapes or tubes, cardboard, rubber or fabric hose, wood and thin metal (0.025 mm), brittle materials like glass, crack or break.

The advantages of WJM include: (1) minimum loss of materials, thus appropriate for exotic materials; (2) no thermal damage, any shape or configuration; (3) fewer dies with CNC/robotic control; (4) easy automation; (5) quiet safety operation with no pollution problem; and (6) smooth cut, avoiding secondary operations.

### 3. Abrasive jet machining (AJM)

The material removal is by a high-velocity gas stream carrying abrasive particles of about 10 to 50 microns size at 150–300 m/s. The abrasives, having sharp edges, are of $Al_2O_3$ or SiC. The carrier gas medium is air, $CO_2$ or nitrogen at 2 to 8 kg/cm$^2$ and about 0.01 m$^3$/min. The nozzle material is tungsten carbide or synthetic sapphire, of 0.05 to 0.125 mm, and the surface roughness depends on the size of abrasive, for example, 14 to 20 rms to 27$\mu$ $Al_2O_3$ or SiC.

The applications of AJM include drilling, slotting, sawing, cutting, cleaning and/or deburring operations, specially on hard and brittle materials. The examples of such materials are: semiconductor materials, like germanium, silicon, gallium, etc. crystalline materials like quartz, sapphire, mica, glass, etc., thin sections of hardened metal and ceramics. The advantages of AJM are cooler cutting action, where the carrier gas also serves as a coolant, and operation free from chatter and vibration problems, due to non-contact between tool and workpiece.

The limitations of AJM include: lower material removal rates (16 mm$^3$/min. in glass), embedding and retention of abrasives in workpieces, taper or spray cutting, constant operator attention, impractical to recycle the abrasives, requires a dust collection system, impractical for heavy deburring or large material removal, not preferable for large surfaces and feasible practical control continued to very small areas of 0.25 mm diameter.

### 4. Chemical machining (CHM or CM)

Here the material removal is by acid or alkaline etchant's chemical attack or action, thus dissolving metal or alloy chemically. The unwanted surface areas are covered by an acid or an alkaline resistant material, serving as a maskant or resist on the workpiece. The maskant or resist is applied to the part by dip, flow or spray coating and is of about 0.03 to 0.15mm thick. A scribe knife is used to peel away the resist, removing it from the areas to be etched. Commonly used maskants are vinyl, neoprene and butyl base materials, polymers and polyethylene. These offer considerable chemical resistance allowing an etching depth of 12mm or even more.

The application examples include aluminium, beryllium, nickel, magnesium, titanium and its alloys, various steel and stainless-steel alloys, and refractory metals like molybdenum, tungsten, columbium and zirconium. The parts can be flat, preformed or irregular, and the metal can be removed either from the selected areas or from the entire surface itself. The process is appropriate for extremely large parts, workpieces with many irregularities, multiple-level steps, by removing additional maskants in steps, and etching depth in excess of 1.25 mm. The process is also called chemical milling, and is suitable for structural, aircraft and missile parts. Tolerances upto $\pm$ 0.13 mm and surface roughness values of 0.8 to 4 $\mu$ are possible.

However, the process is not advisable for thin materials that may get distorted during scribing and peeling, for parts that require high-accuracy, such as razor head or motor laminators.

### 5. Electrochemical machining (ECM)

The material removal by ECM is based on electrolysis using electrical and chemical energies. ECM is also called as "anodic thinning or dissolution process". Here, the workpiece is made the anode and tool the cathode, and the electrode gap, being of the order of 0.025 to 0.25 mm, is filled by the electrically conductive electrolyte. A low voltage, (15 to 20 V) and a high-density d.c. current (about 100 A/cm$^2$) is made to pass through the electrolytic cell. The electrolyte is pumped through the electrode gap at high pressures, of about 20 kg/cm$^2$. A temperature of 100 to 150°F improves its conductance.

The workpiece material dissolves by electrolysis in the form of ions (e.g. metal hydroxide) swept away by the high-velocity electrolyte. The flowing electrolyte also removes the oxide film or passive layer formed at the anode, that tends to lower electrical conductance in the cell. The cathode is not affected otherwise in the process.

The process is suitable for electrically conductive parts. The electrolyte can be an aqueous solution of NaCl, $NaNO_2$, $NaNO_3$, $KNO_2$, $KNO_3$ or $H_2SO_4$ (about 10–15% conc. by weight). The tool cathode, being unaffected, is made of a soft material like brass, copper, titanium, stainless steel, sintered Cu-W, aluminium or graphite. Downfeed of tool is about

0.5 to 1.8 mm/min. depending on work material. Tolerances of ± 0.125 mm and surface roughness values of 4 to 50 rms are practical.

The material removal is dependent on valency of the metal or alloy as governed by Faraday's laws, and not on its hardness. Due to non-contact between workpiece and tool, there is no induced mechanical residual stress or burr and, in addition, no thermal damage due to low operating temperatures. There is no 'tool wear'. And the process can be easily automated, since the operating parameters, i.e., voltage, current, feed rate, electrolyte pressure and temperature, can be measured and controlled.

The notable feature of ECM is machining on tough alloys or exotic materials of otherwise poor machinability aspects in traditional machining, and also on heat-resistant or heat treated alloys. In addition, the soft tool material enables complex three-dimensional features on workpiece, though the tool downfeed is unidirectional. The process has reasonably high metal removal compared to EDM or CHM, especially on hard and tough alloys, and can as well tackle thin, delicate or fragile parts. Specific applications of USM include: cavity or die sinking, hole sinking (through or blind), trepanning, planing and surfacing, deburring, turning and external shaping.

The material removal is largely by electrolysis limited by current efficiency. The electrochemical reactions are: (i) formation of metal ions: (e.g. $Fe^\circ \rightarrow Fe^{++} + 2e^-$) at anode, (ii) hydrogen evolution ($2H^+ + 2e^- \rightarrow H_2 \uparrow$) and hydroxyl ions ($2H_2O + 2e^- \rightarrow 2(OH)^- + H_2 \uparrow$) at cathode, and (iii) precipitate ($Fe^{++} + 2(OH)^- \rightarrow Fe(OH_2)$) in the body of the electrolyte. The removal is determined by the following Faraday's Laws: The mass of substance dissolved is proportional to (i) the current $I$, and (ii) its chemical equivalent (atomic mass $N$/valency $n$) or one gram equivalent weight for one Faraday (96500 coulombs or amp-sec). If $d$ is the density in gm/cm$^3$, $t$ is time in seconds, and $\eta$ is the current efficiency, the volumetric removal $V_m$, combining both the Faraday's Laws, is given by

$$V_m = \frac{It}{96500} \times \frac{N}{n} \times \frac{1}{d} \times \eta$$

For example, for iron as workpiece, $N$=56, $n$=2 and $d$=7.87 gm/cm$^3$. Assuming, $I$ = 100 amp., $t$ = 1000 s and $\eta$ = 100%,

$$V_m = \frac{100 \times 1000}{96500} \times \frac{56}{2} \times \frac{1}{7.87} \times 1.0 = 3.69 \text{ cm}^3.$$

For alloys,

$$\frac{N}{n} = \frac{100}{(x_1 n_1/N_1) + (x_2 n_2/N_2) + \ldots}$$

where the suffices refer to different elements and $x$ refers to percentage of the element. For example, for Nimonic alloy of 20% Cr, 62% Ni and 18% Co (the valencies being 6, 2 and 2 respectively, for Cr, Ni and Co),

$$\frac{N}{n} = \frac{100}{(20 \times 6/52) + (62 \times 2/58.71) + (18 \times 2/58.93)} = \frac{100}{5.03}.$$

### 6. Electric discharge machining (EDM)

The material removal here is by means of electrical sparks or discharges between the electrode tool and workpiece in a dielectric fluid medium. The material is melted and vapourised by the sparks, and the particles are subsequently removed by the flowing dielectric fluid.

A power unit supplies the direct current in a pulse form in different voltage ranges. These are based on different power circuit designs, and typical among them are resistance–capacitance circuit type, rotary impulse generator type, controlled pulse generator–vacuum tube type and controlled pulse generator–transistor type. Spark discharge frequencies of 500 to 10,00,000 pulses per second at voltage levels of 100 to 130 V are common.

The dielectric fluid acts as an insulation between tool and work upto its ionization potential, flushes away the eroded particles and also serves as a coolant. The hydrocarbon oils like kerosene, transformer oils, and other petroleum distillate fractions can be used as dielectric fluids. Distilled or deionized water is used in micromachining and even compressed gas can be used for special applications.

When the voltage level reaches the ionization potential value of the dielectric, it breaks down its insulation barrier. Subsequently sparks jump over the electrode gap. Each of these sparks removes a small amount of material from workpiece leaving a cratering finish. The material removal is dependent on current density and frequency. Higher current density at lower frequency leaves a rougher surface, and conversely, lower current density at higher frequency improves the surface.

The tool electrode is of an electrically conductive material and often of a softer one which enables a specific cavity shape/configuration and size, imparting a three-dimensional shape to the workpiece. There is tool electrode wear during sparking. The tool is normally the cathode and work the anode, the 'straight polarity'. However, the 'reverse polarity' is sometimes preferable. Typical tool electrode materials are brass, copper, steel, zinc, aluminium, nickel, graphite, and molybdenum for larger areas, and copper–tungsten and silver–tungsten for smaller areas.

The ram carrying the tool electrode is servo-controlled, based on lead-screw, gearing, hydraulic cylinder or any other similar mechanism. The feed, controls and maintains the appropriate electrode gap.

Surface roughness is about 1.6 to 3.2 $\mu$m and upto 12.5 $\mu$m in roughing. The texture consists of a series of overlapping small craters, and recast and thermally-affected layers. The surface residual stress is upto 25 $\mu$m deep. This affects the tensile strength and reduces the fatigue strength, and hence requires a post-treatment operation. Inter-granular attacks are also common in exotic alloys. However, the rehardened layer has a high wear resistance, though at the cost of strength.

The applications of EDM are largely machining on exotic metals and alloys, refractory metals, carbides, hardened steels, and also on the parts requiring complex geometries. It is also appropriate for burr-free, machining and machining on delicate workpieces because of the absence of cutting forces. Typical examples include stamping dies, header dies, extruding dies, wire-drawing dies, forging dies and moulds.

**7. Laser beam machining (LBM)**

LASER is an acronym for Light Amplification by Stimulated Emission of Radiation, and is based on the phenomenon called, lasing action, where an electro-optical device converts electrical energy into electro-magnetic energy. When an atom excited to a higher energy level is struck by a higher energy electron (an unstable state), it will tend to revert to its normal energy level by emitting electromagnetic radiation. However, when the same atom at its excited state is struck by a photon of same energy as to be emitted, there is a simultaneous emission of two photons of same energy, in the same direction and phase.

The laser system comprises a reservoir of active atoms, a pumping source to excite the active atoms, and a resonant cavity to provide feedback for laser oscillations, acting as an amplifier. A cascade of identical photons is the output, the laser beam. The lasing property is significant only in certain materials or media. The solid-state and gas lasers are used in manufacturing.

In the solid-state laser, the lasing medium is a crystalline material with a doping additive. The examples of lasing medium are: ruby laser ($Al_2O_3$ with approximately 0.05% chromium as dopant), single crystal rod of yttrium aluminum garnet (YAG) containing ions of neodymium (Nd:YAG laser) and neodymium-doped glass (Nd:glass or simply glass laser). The gas lasers employ a single gas or gas mixure contained in an optically transparent tube, and typical types are He–Ne, Argon and $CO_2$ (a mixture of $CO_2$, $N_2$, He). These are available in a range of capacities such as 400W to 25KW, or 25 to 100 J.

In materials processing, the laser acts mainly as a source of heat. Due to the high energy at the focus, the laser is used for cutting, drilling, welding and surface treatment like hardening and alloying.

(i) Laser cutting involves 'drilling' a hole first through the part, then moving along a programmed path of the shape to be cut. Cutting speed depends on the part material, its thickness and physical characteristics, and power of the beam. $CO_2$ laser of 400W to 1.5 kW as well as YAG laser are appropriate. Thus the laser serves as an alternative to punching or blanking and oxyacetylene or plasma-arc cutting. The examples include steel, titanium, nickel, certain refractory metals and many plastics. Aluminium and highly reflective metals need a coating to absorb beam energy. Sample speed is 25 m/min. for 1.5mm thick stainless steel.

The advantages of laser cutting are high cutting speed for thin stocks, narrow and square edge kerfs (0.01 to 1 mm) with minimal distortion, noise and vibration-free operation and low-fume generation, no cutting tools and requires only programs, complex shapes with sharp corners and slots, an economic alternative to blanking dies for prototyping for short as well as long production runs, for metals and alloys that are difficult to cut or blank by conventional methods.

(ii) Laser drilling is a cost-effective alternative to drilling, ECM and EDM in 'percussion' drilling of making holes of relatively shallow depths, (0.0025 to 1.5 mm and 25mm). Materials, typically processed are plastics, ceramics, and many metals and alloys which are most difficult to drill otherwise, paper rubber, composites and crystalline materials like diamond.

(iii) Laser welding is also practical since the process is self-quenching when the heat input is fast, concentrated at a very small area. The heat-affected area is kept minimum. The notable features of laser welding include low thermal distortion and small heat-affected zone, absence of contamination, no filler materials, easy automation, feasibility in inaccessible and hostile environments like inside pipes or atomic reactors (similar as well as dissimilar metals), competitive alternative to TIG, plasma arc, and the electron beam in several cases and suitable for joining sheet metals of stocks of 2.5 mm or less thick. A range of metals and alloys like low-carbon steels, stainless steels, titanium and titanium alloys, tantulum, zirconium, silicon bronze and nickel alloys are feasible. However, zinc, galvanized steel, silver, gold, and brass are unsuitable due to volatility of zinc. Certain aluminium alloys, copper, tool steels, and carbon steels are intermediate.

(iv) Surface treatment using lasers of above 1kw power is another notable area. Applications of surface treatment are transformation hardening, surface quenching, cladding, or hardfacing by applying a different material to the surface of a part's substrate, surface alloying or coating, etc.

(v) Other applications of laser beam machining are laser marking, and are in metrology or inspection devices.

## 8. Electron beam machining (EBM)

The EBM method focusses a high-speed stream of electrons on the part generating thermal energy, thus melting and/or vapourising the material. The electron beam is generated in an electron gun comprising hot tungsten filament cathode for emitting high negative-potential electrons, a grid/bias cup acting also as cathode, and an anodic aperture at ground potential allowing accelerated electrons to pass through. The electron beam emitted from the tungsten filament cathode is accelerated towards the anode due to high potential difference. The extent of negative bias in the grid cup controls the beam current or the flow of electrons, focussing electrostatically by its design to enable a convergent beam, avoiding collision with the anode. The final focussing is by electromagnetic lens system by focussing coils. The highly accelerated steady electron beam is produced and focussed on the part at the vacuum of $10^{-4}$ mm Hg or more ($10^{-3}$ Torr). The system comprises appropriate workholding and XYZ axes controls within the vacuum chamber, that are well shielded to protect against random X-ray emission.

The advantages include electron beam as the most precise cutting tool that can process any material, metal or non-metal that can exist in vacuum, thus highly appropriate for micromachining (drilling 0.05 to 1.25 mm dia. of depth to diameter ratios of 200:1 and 0.025 mm slots), high cutting speed of about 50 to 600 mm/min., easy process control automation over a range of input energy, absence of 'tool wear or pressure' resulting in distortion-free machining of thin fragile parts, absence of metallurgical or physical damage with no heat-affected zone.

However, vacuum requirements confining to batch processing of small sized parts, high equipment cost and operator skill, low removal rate (1.64 $mm^3$/min. thus limited to small cuts and thin parts e.g. 0.25 to 7 mm), and tapering and divergence effects are the limitations of the process.

The applications of EBM are similar to that of LBM and include micro-drilling on stainless steel, tungsten, alumina, quartz, etc; cutting slots, precision and contamination free welding of exotic or dissimilar materials; surface hardening or beam treating for ferrous alloys; and glazing or fusing of superficial layers at an extreme rate, resulting on subsequent cooling in a very hard, though rough, part surface.

## 9. Ion beam machining (IBM)

IBM is an atomic-bit machining process providing very high precision and resolution. The process employs argon (Ar) ions or other inert gases with high kinetic energy of about 10 keV. The gas is fed into a vacuum chamber ($10^{-2}$ Torr or 10 Pa) and is ignited by the application of a high-frequency (about 10 MHz) electric potential. The gas is ionized by the bombardment of electrons emitted from a heated filament cathode. The argon ions are extracted into the machining chamber using a grid set or 'lens' system present at the top of the machining zone. Masking of the part is needed for selective machining or etching. The ions serve as 'tools', bombarding and ejecting atoms from the part surface by elastic collision. This phenomenon is called 'ion sputtering'. For example, the depth of penetration of an ion at 1 keV is about 5 nm. The sputtering rate is proportional to ion current density and sputtering yield, the ratio of number of sputtered atoms to incident ions. Ion energy of 300 to 500 eV are typical and the yield of argon ions is about 0.1 to 10 atoms/incident ion.

It is to be noted that the theoretical limit of accuracy in machining is of the size of an atom or molecule of the part material (atomic lattice separation is about 0.2 to 0.4 nm). Thus, also called as 'extreme technology' or 'nano technology', IBM provides ultra-precision machining capability of the order of 1 nm. This is a progression from the micro-technology zone of 1 $\mu$m accuracy capability.

However, the transition requires quality machine tools or the processing equipment, and measuring devices for dimensions and surface quality are integrated to provide high-accuracy acceleration/velocity and position-loop control between 'tools' and workpieces, at very high speed. The dimensions of parts or elements of parts may be as small as 1 $\mu$m. The resolution and repeatability of the machines should be in the order of 0.1 $\mu$m or 10 nm to even less. For example, integrated circuit (IC) dimensions are specified to 0.1 $\mu$m requiring ultra-precision machining-accuracy capability of the order of 5 nm.

The IBM is appropriate for the 'thin-film technology' of semiconductor industries, where the thicknesses of layers of different materials like $SiO_2$, Al, etc. on workpieces are of the order of, say 100–900 nm, a typical feature of transistor circuit elements. For achieving this precision, individual atoms have to be controlled and positioned where required.

Typical IBM applications include aspherizing of lenses, sharpening of diamond indicators, diamond microtone knives and cutting tools, optical diffraction grating and IC pattern etching. It is suitable for semiconductor industry for machining patterns even in sub-micrometer field. Practically, it is possible to machine almost any material and the removal can be controlled using masks, texturing surfaces, surface cleaning, smoothing, etc. in glass, silica, diamond or other similar materials.

## 10. Plasma beam machining (PBM)

A gas treated to a sufficiently high temperature to become partially ionized and hence electrically conductive, is called *plasma*, the temperature being upto 27800°C. The gases are constricted in a narrow column in a typical plasma torch.

In the plasma torch system, a cool inert gas such as nitrogen or a mixture of argon and hydrogen (65%/35% or 70%/30%) is forced through a small orifice of the torch under pressure. The torch is connected to a d.c. power suppply and the gas is partially ionized by the discharge of high-voltage arc between the tungsten electrode (cathode) and the tip of the torch through which the gas flows. When this pilot arc contacts with the anodic workpiece, a transferred or main arc is formed, shutting off the pilot arc. A short stand-off distance is maintained between the nozzle and workpiece. The gas is heated intensively resulting in a high-velocity, well-collimated plasma jet of very high core temperature. Often oxygen is injected into the workzone to enhance heating by exothermic oxidation. The molten metal is blown out of the cut by the high-velocity gas stream.

Also called plasma arc machining (PAM), PBM is appropriate for conductive as well as non-conductive materials. In the plasma arc beam method, the workpiece is made anode, suitable for conductive parts while in the plasma jet beam method, the nozzle-system itself is used as anode, thus suitable for non-conductive work materials.

Plasma is used to cut metal upto 100 mm thick. Typical materials that can be cut by plasma include brass, bronze, nickel, aluminium, copper, cast iron, steels, molybdenum, magnesium, titanium, monel and inconel. The process parameters are currrent of 30 A–250 A, velocity jet of 600–900 m/sec, cutting speed of 1000 cm/min., nozzle orifice area upto 30 mm$^2$ and kerf width of 1.5 to 2.5 mm.

The low-current, low-speed systems operating at 50–100A and up to 400 A are suitable for most non-ferrous metals and stainless steels of up to 25 to 75 mm thick. The gas employed is nitrogen or mixtures of argon/nitrogen or argon/hydrogen, and shielding is by $CO_2$ or compressed air.

Surface characteristics depend considerably on work material properties. The surface material is heated up to the melting point and allowed to cool. The depth of heat-affected zone is about 0.75 mm. Depending on the application, this hardened layer is considered beneficial or may have to be removed.

Merits of the process are equal effectiveness on any metal without depending on its hardness or refractoriness, suitability on electrically non-conductive material by process modifications, and requiring only simple support structures without any rigorous fixture. The disadvantages of the process are high-surface roughness, and metallurgically affected surface layers of up to about 3 mm that may require secondary machining operations for removal.

### 11. Wire-electric discharge machining (Wire-EDM)

In this process, a vertically oriented wire electrode is fed laterally into the part or *vice versa*, like a bandsaw (Fig.B.2). The wire speed is about 2.5 to 150 mm/sec. and the new wire is constantly fed into the job, thus the electrode wear factor being not so relevant. The power supply is about 55 to 60 V and 1 to 32 A, at pulse frequencies of 180 to 300 kHz and pulse durations, 1 to 100 $\mu s$. Wire tension is about 50%–60% of the tensile strength of the wire. Typical wire materials that can be used are molybdenum, tungsten, copper and brass. 'Stratified wire' of copper core with thin surface layer of zinc, and aluminium coated brass wire are among others. Normally, the machines are provided with CNC systems of 4 to 6 axis controls for the worktable and the travelling wire. The tapering or tilting of workpiece is upto 30°. Thus, flexible and fast machining of particularly, intricate three-dimensional geometries described by a set of straight lines (turbine blades), is easy.

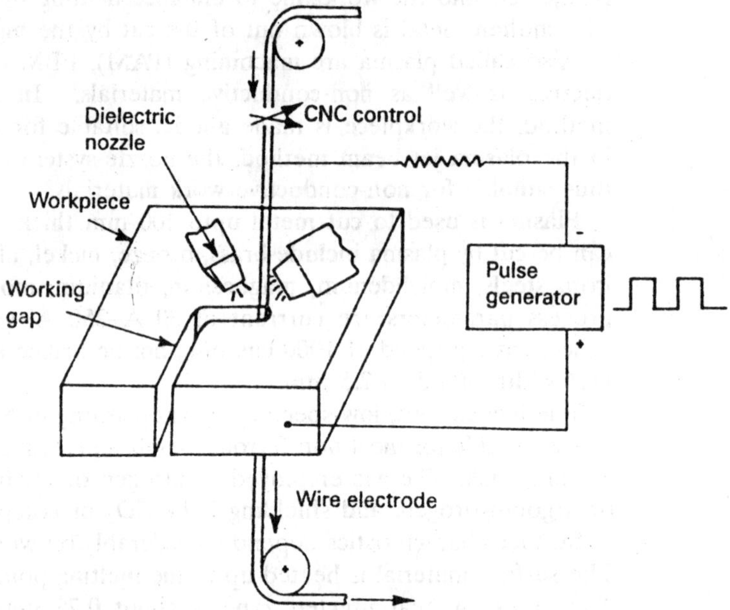


Fig.B.2 Wire-electric discharge machining

Deionized water is generally used as a dielectric, and the deionization is by circulating the water through an ion-exchange resin. The degree of deionization is measured by its specific resistance. Lower the value of resistance, faster will be the cutting speed. Additionally, oil, and rarely air, or plain water are also used. Deionized water provides faster cutting than oil and is also fire proof, a property useful particularly in untended operations. However, oil produces better surface finishes that improve die life by 3 to 4 times in steel discs cut by this process.

The process is suitable for electrically conductive heat-treated metals, sintered or cemented carbides, and other ultra-hard materials like electrically-conductive ceramic materials like SiC, $ZrB_2$ and $TiB_2$, $B_4C$, CBN and PCD. Typical applications of this process are cutting of punches, dies, stripper plates, patterns and moulds in very hard materials. A punch and a die from the same material, simultaneously, is possible, because tapers can be cut easily by shifting the working plane.

## 12. Electrochemical grinding (ECG)

ECG is a process in which the material removal takes place by a combination of electrochemical and mechanical actions. It is also called as electrolytic grinding. The electrolytic cell is formed by the part or workpiece as the anode, and the electrically conductive metallic bond of the wheel as the cathode It is connected to a d.c. power source, being separated during grinding by the non-conductive abrasives. The electrolyte is introduced in the electrode gap. The process is appropriate for grinding hard and exotic alloys including cemented carbides, and Diamond wheels are popularly used, though $Al_2O_3$ and SiC wheels can be used for less harder materials. The abrasives remove the oxide film or passive layer generated during anodic dissolution and also contribute to mechanical material removal to a limited extent by direct abrasive action (Fig.B.3).

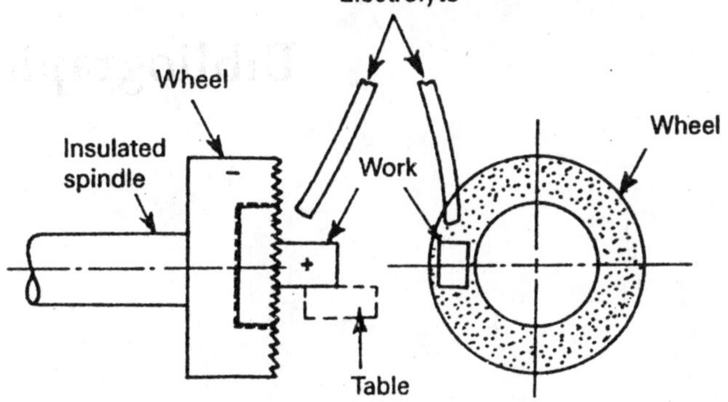


Fig.B.3 Electrochemical grinding

The electrolyte should have the properties like high electrolytic aggressiveness for material removal, high electrical conductivity, ability to dissolve reaction products, durable no detrimental physiological reactions such as skin rash, and chemical passivity towards the machine or rust inhibition. Electrolyte mixtures of nitrates or nitrites of potassium or sodium in water are the commonly used elecrolytes with 10 to 15 per cent concentration. The applied voltage is about 5 to 20 V d.c. at current densities of up to 100 $A/cm^2$.

The advantages of ECG as a production process include high removal independent of material hardness or toughness thus appropriate for superalloys, no induced stresses in the workpiece, reduced heating of workpiece and thermal damage, high surface finish, no burrs produced and reduced wheel wear, especially important with costly diamond abrasives that are expensive. The process is also preferred to mechanical or traditional grinding, for machining of cemented carbides, and has broad applications with extremely hard or difficult to grind thermal resistant alloys. It is also used for alloy and stainless-steel grinding.

# Bibliography


1. Venkatesh, V.C. and H. Chandrasekaran, '*Experimental Methods in Metal Cutting*', Prentice-Hall of India, New Delhi, 1982.

2. Arshinov, V. and G. Alekseev, '*Metal cutting Theory and Cutting Tool Design*', Mir Publishers, Moscow, 1979.

3. Bhattacharyya, A., '*Metal Cutting Theory and Practice*, Central Book Publishers, Calcutta, 1984.

4. '*Turning Handbook of High-efficiency Metal Cutting*', General Electric Company, USA, 1980.

5. Kane, G.E., Editor, '*Modern Trends in Cutting Tools*', Society of Manufacturing Engineers, USA, 1982.

6. Follettee, D., '*Manufacturing Fundamentals, A Basic Approach to Metal Cutting*', Society of Manufacturing Engineers, USA, 1980.

7. Shaw, M.C., '*Metal Cutting Principles*', Oxford, Clarendon Press, 1984.

8. Boothroyd, G. and W.A. Knight, '*Fundamentals of Machining and Machine Tools*', Marcel Dekker, New York, 1989.

9. CIRP Unified Terminology', *Annuals of the CIRP*, **34**(2): 643–663, 1985.

10. ISO 3002/1 (August 1982), ISO/DIS 3002/3(March 1983), ISO/DIS 3002/4 (April 1983), International Organisation for Standardisation.

11. Lindberg, Roy, A., '*Processes and Materials of Manufacture*', Prentice-Hall of India Ltd., 1990.

12. Appold, Feiler, Reinhard and Schmidt, '*Technology of the Metal Trade*', Wiley Eastern Ltd., 1982.

13. '*Tooling for High Productivity Metal Cutting Carboloy Systems*', Catalog, General Electric Company, USA, 1986.

14. '*Total Capability Tooling Manual*', Valenite, USA, 1986.

15. '*Kennametal/85*', Catalog on Metal Cutting Tools, Kennametal Inc., USA, 1985.

# Answers to exercise problems

## Chapter 2

2.1(a) $\lambda_s - \gamma_o - \alpha_o - \alpha_o' - k_r' - k_r - r$ (ORS)
$0° - 28°30' - 6° - 6° - 8° - 75° - 1$ mm (ORS)

(b) $\gamma_p - \gamma_f - \alpha_p - \alpha_f - k_r' - \psi - r$ (MRS)
$8° - 27°40' - 22°6' - 5°15' - 8° - 15° - 1$ mm (MRS)

(c) $\gamma_m = 28°30'$, $k_\gamma = 75°$

2.2 $k_r = 60°$, $\gamma_p = 5°4'$, $\gamma_f = 8°42'$
$k_r = 90°$, $\gamma_p = 0°$, $\gamma_f = 10°$

2.3 $\gamma_o = -11°6'$, $\lambda_s = 1°12'$

$\gamma_n \simeq -11°6'$, since $\lambda_s$ is very small

2.4 $\gamma_p = 7.98°$, $\gamma_f = 10.46°$, $\gamma_n = 12.12°$

or $\gamma_p = 7°59'$, $\gamma_f = 10°28'$, $\gamma_n = 12°7'$

2.5 $\gamma_o = 15°30'$, $\lambda_s = 4°6'$

2.6 $\gamma_o \simeq 10°$; $\gamma_f = 6.23°$ or $6°14'$, $\gamma_p = 9.32°$ or $9°19'$

## Chapter 3

3.1 $\gamma_o = -10°$, $\phi = 19°53'$, $\epsilon_s = 3.337$

If $\gamma_o = +10°$, $\phi = 22°30'$, $\epsilon_s = 2.636$

3.2 $\gamma_o = -5°$, $\phi = 24°26'$, $\epsilon_s = 2.799$

If $\gamma_o = +5°$, $\phi = 26°16'$, $\epsilon_s = 2.415$

3.3 (a) Chip formation by deformation is associated with increase in thickness of cut layer and reduction in length.

(b) $\gamma_o = 0°$, $\Lambda_h - 2.7714$, $\phi = 19°50'$, $\epsilon_s = 3.133$

If $\gamma_o = +20°$, $\Lambda_h = 2.7714$, $\phi = 21°9'$, $\epsilon_s = 2.605$

3.4 $\Lambda_h = 2.194$

| Rake angle, $\gamma_o$ | Shear angle, $\phi$ | Shear strain, $\epsilon_s$ |
|---|---|---|
| −10° | 22°36′ | 3.042 |
| 0° | 24°30′ | 2.650 |
| +10° | 26°0′ | 2.337 |

3.5 $\lambda_s = 4°1'$, $\gamma_o = 15°30'$, $\gamma_n = 15°26'$,

$\Lambda_A = 2.2$, $\Lambda_n = 2.1952$, $\phi_n = 26°34'$

## Chapter 4

4.1 $\Lambda_h = 0.2514$, $\phi = 22°54'$,

$V_f = 5.97$ m/min., $V_s = 12.57$ m/min.

$\mu = 1.5278$, $\delta = 56°48'$

4.2 (a) $\lambda_s = 0°$, $\gamma_f = 8°$

(b) $\gamma_o = 11°14'$, $\mu = 1.06$

(c) $F_\gamma \doteq 427$ N, $v_f = 36.36$ m/min.

$e_f = 155.28/A_r$ N/mm$^2$

($A_r = h_D b_D$, the uncut area,

$h_D = f \sin k_r$, where $f$ = feed, mm/rev.,

$b_D$ = depth of cut in turning, mm).

4.3 $\Lambda_h = 1.95$, $\phi = 29°$

(a) $F_{sh} = 187.46$ N, $F_{shN} = 303.82$ N

(b) $F_\gamma = 223$ N, $F_{\gamma N} = 285.6$ N

(c) $\mu = 0.78$, $\delta = 38°$

(d) $l_c = 800$ N/mm$^2$

(e) $v_s = 208.3$ m/min., $l_s = 514$ N/mm$^2$

(f) $v_f = 102.56$ m/min., $l_f = 285.8$ N/mm$^2$

4.4 $\phi = 11°19'$, $\delta = 45°$

$F_c = 207.8$ N, $F_{cN} = 207.8$ N,

$F_f = 207.8$ N, $F_D = 0$

$v_s = 40.8$ m/min., $v_f = 8$ m/min.

$F_{sh} = 163.02$ N, $F_\gamma = 207.8$ N

$l_c = 519.5$ N/mm$^2$, $l_s = 415.6$ N/mm$^2$, $l_f = 103.9$ N/mm$^2$

## Chapter 6

6.1 Tool-life equation:

$vt^{0.475} = 461.4$

At $v = 150$ m/min., $t = 10.65$ min.

6.2 Tool-life equation: $vt^{0.5} = 126.5$

At $v = 60$ m/min., $t = 4.442$ min.

6.3 $v_1 = 44$ m/min., $v_2 = 28.3$ m/min.,

$t_1 = 10$ min., $t_2 = 90$ min.

Tool-life equation: $vt^{0.2} = 69.58$

For $t = 45$ min., $v = 32.5$ m/min.

6.4 Generalized tool-life equation:

$vf^{0.383}t^{0.178} = 145.7$

At $v = 150$ m/min., $f = 0.175$ mm/rev.

$t = 36.19$ min.

## Chapter 7

7.1 *Tool-life equations*

M Grade : $vt^{0.466} = 692.4$
P Grade : $vt^{0.55} = 712.5$

For $t = 40$:

M Grade : $v_{40} = 124.1$ m/min.
P Grade : $v_{40} = 93.67$ m/min.
M Grade carbide is better.

7.2

| Feed, mm./rev. | 0.20 | 0.22 | 0.24 |
|---|---|---|---|
| Cost, Rs./cm$^3$ | 0.053 | 0.048 | 0.080 |

Optimum feed = 0.22 mm./rev.
Minimum cost = Rs. 0.048/cm$^3$

7.3

| Speed, m/min. | 10.65 | 12.6 | 15.3 |
|---|---|---|---|
| Cost, Rs./cm$^3$ | 0.515 | 0.419 | 0.473 |

Optimum speed = 12.6 m/min.
Minimum cost = Rs. 0.419/cm$^3$

7.4 *Optimum cutting velocities*:

Cutting fluid I : $(V_o)_{I} = 152$ m/min.
Cutting fluid II: $(V_o)_{II} = 186$ m/min.

*Tool life for minimum cost*:

Cutting fluid I : $(t_o)_I = 40.8$ min.
Cutting fluid II: $(t_o)_{II} = 24.5$ min.

*Relative cost ratio*: $(TC_o)_I/(TC_o)_{II} = 1.067$

Cutting fluid II is better.

7.5 For maximum production rate, the ratio of cutting velocities:

$(v_o')_I/(v_o')_{II} = 0.964$

Cutting fluid II is better.

7.6 *Tool-life equations*:

HSS : $vt^{0.34} = 100$
Carbide: $vt^{0.34} = 413.5$

*Minimum cost criterion*:

HSS: $(V_o)_I = 39.35$ m/min.
$(t_{co})_I = 7.987$ min.
$(TC_o)_I =$ Rs. 60.51

Carbide: $(V_o)_{II} = 69.45$ m/min.
$(t_{co})_{II} = 4.525$ min.
$(T_{co})_{II} =$ Rs. 37.71

Carbide is a better choice.

## Chapter 11

11.1 $k_r' = 15°34'$, $R_{max} = 12\ \mu m$
11.2 $R_a = 0.11\ \mu m$, $R_{max} = 0.42\ \mu m$

## Chapter 12

12.1 $h = 0.78$ mm., $l_o = 1.74$ mm.
12.2 If $\sigma = 45°$, $l_o = 2.7$ mm; $\sigma = 60°$, $l_o = 3.8$ mm; $\sigma = 30°$, $l_o = 1.8$ mm.

## Chapter 13

13.1 $\lambda_s = 1°25'$, $\gamma_o = 13°48'$, $\gamma_n = 13°48'$, $W = -84°36'$, $\theta = 47°54'$, $\lambda_{sm} = -8°25'$, $\gamma_{fm} = 9°6'$, $\gamma_{pm} = 6°54'$, $k_{rm} = 79°36'$. Since $\eta = 0$, $\gamma_{fe} = \gamma_{fm}$, $\gamma_{pe} = \gamma_{pm}$, $k_{re} = k_{rm}$, $\lambda_{se} = 5°9'$, $\gamma_{oe} = 10°10'$, $\gamma_{ne} = 10°8'$.

13.2 $\gamma_p = -2°14'$, $\gamma_f = 10°55'$, $W = -84°36'$, $\theta = 80°54'$, $\lambda_{sm} = 1°11'$, $\gamma_n = 9°57'$, $\gamma_o = 10°$, $\lambda_s = -5°$. Since $\eta = 0$, $\gamma_{ne} = 4°37'$, $\gamma_{oe} = -4°38'$, $\lambda_{se} = 0°50'$, $\eta = 0.9°$, $\gamma_{ne} = -3°44'$, $\gamma_{oe} = -3°45'$, $\lambda_{se} = 0°38'$.

# Index